Evidence for Truth: Miracles and Angels

Evidence for Truth:
Miracles and Angels

Victor Pearce
B.Sc. (UCL), Dip.Anth. (Oxon), MRE, D.Ed., FRAI, CF

Series Editor: David Page

eagle

Bath, England

Other books in this series by Victor Pearce:

Evidence for Truth, Vol. 1: Science
Evidence for Truth, Vol. 2: Archaeology
Evidence for Truth, Vol. 3: Prophecy

Other titles by the same author:

Who Was Adam?
Origin of Man
The Science of Man and Genesis

Copyright © Victor Pearce 1999

Reprinted 2003

The rights of Victor Pearce to be identified as author of this work has been asserted by him in accordance with the Copyright, Design and Patents Act 1988.

British Library Cataloguing in Publication Data. A catalogue record for this book is available from the British Library.

Published by Eagle Publishing Ltd, 6 Kestrel House, Mill Street, Towbridge, Wilts BA14 8BE

Scripture quotations unless specified are the author's own translation from the Greek or Hebrew text. Those noted NIV are taken from the Holy Bible, New International Version. Copyright © 1973, 1978, 1984 by International Bible Society. Used by permission of Hodder & Stoughton, a Division of Hodder Headline.

Typeset by Eagle
Printed by CPD, Wales
ISBN No: 0 86347 336 9

CONTENTS

List of illustrations   10
The Principles Behind this Series   11
About the Author   13
Foreword   15
Introduction   17

1.   **Angels**   23
      An Apparent Miracle in India   23
      Could it Have Been a Miracle?   25
      God's Timing   26
      An Angel in Uniform   26
      Banks collapse at Adamieh   27
      Return Time Also Important   28
      Angels in the Bible   29
      Manoah Meets a Man   29
      Angels in Plain Clothes   30
      From Latvia to London   30
      Strange Man Appears   31
      Wrong Carriage to Rotterdam   33
      Angel's Grocery List   34
      Another Disappearance   35
      Angels in Public Service   36
      Could it Be Angels in Uniform?   36
      Those Stairs Again!   37
      The Unknown Doctor   38
      From Hate to Healing   39
      More Plain Clothes Angels   41
      Runaway Pram   41
      The Welsh Mountain Angel   42
      A Voice in the Ear   42

2.   **Visions**   45
      Deathbed Visions   45
      The Story of Ohn Maung of Burma   45
      From Germany   46
      Vision of Sister's Death   47
      Strangeways Prison Vision   48
      She Saw Jesus   48
      Is Science Contrary to the Bible?   50
      Near Death Experiences   51
      Glimpses of Glory   51

Saw Hell and Didn't Like It   52
Dave Cole's Testimony   55
Troubles Traced to Ouija Board   57
Mrs Jang's Story   58
John Naylor, Aged Forty   59
Don't Weep for Me   59
Death at Birth   60
We Held a Women's Meeting   60
A Twin Experience   61
Kathleen   61
Other Women   62
Men and Death   62
John Had a Vision   63
Family Experiences in Old Age   63
Children at Death   66
Out of the Mouth of Babes   66
An Historical Account   67
Recognition in Heaven   68

3.   **Divine Guidance**   69
Guided to an Atomic Time   69
Why I Returned to University   70
First Impressions – Brachiators   72
Flatheads   73
Oxford and Evans-Pritchard   74
Piltdown Fraud   74
Experts on Archaeology   75
The Devil Was not Pleased   76
Guidance to a Dying Man   77
Guidance to Land for a Hall   79
Women Messengers   80
The Alarm Bells Ring   82
Messenger Unknown   83

4.   **Guidance by an Audible Voice**   85
Voice Avoids Accident   85
Urge to Go Back Home   86
Nearly Ashes to Ashes, But For the Voice   86
A Strong Authoritarian Voice   87
The Ecstatic Dance   88
The Little Book   89
Guess Who!   89
The Voice in the Night   90
A Voice in China   92

	Guidance to an Unknown Destination	93
	Praying for Healing	94
	An Illness for a Purpose	95
5.	**People We Would Be Surprised to See in Heaven**	**97**
	Seven Nazi War Criminals	97
	One Who Saw Jesus	98
	Those who Refused	100
	The Chaplain	101
	Twenty-two Signatures of Appreciation!	103
	Sauckel the Slave-Driver First	106
	Attitudes Begin to Change	107
	Progress	108
	The Lord's Supper	108
	Counteracting Nazi Brainwashing	109
	From U-boat to Pulpit	110
	The Scenes at the End	110
	Disgraced but not Rejected	112
	A Cruel Japanese War Crime Tyrant	112
	Translation of the Former Tyrant's Last Letter	114
6.	**Angels in War (The First World War)**	**117**
	New Light on the Reasons for Supernatural Intervention	117
	Hidden Mysteries behind the Two World Wars	117
	I Saw the Zeppelin in Flames	120
	Angelic Intervention Reports	121
	The First Angelic Intervention	122
	The Sound of Marching	122
	Newspaper Reports	123
	It's Happened Before!	125
	Unbelief Leads to More Evidence	126
	Debated in the Churches	126
	The Stampede	128
	Newspapers Continue the Debate	128
	The Reason for Supernatural Intervention	129
	Charter for a Jewish Commonwealth	130
	How the Churches Got Excited in 1917	131
	The Second Angelic Intervention	131
	The White Cavalry of Bethune	131
	Letter from Mrs Peggy Main of Ascot, Berkshire	132
	The Vision as Seen from the British Area	133
	Only the First Stage, Making a Second War Necessary	134
7.	**The Second World War Miracles**	**137**
	The Supernatural Events Resulting from National Prayer	137

Angelic Appearances   137
Victories after each National Day of Prayer   138
Seven National Days of Prayer in Six Years   138
Drama of the Little Boats   140
The Cabinet's Words of Encouragement   142
Tunbridge Wells Empty!   142
Tennis Courts Empty!   144
The Answer   145
Remarkable Guidance for the Fourth Day of Prayer   145
Significant Events after the Fifth National Day of Prayer   147
Italy Surrenders, Mussolini Murdered   147
Military Leaders Testify to God's Help   148
The Miracle of Malta   149
Four Days to Save HMS *Illustrious*   151
The Sinking of the *Bismarck*   152
The Miracle of the Fog   152
The Impact of Public Prayer and Faith of Leaders   153
Prayer and the Angels   155

8. **The Unseen Battle for Nations**   157
Prayer and the Angels   157
Greece Was to Be Next   157
As Soldiers of Jesus Christ, How Do We
  Engage the Enemy?   158
Satan's Devices   159
The Mystery of Micaiah   160
Author's Wartime Predictions which Came True   161
Shock of the Atom Bomb   163
Jewish Scientific Weapons Turn the Tide   164
The Hidden Hand   164
Atomic Weapons and the Startling Accuracy of Jesus   165
Angels and Israel   167
Something Symbolic about the Discovery of the Scrolls   167
The White Cavalry for Israel   168
What Had Caused Such a Dramatic Reversal?   168
The Six Day War Was Also Significant   169
The Sign in the Sky in 1973   169
Elijah and Angels   170

9. **What Happens after Death**   173
Winning Back the Ashes   173
The Bema Court   174
Is There a Soul?   175
Sleeping Seed   176
Ghost in a Machine?   177

Saved Today   177
With Christ?   178
Overcoming Embarrassment When Visiting the Dying   179
Taking Away the Fear of Death   180
After Death – Christ's Experience   181
Why Raise the Body?   182
Life After Death   182
The Cruelty of Reincarnation Belief   182
What Happens After Death   184
Heaven Is Beautiful   185
Concern for Loved Ones   185
Reflected Glory   186
Disabled in Body or Character   186
Problems of the Body   187
Your Improved Character   188
With Christ   188
Marriage in Heaven?   189
Separation   190
Scripture Teaching of Life After Death   191
Visions not Enough   192
Satan Unmasked   193
Satan's End   194
Peter's Glimpse of Glory   196

10.   **Strange Miracles**   **197**
A Prayer that Felled a Tree   197
Hot Air Whale and the Ghost from the Sea   198
Why Fireballs Hit a Cathedral   201
York Minster Transept on Fire   201
Ayatollah's Writing on the Wall   204
UNO Conference at Lake Success (Confronted
  by an Angel)   205
Grotesque Figures   207
Is this the Millennium?   210
The First Calendar Millennium   212
The Second Calendar Millennium   213
The Third Calendar Millennium   213
Birthday Millennium   214
Conclusion   214

List of Illustrations

Fig. 1.1.   'Scientists believe' article published in 1988.   21
Fig. 1.2.   Thousands of Indians marching to baptism   25
Fig. 3.1.   Author's notes on atomic time   70
Fig. 3.2.   Author holding plans of Bucknall Church Hall   80
Fig. 5.1.   Nazi chiefs in the dock   97
Fig. 5.2.   Twelve Nazi leaders to hang   98
Fig. 5.3.   Newspaper article on The Goering story   99
Fig. 5.4.   Captain Henry F Gerecke, American padre to
             Nazi war criminals   101
Fig. 5.5.   Letter containing 22 signatures of Nazis on trial
             for war crimes   104
Fig. 5.6.   Cartoon of Hitler changing a cross into a swastika   108
Fig. 5.7.   Newspaper cutting of 'The man Hitler fears most'   111
Fig. 6.1.   War memorial at Llanelli   119
Fig. 6.2.   Author's picture as prize winner in a beautiful
             baby competition   120
Fig. 7.1.   Newspaper cutting of Sussex vision of Christ   138
Fig. 7.2.   Newspaper cutting of Ipswich vision of Christ
             on the cross   139
Fig. 7.3.   Cover of 20-page leaflet for prayer in time of war   139
Fig. 7.4.   George VI calls the nation to prayer   140
Fig. 7.5.   The author's father-in-law's motor yacht
             used in the Dunkirk evacuations   141
Fig. 7.6.   The town that stood still – local traders
             stop to pray   142
Fig. 7.7.   Circular letter from the Ministry of Information
             to all clergy to prepare people for shock   143
Fig. 7.8.   Map of German invasion plan   146
Fig. 7.9.   Monty's Alamein message   147
Fig. 7.10.   Testimony of Emperor Haile Selassie of Abyssinia   148
Fig. 7.11.   Supporting the King's call to prayer during WW2   149
Fig. 7.12.   Statement of faith by leaders of the armed forces   150
Fig. 7.13.   Tips on how to pray during WW2   150
Fig. 8.1.   The Miracle of D-Day, map showed that Russia
             did reach Berlin first as prophesied   162
Fig. 8.2.   Newspaper cutting of post-war Europe   163
Fig. 10.1.   Author standing beside fallen tree   198
Fig. 10.2.   The fish-man god Nina   199
Fig. 10.3.   York Minster after fireballs attack   202
Fig. 10.4.   Newspaper report of Ayotollah's cross on the wall   205

THE PRINCIPLES BEHIND THIS SERIES

WE HAVE MORE EVIDENCE TODAY that the Bible is true and accurate than ever before, but the facts have been denied to the public and even to many church people. Evidence and the Bible text have convinced Dr Pearce that the Bible is true from the beginning. It is his purpose to reveal all the undeniable facts:

1. That the Creator of the world is also the Author of the Word. He fully inspired all the 41 writers of the Bible who contributed to the sacred Scriptures over a span of 1,500 years. This is the only explanation of the accuracy and cohesion of the Bible.
2. That the message in the Bible concerning spiritual truth is true, as is also its history, prophecy and science. All are completely true, reliable and factual. This has been confirmed by research.
3. That those who doubt, do so because they do not have the facts, or do not wish to have them or believe them.

Those who have attended the author's lectures have included atheists and agnostics who thought that they had explained everything without God, but as the result of his teaching, have become convinced and converted and blessed.

Dr Pearce has found it is possible to explain science, archaeology and prophecy in simple ways which thrill the student.

Psalm 119:160 'Your Word is true from the beginning.'
Psalm 119:18 'Open my eyes that I may see wonderful things out of your law.'
Psalm 119:42 'Then I shall have an answer for him who taunts me.'
1 Peter 3:15 'Be ready to give an answer to everyone who asks you for a reason for the hope that is in you'.

In this his fourth book of the series, the author demonstrates facts beyond the natural world by providing accounts of supernatural experiences involving visions, angels and other miraculous events. The Creator is seen in his works, his Word and his intervention in the affairs of mankind.

ABOUT THE AUTHOR

DR VICTOR PEARCE had factory experience as an apprentice and later as a personnel officer and so knows the type of discussion typical of the factory floor and in the office. His experience as a teacher in comprehensive and grammar schools, also his training and lecturing in universities, gives him additional insight to academic views on science, archaeology, theology, anthropology and philosophy. He became an honours graduate of London University in anthropology, through University College, and specialised at Oxford in prehistoric archaeology. He travelled to archaeological digs and conducted research around the Mediterranean including Turkey and the Levant and also in the USA. He read theology at the London College of Divinity; is a Prebendary of Lichfield Cathedral; was Rector of one of the largest Anglican parishes in England; has had 25 curates, built two churches and several halls (one by voluntary labour). He was a member of the Diocesan Synod; was chairman of an ad hoc committee of the Education Council for a new religious syllabus and a visiting lecturer in two Bible colleges. Because this combination of skills with geology and fieldwork is unusual, Victor Pearce is able to offer a unique ministry. He has been much used of God in the conversion of atheists and agnostics who become surprised and fascinated by the facts which previously had been denied them.

He is author of *Who was Adam?*, *Origin of Man, The Science of Man and Genesis* and a contributor to the *Dictionary of the Church* and writes in various periodicals. He has lectured on evidences for biblical truth in university unions and schools. He was a broadcaster for Hour of Revival Association and Transworld Radio for 18 years and now broadcasts daily in Europe for United Christian Broadcasters. His main subject is the accuracy of the Bible as corroborated by the science of man (anthropology) and archaeology. His organisation is inter-church and the staff includes people from most denominations.

This latest book draws on material from the author's personal experiences and those of his listeners and readers.

FOREWORD

Popular accounts of heroes, history and heritage have been dominated by writers who decline to take account of divine intervention. Facts are recorded without reference to the hand of God. School textbooks are written (or rewritten) from a secular viewpoint. Whole generations have grown up in the twentieth century without an awareness of God's intervention in, for example, the defeat of Napoleon, the saving of Malta or the use of angelic forces in World War I. Personal testimonies abound of miracles, answers to prayer and angelic guidance but few gain wide acceptance in the public domain. After two World Wars, leaders have tried to put behind them both the atrocities of man and the interventions of God. Mankind easily or willingly forgets the sovereignty of God in world events and in everyday affairs.

So we find, at the dawn of the twenty-first century, Western civilisation has become as morally and spiritually bankrupt as in the early eighteenth century when crime, cruelty and carnality replaced the respect for God, people and property of the Puritan era. But in many ordinary people of today there is a yearning for spiritual values and an interest in the supernatural. Theologians inform us that we live in a post-modern age where dependence on monetary controls, material wealth and secular beliefs has proved inadequate in a changing and confusing world. In the rush to build a new world order for the third millennium, spiritual needs must be met and the voice of God must be heard clearly while there is yet time before his Messiah comes again.

The author of this additional book in the *Evidence for Truth* series believes that the God of history – including recent history – can and does determine world events and meet the spiritual needs of ordinary men and women. Victor Pearce, having thrilled and encouraged us in his first three books with his scientific, archaeological and biblical facts about God's purposes and intervention in the human race, now presents facts of a supernatural nature. He recounts for us many events of the twentieth century which confirm God's divine hand in the affairs of our planet. Many were recorded in the newspapers at the time but have long since been forgotten by the media and teaching establishments of today. Other events have never been recorded before and describe 'minor miracles' in the lives of ordinary men and women who have trusted in the power of prayer and the salvation offered through the Lord Jesus Christ. Some are the personal experiences of the author, others are from listeners to his radio broadcasts who have written in with accounts of supernatural provision. All can be verified and authenticated.

One of the earliest records of a miracle in the Christian era was in AD 175 when the soldiers of the Twelfth Roman Legion, facing defeat in war, dropped to their knees and prayed for deliverance. A thunderstorm occurred causing such a sea of mud that it ruined the onslaught of the enemy and convinced Emperor Marcus Aurelius that a miracle had happened. In the fourth century, it is recorded that Emperor Constantine trusted in God in battle and saw in the sky a flaming cross inscribed 'By this, conquer'. Although some question the accuracy of such accounts, we will find much encouragement in the true stories documented here. By no means all are war stories. Many record answers to personal problems which testify of a loving God who cares. Read on and allow Volume 4 of *Evidence for Truth* to rekindle and strengthen your faith at a time when church and state often fail to provide the spiritual answers to life.

David Page, Series Editor
Kettering, May 1999

INTRODUCTION

ATTITUDES REGARDING THE MIRACULOUS AND MARVELLOUS

The Change in the Scientific Outlook Concerning Miracles

Earlier in the twentieth century a favourite subject used to be: can miracles be accepted as scientifically possible? It was thought that the universe was rigidly bound by its laws. Miracles were ruled out as impossible because they contravened those laws. Now with better telescopes and advanced microscopes scientists are detecting phenomena for which their theories had not catered. More powerful telescopes have caused the astonishing confession that science is only able to detect the existence of one per cent of reality. Ninety-nine per cent of what exists cannot be detected even with the most advanced scientific instruments. It has become acknowledged that there is a real world beyond the detection of our five senses of sight, hearing, touch, smell and taste, or even a sixth sense. The accounts which I give in this book of the miraculous and marvellous bring into focus a small part of the vast hidden reality.

Scientists have also acknowledged their limitations due to their failure so far to bring into working harmony the two theories of relativity and quantum mechanics. They seem to conflict. I believe the scientific solution is in Jesus Christ 'by whom all things hold together' (Colossians 1:17). My point is this: all these discoveries have made scientists much humbler in their approach to the supernatural. Professor O'Sullivan made the remark that science has become more mysterious than religion to the extent that 'it is becoming increasingly difficult to imagine what we are talking about!'

One of the greatest paradoxes of modern times has been that in an age dominated by science and technology, when mankind is supposed to be guided by rational thought and where countless commentators attempt to explain away any existence of the supernatural, people persist in a fascination with the paranormal and the unexplained. In fact it would seem that as our world becomes increasingly soulless and everyday life becomes less satisfying for those in the richer nations, many people are 'searching for something' in the daily round of working, eating, socialising and leisure activities. Often this has involved an interest in the religious practices of less developed nations who would appear to have a more 'spiritual' outlook on life compared with institutionalised Christianity.

It seems that the richer nations who were once predominantly Christian, are those that are also the most materialistic and unspiritual and apparently unable to supply the needs of those who thirst for more depth and meaning to their existence. Yet even in our supposedly unspiritual rich nations ordinary people are having experiences that can only be described as supernatural or spiritual and it is becoming apparent that these experiences are a far more common and widespread phenomenon than has been previously imagined.

Perhaps it is because we do not wish to appear to be 'odd' in any way that we usually keep these experiences to ourselves and only admit to them when prompted by some braver soul who recounts a similar experience to our own. It may also be that our 'educated' and 'rational' upbringing persuades us that we only imagined these experiences, and we try to dismiss them as the product of an overactive imagination. However there can be no denying that there have been many well-publicised accounts of people who have had supernatural, spiritual or paranormal experiences and that these experiences have had a marked and often life-changing affect on the people concerned. Furthermore, the people who have recounted such experiences are from all walks of life, and cannot all be placed into the 'odd' or 'unstable' category.

That Uncomfortable Feeling

Despite this there is still the tendency for people in Western civilisation to be uncomfortable with these supernatural events. Perhaps it is because we do not like to be reminded that our existence in this life is only transitory, or maybe it is the tendency of mankind in general to be comfortable with what we know and to distrust anything that shakes the status quo.

Whatever the reason, there is a genuine mistrust of the very spiritual experiences that should be welcomed into our lives and investigated as a source of inspiration, hope and guidance for a life that is to come.

This strange reluctance to embrace the evidence of an existence beyond ours that is more dynamic and permanent, even extends to the Christian Church in general, despite the growth in the charismatic experiences of many Christians of all denominations. It would seem that even a faith that has the spiritual world and its values at its very heart, is often ready to accept a level of spirituality that it can be comfortable with, and does not challenge too deeply our placid existence. There would appear to be two main reasons for this.

Firstly, Christianity has become too closely associated with Western materialism, where time and money have become the driving forces and the 'Protestant work ethic' has given a superficial credence to the provisions and benefits of life: this in turn excludes meaningful interaction with the spiritual world and its values. Many of the values that we hold dear are no longer Christian values, but those of a culture that has grown up over the decades alongside Christianity and has become entwined with it.

Secondly, in our Western culture there has been a long-standing mistrust of all things that cannot readily be understood within our intellectual framework, or explained by the workings of this world. This, coupled with the religious background of a Church that histori- cally depicts cherubs and angels as cute fluffy winged creatures, has led to an association of all things overtly supernatural with doubtful practices rather than with good. Also the tendency to concentrate on parts of the Scriptures that we can understand and feel comfortable with has led to a misunderstanding of the supernatural way in which God works, whereas even a superficial expedition through the Scriptures should convince the most sceptical reader that Christianity and its Judaic roots are firmly set on spiritual principles and experi- ences.

However, the tide seems to be turning. The majority of people still believe in a Creator God, despite the continued efforts of certain sci- entists and secular broadcasters, and there is a growing need in all sec- tions of society to know 'what happens next' when faced with an increasingly uncertain world. This coupled with the growing under- standing of the spiritual dimensions of the Bible by Christians has led to a readiness to re-examine our attitudes to the relevance of spiritual experiences in our lives, and to an increased understanding that being aware how God works in the supernatural is an essential part of the Christian life.

This new awareness is reflected in the great interest shown in my series of broadcasts which told of miraculous and marvellous events in modern times. Some of these were experienced by myself as I travelled around the world, others were the accounts of experiences sent in by listeners. These accounts are of a variety of supernatural interventions, guidances and deliverances that have come through different means, such as the hearing of a voice, an overwhelming conviction or pres- ence or sometimes an encounter with an 'angel in plain clothes' as I have called them.

Why Some and not Others?

Why some people have these experiences while others seem to have a completely 'ordinary' life, is one of the apparently complex issues that divides opinion and causes some argument about the validity of these experiences. However, as with many of the issues concerning the way God works, the answer is often quite simple. One view is that if you are not open to the spiritual aspects of Christianity, then God is unable or unwilling to operate in that area of your life; he will not and does not intrude into your sovereignty unless there are overriding reasons to do so. Even then in the well-known cases, such as that of St Paul's conversion on the road to Damascus, there has to be a response of 'Yes I will do as you say' before he can proceed with his plan.

It may seem that there is an issue of unfairness when some people are spared from a disaster when others are not, or when one nation would appear to have been aided in a conflict or war, but in these instances it can be shown that there has been a clear purpose behind these interventions that involves far more than the lives of the individuals concerned or the fate of a nation. It has to be remembered that often these interventions or visions include information concerning the fate of the individuals concerned that are not always pleasant. St Paul knew through prophecy that he was to be imprisoned without knowing that this was when he would write the majority of his superb letters to the churches. He had to accept it as God's plan for him before it produced results which have blessed and guided Christians for nearly 2,000 years.

This collection represents a wide range of experiences, from the personal and seemingly unimportant to those that have affected thousands of lives and the course of history.

There is one common theme however, that of God's intervention and control in the course of this world's events at all levels, where he chooses, on the one hand, to answer the prayers of ordinary individuals, and on the other hand, where he acts in the course of history to bring about his sovereign purposes.

Victor Pearce
Kidsgrove, May 1999

Scientists believe

CAN scientists believe in miracles? The question keeps coming up, as we hear that the Bible's view of the world is one that we can't accept in today's "scientific" age.

Can scientists accept that things like the resurrection of Jesus or his virgin birth could happen?

If you don't read The Times you may have missed the letter which was sent in answer to the discussions about the bishops' views on miracles. It came from six Fellows of the Royal Society and seven university professors, all experts in scientific fields – and all members of the Research Scientiest Christian Fellowship or the Christian Medical Fellowship.

The boffins said:

"It is not logically valid to use science as an argument against miracles. To believe that miracles cannot happen is as much an act of faith as to believe that they can happen.

"We gladly accept the Virgin Birth, the Gospel miracles, and the Resurrection of Christ as historical events. We know that we are representative of many other scientists who are also Christians standing in the historical tradition of the churches.

"Miracles are unprecedented events...it is important to affirm that science (based as it is upon the observation of precedents) can have nothing to say on the subject. Its 'laws' are only generalisations of our experience.

"Faith rests on other grounds."

(Release Nationwide)

THOUGHTS

"In a world where we might destroy ourselves totally at any moment, and where millions starve while we burn tonnes of grain, our confidence in reason evaporates... We set our hopes on human reason; and human reason is not enough to save us from power and passion, greed and envy."

"We cannot manipulate God. We cannot take a detached, impersonal view of whether he exists or not... There are questions – about our personal relationships, the values we have and the meaning of our lives – which the natural sciences cannot, and do not wish to, explain."

Prof Keith Ward, in The Turn Of The Tide (BBC Publications).

Figure 1.1. 'Scientists believe' article.

1 ANGELS

AN APPARENT MIRACLE IN INDIA

The first remarkable event I have to tell you about happened to me in India very recently. As I think about it the only explanation possible, it seems to me, is that it was a miracle.

The Indian roads are virtual death traps, especially in the cities. The government has expressed its great concern at the very high casualty and death rate, and the city of Vijayawada where I was staying is no exception. The city is near the east coast, about sixty miles north of Madras.

Opposite my hotel was a broad main road which was filled throughout the day with all varieties of Indian traffic sounding their horns, hooters or bells, all going as fast as the heaving mass would allow – with constant screeching of brakes to avoid at the last second, by centimetres, a vehicle or the people weaving in and out to cross all along the road. There was an unending avalanche of mopeds, tricycles, peddle-rickshaws on three bicycle wheels carrying up to eight people, motor-rickshaws, cars, vans, people-packed dilapidated buses, and lorries belching smoke.

This river of death flowed relentlessly on, all crammed together, often turning onto the wrong side of the road, meeting traffic head on, and avoiding it only at the very last second. No pedestrian crossings were visible and if there had been they would be totally disregarded as would any traffic police.

Usually I tried to avoid crossing the road, but on this occasion I had to in order to reach a currency exchange bureau to obtain rupees. Such an adventure needed careful thought. I chose to benefit by the regular custom at 9 am each weekday morning of about thirty or forty lady students crossing to their college on the opposite side. For this a white-helmeted traffic cop would appear with a whistle. The traffic just had to stop for such a crowd of graceful young ladies in beautiful richly-coloured saris which were so clean in spite of the muddy rubbish-strewn streets.

The traffic cop arrived as scheduled, held up his white-gloved hand and blew his whistle. A surge of female colour, with me trying to look like one of them, dared the traffic to invade, and crossed. Safe and sound in life and limb I reached the opposite kerb as the frustrated vehicles whipped round the last student missing her by three millimetres or less.

When I had finished my business I made my way back along the disjointed pavement avoiding the short breaks in it and skirting the occasional heaps of rubbish. I put some coins into the hands of some chuckling children who ran to give it to their young mother with a look of accomplishment. She was making her home on the hard pavement and suckling her latest baby. She looked astonishingly clean in spite of many nights on the flagstones. Perhaps, I thought, she was one of those recently widowed by the suicide of about seventy cotton farmers whose crops had failed and so were unable to pay off their government mortgage for the purchase of seed.

I passed on by an open unfinished concrete building, which had been abandoned for years. The naked reinforced concrete pillars looked ashamed that they supported bare concrete floors open to the public gaze, which revealed that several destitute families had gratefully occupied those hard floors and made them their home. They lacked furnishings and furniture so far as one could see. For their ablutions there was a pool by the side replenished by the rains. In front of the desolate site was a modern poster-board. It advertised electronics, and asked in bold letters: ARE YOU COMPUTER LITERATE?

It was but a few metres on now to the place where I had crossed the flow of impervious automated ironmongery. I hoped desperately that the traffic policeman had remained there with his white crash helmet and whistle.

My heart sank. He was not there. My eyes searched among the heads of people on the pavement for a sign of his white enamelled safety helmet. I looked back at the streaming, hooting traffic. Could I venture? Could I dodge those lethal lorries, and perilously impelled machines charging at me and swerving to fill every niche between rival vehicles?

Now I understood how Moses felt when he stood with the Red Sea blocking his escape, and thousands of escaped Israelite slaves blaming him for getting them trapped, until a path was blown open by a gale which blew all that night. It was sent by God, Scripture says, so I stood there fearful, saying, 'What shall I do Lord? What can I do?'

Then I said, 'Lord, make me a pathway.'

I had hardly finished the word 'pathway' when an astonishing thing happened. The road completely emptied before me. All the traffic flowed away to right and left. Nothing followed them, nothing came from the right and nothing came from the left. I walked dumbfounded into the middle of the empty road. I stood there and looked to my right to see where the traffic had gone. There was not a vehicle in sight. I tried to see what was holding them up. My sight is good and I could see about a mile along that straight main road, but it was too far to make out what the blockage was.

Then, still standing in the middle of the road I looked in the other direction, to my left. The road again was completely empty for about a mile: again I could not see what was holding them up.

While I was standing there in amazement, God seemed to give me a prod, 'Victor! don't just stand there, get across!'

I reached the other side, and the traffic began to flow again. My heart welled up with praise: I was thrilled with the thought that God was supreme here in India.

And so it was to prove by later events, because in the week that followed, thirty thousand found peace and joy and salvation.

Figure 1.2. Thousands of Indians marching to the river for baptism after the author's evangelistic meetings in 1997. Victor Pearce (to right of cameraman) heads the parade next to the president of the Gospel Association of India, Yesupandam Bandela.

Could it Have Been a Miracle?

Afterwards I began to think about the remarkable happening. Could it have been a miracle or was it, as with some miracles in the Bible, God using natural means? In the crossing of the Red Sea for example, the passage says:

> Moses stretched out his hand over the sea; and the Lord caused the sea to go back by a strong east gale all that night, and made the sea into dry land, and the waters were divided. So the Israelites went through the midst of the sea on dry ground. (Exodus 14:21,22)

So, I thought, perhaps a traffic hold-up occurred simultaneously at opposite places. God would have used natural means as with Moses, but even so that was miraculous.

Then I thought, what about all those side roads emptying into the main road? There must be at least six of them each way, making twelve. They were always bursting with traffic seeking to join in the main flow. Something must have held up those roads also. With the two main road blockages that would have needed fourteen blockages all instantaneously. *There are not enough policemen to do that.* It looked more like a legion of angels did it! Or some kind of spiritual mechanics!

God's Timing

There was another lesson I learnt from that experience. It was God's instantaneousness of timing. The space opened up before me the moment I said in my mind the word 'pathway'. And that instantaneous resulting action must have taken place in fourteen places at once.

I have noticed God's instantaneousness on some other occasions which I will tell you about. They were quick as thought itself. But first, another Indian experience.

AN ANGEL IN UNIFORM

The experience on that Indian road of traffic stopped by prayer for a mile each way, made me take a second look at another incident that same year, 1997, in India. Had I met an angel in airport uniform?

I'd flown from England to Bombay where I was to catch another plane to Hyderabad. This required transport from the international airport to one of the domestic airports. It was the Jet Airport I needed, but the driver stopped at the wrong one and put me down at Indian Airways.

I did not know that there were different airports so I lined up in all innocence at the check-in desk to await my turn. My ticket was in a closed folder in my hand and no labels displayed my route as yet, so I was greatly surprised when, out of the corner of my eye, I saw an officer over the far side of the hall began to walk rapidly my way. She was smartly dressed in airport blue uniform and I realised she was making straight for me. She reached me and said urgently, 'You are at the wrong airport! You should be at the Jet Indian Airport, not here. Come quickly! Hurry, or you'll miss your plane!'

'I don't know how to reach it!' I said.

'Come! I will show you. Quick! This way! Go to the right and out of that door there. Then cross over the square and the airport is on the other side.'

I was confused: 'What? Out of that door and then to the right? But how far is it?'

She took hold of my hand and pulled me towards a youth with a trolley. I hadn't noticed him before. He took my baggage and put it on the trolley.

'Hurry! Hurry! This youngster will show you the way.'

The youth whizzed along, out of the obscure exit which I certainly would have missed, and along the road to a gardened square.

At the square he stopped.

'I can't go any further with you, but its just over there. You'll find it.'

He turned to go.

'Wait!' I said, 'What about your tip?'

'I don't take a tip, thank you.'

'What, no tip!'

He completely ignored a rupee note which I held out to him. How unusual, I thought, usually these porters argue for as big a payment as they can get out of you.

I just managed to catch the plane, and when I'd settled into my seat, I began to think about the incident. There were one or two strange things about it. First, how had the uniformed lady known I was at the wrong airport? She couldn't see the ticket which was covered. Also I could have been German, French or Italian. How had she known I was English?

Thirdly, that's the first Indian porter I've known to refuse a tip. Had I been rescued by an angel in uniform, and an angel youth?

Had I not been rescued and put on the right plane, I would have missed these meetings attended by 45,000 Indians to whom I brought the Good News of Jesus Christ.

BANKS COLLAPSE AT ADAMIEH

The precise timing of miraculous events reminds me of one of my visits to the River Jordan in Palestine.

A few miles north of Jericho, the river flows rapidly like a winding snake between soft steep banks. I visited this place which is called Adamieh. I wanted to see where these 'mobile clay' banks had collapsed and blocked the river in Joshua's day, 1400 BC. It was at the town of Adam, the scripture says. That's why it's called today, Adamieh. The account in Joshua 3:16 tells us that suddenly, far up the river at the town of Adam, the water, 'began piling up as though against a dam! And the water below that point flowed on to the Salt Sea until the river bed was dry . . .' (Living Bible). 'Then the priests who were carrying the ark touched the water with their feet, the river stopped flowing. It was held back by a dam which had heaped up.'

Exactly the same thing happened again this century, in 1962. It illustrated how it occurred in Joshua's day as described in Scripture, at the same place in the same way. In this century's incident the collapsed banks dammed up the river for as long as twenty-two hours. In biblical times, it must have blocked up the flow for just as long because nearly a million Israelites had to cross over and camp before the walls of Jericho.

The Bible is quite open about the natural means God used to stop the Jordan flowing, but think of the timing! That was miraculous! It was timed so minutely that the waters' edge shrank away from the feet of the priests the moment they dipped their feet into it. They walked steadily forward carrying the sacred ark of the covenant on the poles borne on their shoulders. The soldiers followed on, and then the thousands of Israelites behind them. The timing of the natural miracle was perfect. Time had to be reckoned for the rate of flow emptying the river bed down the eight miles to where the ark was being carried relentlessly forward.

In all such things there are also spiritually comforting thoughts. The River Jordan has long been used as symbolic of death through which we have to pass to reach the promised land of heaven. The fear of death shrinks away before the gold-covered ark. Why? Because of its meaning. In that sacred box were the ten commandments which we, as sinners, have broken. But above them was the mercy-seat upon which was sprinkled the atoning blood of a lamb – depicting the blood of Jesus. So the shed blood of the Lamb brings forgiveness for those broken laws if we believe, and the waters, symbolising fear of death, shrink away as the believer reaches heaven.

Return Time Also Important

The timing of the return flow of the water was just as precise, for I read in the Bible these instructions: 'Come up from the river bed!' the Lord told Joshua.

So Joshua issued the order. And as soon as the priests came out, the water poured down again as usual and overflowed the banks of the river as before [at the spring harvest time]!

(Joshua 4:17, Living Bible)

That's just how it seemed to me on that Indian road. As soon as I stopped standing in the middle of that empty road, the traffic rushed in and filled the road again.

ANGELS IN THE BIBLE

Manoah Meets a Man

So are there any cases in the Bible of angels in plain clothes? Yes, there are several.

Firstly, I think of Samson's parents. That extraordinary story of Samson, the tremendously strong man whose muscles could move monuments, begins with the visit of an angel in plain clothes to his parents.

Before Samson was born, his mother was childless. Israel needed a mighty warrior to deliver them from the dominating Philistines.

One day a man visited the future mother and said, 'I know that you are childless and unable to have children. I have come to tell you that you will become pregnant and give birth to a son. He will begin to deliver Israel from the conquering Philistines. So eat only pure food and avoid intoxicating liquor.'

Apparently she did not recognise her visitor as an angel because when he came a second time, she ran to her husband and said, 'Look! The man who appeared to me the other day has come again!'

So Manoah, the woman's husband, went out to him and said, 'Are you the man who spoke to my wife?'

He said, 'I am.'

Manoah said, 'When your words come true and a boy is born, what kind of life must he lead and what is he supposed to do?'

The visitor avoided the question and merely replied, 'Make sure that your wife obeys my instructions and avoids intoxicating drinks.'

'What is your name?' asked Manoah

'Why ask that, seeing that it is wonderful?'

'May I make you a meal?' said Manoah.

'No: make it an offering by fire to the Lord instead.'

The following events show that although the visitor was in ordinary dress he was an angel or more. Manoah burnt the meat as a sacrifice to God and then, to his surprise, the man ascended up in the smoke, and Manoah and his wife then knew that this was an angel of God.

Manoah said, 'We will certainly die because we have seen God.'

But his wife said, 'If the Lord had meant to kill us, he would not have accepted a burnt offering, or revealed what he was going to do.'

The wife did conceive and Samson was born. He became the man famed for exploits of strength, and not least was full of fun and loved riddles. Guess the riddle and get a prize, he'd say.

He was clever on improvisation too. The Philistines had taken all the swords away from the Israelites, so Samson made a sword out of the jawbone of an ass – that's been the butt of some jokes from Bible sceptics. But, surprise, surprise, the archaeologists found in ancient

Philistia one side of the long jawbone of an ass with the row of teeth filed down sideways to a sharp murderous edge. So Samson was certainly no ass!

ANGELS IN PLAIN CLOTHES

From Latvia to London

Some incidents could be put down to being only remarkable coincidence, but do you think that the following example of an 'angel in plain clothes' excludes any such explanation?

This personal experience was sent to me by a lady, with permission to use it:

> Having listened to your broadcasts I wished to relate my own experience. Originally I come from Latvia, one of the Baltic States, but I am now a British Citizen. One grey and rainy morning I left my home in Latvia, left my parents, all loved ones, friends, church and country to come to the UK in order to prepare myself for a special vocation.
>
> From Latvia I had to travel through Lithuania, Germany, Netherlands and Belgium. Then from Brussels to Ostend in order to cross the Channel to Dover. From there it was to London to my final destination all on my own and hardly out of my teens.
>
> It was getting late when I arrived in Brussels, a porter saw me off the train and a taxi brought me to the station from which I could get a train for Ostend. The taxi man left my luggage just outside the station and was gone. I was looking for a porter, but there was none.
>
> Announcements were made over the public address system which I did not understand. People rushed to the gates. Was it my train?
>
> I was nervous, but without a porter I could not move, and anyway I did not hear Ostend mentioned in the announcements.
>
> The station emptied within a few minutes and I felt dreadfully alone. I was very tired having travelled all day and night, and for the last two nights I had hardly slept. Also on the last night at home I had hardly slept a wink.
>
> Just across the station road was a large lumber-yard in which several workmen were checking and marking timber which was scattered all over the yard. As I watched them I thought perhaps one of them might help me with the luggage to the railway gates, and they might know when there was a train to Ostend. Two of the men were working near the road.
>
> I could not speak French or Flemish, and beside my native language I could speak only German.
>
> 'Perhaps they could understand some German,' I thought.
>
> But I was afraid to approach them. I could be robbed! I was afraid of that in the train during the nights. It would be worse if my handbag was snatched for that contained my Latvian passport and visa to enter the UK, as well as tickets made out for the whole journey. Perhaps the Ostend train

had already left before I'd reached the station!

What then?

Not a porter or guard was to be seen. The station seemed deserted. Night was coming on and I was very nervous, so there at the entrance to the station surrounded by three suitcases and with a guitar in my arms I closed my eyes and prayed: 'Lord send someone who can speak German and who can help me!'

I did not expect anyone in those parts to be able to speak one of the Baltic States languages. It was the first time out of my own country and so far from home although I knew they were praying for me at home.

Strange Man Appears

I turned my eyes towards the lumber-yard again. It was still daylight and I could still see the yard plainly. It was then that I became aware that there was another man in the middle of the yard who was quite different from the workmen. In fact you could have taken him for a business man whom you would not have expected to see in the middle of the timber-yard. He wore a three-quarter-length coat and a rimmed hat. He looked as if he ought to have been carrying a briefcase, but he had nothing in his hands.

I watched him as he made his way through the yard to the station, but I was puzzled. *How did he get into the timber-yard? It was blocked off by a high brick wall!* How strange, I thought. They are treating him as if he does not exist. I would have thought they would have asked what he was doing there.

He did not speak to them either. He came on to the station road and walked to the station entrance to the right side. I was standing on the left, so without going any further into the station, he turned and came to me and politely asked in German, 'May I help you? I saw you standing alone.'

He sounded so sympathetic and kind, which was a great relief to me. 'I am looking for a porter because I want to get the Ostend train.'

'Your train has gone I'm afraid and there is no other train tonight.'

I was stunned and couldn't think what to say. So he suggested, 'You could stay the night in a hotel and then get the train in the morning.'

'But I don't know of a hotel and I'm a stranger here, besides will there be a place open so late?'

I was panicking.

'I know of a small private hotel in the suburb,' he assured me. 'Would you permit me to take you there?'

'But we should need a taxi.' I said in delaying action fearing that I might be taken for ride in an unwelcome sense.

'We don't need a taxi. It's only a ten minute walk – we can walk it easily.'

'But we'll need a porter for all my baggage,' I objected.

'We don't need a porter. Let us leave your heavy suitcases in the left-baggage office for when you come back in the morning. We need not put your small case in because there are things in it that you'll need tonight. The baggage office is on the other side of the station.'

With that he lifted up the two heavy suitcases as if they were as light as a feather, even though he was medium height and did not look particularly athletic. I picked up my small case and guitar and followed him. On reaching the baggage office he put the heavy cases on the counter with ease. I left the guitar also.

He seemed to have taken over my affairs. I felt like a little girl again beside my father. My fears were changed to happiness and a sense of security came over me. 'Now I will take you to where you can exchange some money.'

He told me how much of the British money I would have to change to be able to pay for the hotel and then the taxi and porters in the morning. Then he added, 'I will order a taxi and porter for you in the morning, giving him the address of the hotel to which I am taking you and telling him which station he's to take you to.'

I got some Belgian money from a very brightly lit bureau, and from the bright lights he led me into a dimly lit street but no anxious thought crossed my mind that someone might snatch my handbag in the dark. Soon we were on a bridge crossing over to the other side, and to make conversation he told me all about the city, but I was surprised that he never asked me where I was from or why I was going to England. All tiredness and anxiety vanished, peace filled my heart and joyfully I walked beside the stranger who was carrying my suitcase.

We reached the hotel which was in a quiet street, so we stepped onto the veranda. He put down the suitcase and rang the bell. The door opened and a middle-aged lady appeared, and to my surprise my kind stranger did not speak to her in German but what sounded to me like French or perhaps Flemish. I rather gathered that he apologised for lateness, and he must have told her that I understood German because she turned to me and said in German: 'I will show you the rooms.'

The stranger reminded me to take the suitcase with me. They were two nice rooms just off the veranda, one leading into the other.

'Both these rooms are free tonight. You can have either of them.'

'I'll just take the first one – I'm very happy with that.'

'Good, I must go and tell the gentleman who brought you here that you are taking one of the rooms. He must have remained on the veranda.'

She hurried back but then returned looking very puzzled.

'He's gone! Completely disappeared! How could he do that! I've looked out in both directions down the street! There's not a sign of him. I can't believe it!'

She looked searchingly at me as if waiting some explanation, and then she covered her confusion by saying: 'Anyway, he told me he would order a taxi for you.'

'Yes, that's what he told me.'

'Well then,' she added pointedly, 'if he was going to order a taxi he would have to cross the bridge. There is no other way he could get to the station, and in only two minutes he would be nowhere near reaching the bridge, let alone crossing it!'

She looked at me waiting for a solution, but I could offer none. In my bedroom I thought the whole incident through. There was his unexpected appearance in the timber-yard among workmen who were not aware that he was there. It was just after my prayer, 'Send me a helper who can speak German.'

He came and knew I was a not a Belgian girl. His immediate words to me were in German. In addition, he knew that I had no British money and no German marks. Then there was his strength with the baggage, and to cap the lot – his sudden disappearance.

Now wasn't there a case in the Bible where a couple were rescued by an angel in plain clothes?

Thankful, but not tired out, I slipped between snow-white sheets and fell fast asleep.

In the morning the door bell rang and there stood a taxi driver who said: 'Good morning! A gentleman rang me to take you to the station!'

Wrong Carriage to Rotterdam

The details given by the Latvian lady seem very convincing don't they! Yet we are nurtured these days in such an atmosphere of scepticism that even such a case could be unconvincing. Then I remembered a similar experience that Steve Lightle had in his book *Exodus II*. He had to take Bibles into Eastern Europe and Russia.

He'd been given his ticket at Utrecht, Holland, and told to catch the train to Rotterdam and then change trains to go south to the city of Roosendaal. The train came in with five carriages. As the first carriages were all marked up for Rotterdam, he hurried on to the last carriage opposite him assuming that its destination would be the same.

The train went on its journey. Three towns were passed and forty-five minutes later the train stopped at a station. The door opened. A man stepped into the compartment and, going straight to Steve, in perfect English he said, 'Excuse me sir, but you're in the wrong carriage for Rotterdam in order to change your train for Roosendaal. Would you follow me please?'

He stepped off the train. But Steve did not move immediately. He was puzzled. How did he know who he was? How did he know where he was going? How did he know he was English when all the others were talking away in Dutch? But he jumped up quickly when he saw that the train was dividing. The carriage he was in was going off to the Hague – the opposite direction from where he wanted to go, so he snatched up his two bags and rushed after the man. When he was within six feet of him he looked him straight in the eyes and thanked him. He turned to put his bags into the correct carriage and then turned back to ask, 'However did you know about my mistake?' but there was nobody there – absolutely no one!

He was so puzzled that he looked all along the train and scrutinised the low platform. Yes, the man had completely disappeared!

It proved to be vital for him to catch that connection because he learned later that plans had been altered. A later train would have jeopardised the whole mission to take Bibles to those seeking God's truth in a closed country.

Angel's Grocery List

Of course I always search my mind to see if there is some natural explanation for some experiences, both my own and those that listeners have written to me about. Some have seen traditional angels in bright white clothing which I will tell you about later, but it's those appearances of angels in ordinary clothes who usually disappear after they have done their rescue job which leave you wondering whether you have imagined things. What about this story from Switzerland?

In Switzerland there lived a missionary couple known by C.M. Ward of *Revival Time*. This couple were in very great need. Their last coin was spent and all their food had been eaten. The wife was in tears, 'What shall we do! We shall starve!'

'There's only one thing we can do,' said her husband, 'and that is pour out our fears to God, and tell him what our needs are – tell him that our food store is empty. The Bible tells us to be more specific than that. Let's look at the advice to the Philippians; it's in chapter four verse six:

> Don't worry about anything; instead, pray about everything; tell God your needs and don't forget to thank him for his answers. If you do this you will experience God's peace, which is far more wonderful than the human mind can understand. His peace will keep your thoughts and your hearts quiet and at rest as you trust in Christ Jesus. (Living Bible)

'Tell him about everything,' repeated the husband,

'Well then, let's make him a grocery list.'

The wife fetched a piece of paper and made out the following list: 'Lord Jesus we need: 5 pounds of potatoes, 2 pounds of pastry flour, 4 pounds of apples and pears, a cauliflower, and beef for Sunday.'

She completed her list and then remembered to add, 'Thank you, Jesus'.

She then felt much happier and went about her housework.

A few hours later, at about 11.30 that morning, a knock came at the door. The wife wiped her hands quickly and opened the door. A man stood there dressed like a grocer with a long blue apron over his clothes. In his hands he held a basketful of provisions. He smiled and said, 'I have brought what you asked for.'

He pressed forward the basket for her to check.

'But I didn't order anything,' she said.

'Oh yes you did, madam.'

'No, there must be a mistake. I'll call my husband. Perhaps he can explain.'

Her husband came and said, 'I expect you've come to the wrong door. There are twenty-five other doors along here – try one of those.'

'Oh no, I've just brought you what you asked for.'

He pressed the basket onto them. The wife took it in and began to check the contents. She found: 5 pounds of potatoes, 2 pounds of pastry flour, 4 pounds of apples and pears, a cauliflower, and beef for Sunday.

She looked up, her face glowing with surprised joy, to thank him. The man was not there! Her husband said, 'He did not pass this window. He just disappeared. I checked the hallway, but there's no trace of him anywhere!'

Another Disappearance

Do you remember another story of a dramatic disappearance? It was about a man who walked seven miles on badly wounded feet talking to a couple who were in deep distress. He explained everything to them, changing their bereavement into joy, and then he suddenly disappeared.

This couple were walking westward into the rays of the setting sun towards their home seven miles away. They were absolutely shattered. Their great friend who meant everything to them had died a cruel death unexpectedly. Not only had they lost a friend whom they loved more than anyone else, they had lost one who had brought new purpose and a new future to their lives. Now all their hopes were dashed.

As they wept and talked, a man joined them. They couldn't see him clearly because the low setting sun was shining right into their faces, but he sounded so sympathetic and understanding, 'Why are you so distressed?'

They answered, 'Haven't you heard about the terrible things that happened in Jerusalem last week? Why, you must be the only person in town who does not know!'

'What things?' the stranger persisted.

'The things that happened to that wonderful healer from Nazareth. He was a prophet who did incredible miracles and was a mighty teacher highly respected by God and man. But our religious leaders arrested him and handed him over to the Roman government to be tortured to death on a cruel cross. We had built all our hopes on him. We thought he was the glorious Messiah prophesied and that he had come to save us.'

'And now besides all this which happened three days ago, there is a distressing report that his body has disappeared from the rock tomb which was so thoroughly sealed up. Even more confusing is that some women and then some men saw angels in white who told them that the Messiah had risen from the dead.'

The stranger seemed surprised. He asked gently, 'Why do you find it so hard to believe all that the prophets wrote in the Scriptures? Wasn't it clearly predicted that the Messiah would have to suffer all these things?'

The couple were speechless, and so the stranger began to quote passage after passage, starting at the beginning of the Bible, showing that the death and resurrection of the Messiah had been foretold all down the centuries before it happened.

During their two-hour walk he started with Moses' writings fifteen hundred years before.

'Moses wrote about it. God told him how sin had to be atoned for by someone who was without sin, so that believers could be forgiven. David wrote about it in the psalms a thousand years before. Then other prophets starting from seven hundred years before gave all the details.'

By this time they were nearing the end of their journey at their cottage in Emmaus, and so the stranger made as if to go on but Cleopas said to him, 'Won't you come and stay with us because it's getting so late?'

So the stranger went home with them. They prepared a hasty meal and then asked him to say grace. He took a small loaf, broke it and passed it over to them.

Then they realised, 'Haven't we seen that before? Why, it's Jesus!'

Then he vanished clean out of their sight.

You will find this account in the New Testament in Luke chapter 24.

ANGELS IN PUBLIC SERVICE

Could it be Angels in Uniform?

I received a letter from someone who thinks that the only explanation of her experience is that she was helped by two angels wearing London policemen's uniforms! This is the story I've been given permission to tell you.

Don and Beryl retired to America to be near a married daughter. Unfortunately the heat in that particular area did not suit Beryl. The doctor told Don that it was urgent that he should take his wife back to the more temperate climate of Britain. Even there she would probably need heart by-pass surgery. Reluctantly, they acted on that advice, and packed up and journeyed back to England.

Unfortunately there are still a number of London Underground stations which don't have escalators, and at Charing Cross they came to one where they faced some steep steps.

'Let me have the heavier hand luggage,' said Don and went ahead, thinking that his wife could manage the other lighter things, but when Beryl started behind him her heart started pumping painfully. She felt alarmed.

'Lord! Help me! My strength is failing. Please help me!'

In his letter the husband said, 'Of course, I should have looked behind to see if my wife was following me all right. I didn't realise she was hesitating at the foot of the steps. She told me afterwards that as she stood there she suddenly realised that there were two identical Metropolitan policemen, one on each side of her at the bottom of those impossible steps.'

One moved forward, took her arm, smiled at her and began to lift her step by step, leaving her hand baggage which she'd dropped.

'What about my handbag!' she whispered, and looked down to her side. To her amazement she saw the other policeman pick up all her things and carry them up at her side. So she had a policeman on either side of her helping her up those hard cold steps. Slowly they all reached the top and Beryl looked up to see her husband waiting for her. Then she turned to thank her kind escort, but they were nowhere to be seen.

Surprised, she turned to Don and asked, 'Where have those policemen gone?'

Don looked surprised, 'What policemen?'

'There were two policemen. One on either side of me.'

Beryl's eyes continued to search around among the people, but in vain.

'I was definitely helped up those long steps by two policemen!'

Don gesticulated and with a mystified voice said, *'You couldn't have been! I've been standing here waiting for you and watching you come up those steps, and there have been no policeman anywhere!'*

It looks as if they must have been angels in policemen's uniforms, doesn't it? But even if not, it was remarkable how God answered her prayer so immediately.

Those Stairs Again!

On reading this letter my mind went to an occasion which could have been similar. It also happened in a London Underground station.

I had been wheeling along a very heavy case full of appeal forms to deliver at a conference. They were for people to sign to ask the government to grant freedom for Christian broadcasts to be put on the air in Britain. It was all part of a long battle in which several British Christian organisations took part. They were: The United Christian Broadcasters, The Hour of Revival and Good News Broadcasters, as well as some Members of the House of Commons and the House of Lords.

Even though my case had wheels on one end, it was still heavy to pull, and so to get to the higher levels I was banking on the escalators to get my load and myself to the top. At the side stood a notice: OUT OF ORDER! USE THE STAIRS.

I stood dumbfounded. That baggage was far too heavy to yank up sixty steps. 'The devil doesn't want the forms to be delivered!' I muttered. Then I noticed a tall slim man dressed in a suit standing opposite me and smiling: 'If you pull your baggage along that dark tunnel to my left, you'll find an escalator right at the end. It belongs to another tunnel system, but it'll see you to the top safely.'

Now why didn't the notice say that, I thought. I smiled and thanked him. As he smiled back encouragingly I thought, 'He's smiling as if he knows me.' You know there's a difference in the smile of one who knows you from the friendly smile of a stranger. He didn't seem to be a passenger because he made no attempt to go anywhere. Was he a porter? Well, he didn't wear a uniform and he was smartly dressed. Anyway I thank the Lord for solving my problem.

I'm glad to say that after a number of visits to Parliament by myself and friends and especially by Gareth Littler, Managing Director of United Christian Broadcasters a little more freedom was won for Christian Broadcasting, partly due to the intervention of Margaret Thatcher – and also due to an extraordinary incident at the time of the vote.

The House was thinly attended at the time but it became obvious that there were more present who would vote against the revision than those who were for it. However, just before voting was due there was an interruption which caused all of our opponents to leave the chamber, and the revision of the law allowing freedom of Christian broadcasting was approved. The revision removed clauses which would have banned even basic truths of the gospel from being expressed.

The Unknown Doctor

I was chatting with some of our UCB staff in the canteen about some of the letters coming in to me, and one of them, Christine, said, 'I had an experience which puzzled me.'

She had been suffering from a rare disorder of the body's immune system, and she was deteriorating. Worse still, the doctors had told her husband Peter that they did not expect her to improve. She had been working as a keep fit teacher as well as being a pianist and artist. As a physiotherapist her task was physically exacting.

She took a holiday in France, but she collapsed and was brought back for intensive treatment in hospital. Here they tried to diagnose her trouble and also discover what food she was able to eat as she had become allergic to tap water and most foods. Indeed with only five foods left which she could take she became even allergic to the smell of grass, dust and petrol fumes. She said: 'My brain became confused and inflamed. Reading was difficult or impossible, and irrational fears made me withdrawn and suicidal. Severe depression changed my whole personality.'

In hospital while being tested for allergies and receiving treatment for the depression, she was allowed no solids, only artificial slops.

'I was given four meals of a strawberry-flavoured squishy substance each day, and injected with certain foods to see what I was allergic to,' she explained. Was she suffering from myalgic encephalomyelitis? Then they tested her with milk and she seemed to go unconscious, because she didn't remember anything until she woke up.

When she regained consciousness she found that they had put her back in a ward bed. It was in the middle of the afternoon and she felt very hot and sticky and very unwell. It was then that a doctor came and sat by her bedside and stayed with her over an hour speaking encouraging healing words. She said: 'He was so kind and I felt myself being lifted out of depression so that by the time he said farewell, I felt much better and my depression was transformed into optimism, and it became a turning point in my long journey to recovery.'

When the sister came, Christine asked her what the doctor's name was. She looked surprised:

'I don't know who you can be talking about! We have no doctor here who could spare an hour to talk to you. What was he like?'

'Oh, sister, he was so nice and wonderfully kind. He wore a white coat which made me think he was a house doctor. And he had blond hair.'

'Blond hair! Well he wouldn't be a member of our doctors' team for this ward; neither of them have blond hair, but I will ask around.'

She did, but could trace nobody. She searched the registry, but found absolutely no clue. So who could it have been?

From Hate to Healing

Christine completely forgot all about her encounter with the delightful blond doctor. Then the illness began to return, and she gave up all hope of ever recovering, just living a day-to-day existence, and becoming gradually more depressed.

One September, at home, Chris and Peter received a visit from an old childhood friend who'd heard that Chris was ill. Her name, Joy, was certainly appropriate for she came with a happy confidence that prayer would bring healing. Joy was not like this when Chris first knew her. What had happened? She had had a life-changing experience through Jesus, and she persuaded Chris to come to the church she now attended where the people there would pray for her healing.

Chris attended several times and prayers were made but nothing seemed to happen. One morning Christine was quite shocked to find that she felt full of hate for everyone, even her own family, and doctors. That morning Joy called and came into her bedroom with her big loving smile. 'How are you this morning?'

'Horrified,' replied Chris, her voice full of venom. 'I hate everyone.'

'Everyone?'

'Yes everyone, even the doctors who've tried so hard to help me!'

Joy's response was unexpected: 'This is wonderful!' she exclaimed leaping up. She knew that the suppressed suppurating sore had been released. 'You can give it all to God,' she said. 'And he will wash away all this bitterness and heal you. I will send for my friend and we will pray with you.'

The friend came straight away. Chris saw her little car draw up under the window. She had the same shine on her face that Joy had. That look of inner peace. Joy came to the point straightaway: 'Chris, all that hatred you were feeling this morning is poisoning your life. If you want him to, God can change your life and give you a new start.' I could certainly do with one, thought Chris.

'But before you can have a new life you must sort out the old one. You see, God is kind and loving, but he is also holy, and can't have anything to do with us while we're still messed up with the wrong things we've done. That's why Jesus died on the cross. He took your punishment so that God could justly forgive you for all that hatred, and for other things that you have done wrong.'

Chris had never heard anything like it, but she felt that this was the solution. So she asked God to forgive all her unkind thoughts. She thought of Jesus dying for her, and asked him to take over her life and do whatever he liked with it. She didn't care what happened, her life was over anyway.

Immediately, the interference in her head that had been constant stopped, as if switched off. The severe feelings of illness left her as the disease tore upwards out of her body. In rushed a powerful wave of love, joy and peace. She was aware of Jesus, very close and alive. He had healed her.

She was eager to tell the good news at the next church service and as she was about to wrap up her allergy pills to take with her, a quiet voice said, 'You don't need those.' She looked up to see who had spoken, but no one was there. She was absolutely alone.

It was many years after her healing in Joy's house that Christine heard about the activity of angels still helping people in this day and age. She remembered then about the unexplained doctor, and had a fresh revelation of God's love in recognising the angel God sent even before she had given her life to his loving care.

MORE PLAIN CLOTHES ANGELS

Runaway Pram

On hearing that I was recording people's experience of being helped by plain-clothed angels, Kerry Cole of Cross Rhythms Radio told me her story.

Kerry and her husband Chris had acquired a rather large pram for their first baby. Kerry was shopping in Plymouth with a friend and, as there was plenty of room in the pram, she put her purchases in the empty end. This added a fair amount of weight. She wheeled the pram along to peer into an optician's window. There was a test screen which invited closer examination in order to reveal sight problems. Kerry leaned forward to do this and momentarily released her grip on the pram. The weighted pram quickly ran back from her, and gathered speed as it headed towards the high kerb of a dual carriageway filled with speeding traffic. In panic she ran to catch the handle but it sped away from her.

To her horror, the pram was inches off the kerb ready to tip her precious baby under the wheels of the rushing vehicles. There was no one in that area, no one to help. As she dashed forwards, suddenly there was somebody there. It was a man who looked about forty years of age wearing a long brown coat. He was standing right in front of the pram. Kerry's relief was so great that she burst out: 'Praise the Lord!'

She looked at the man who said: 'Yes indeed!' He said it in a tone of voice which was so peaceful that it made her think that he must know the Lord to say it like that.

She turned to her friend who had followed her down, and then turned back to thank the welcome rescuer, to express her deep relief and gratitude and to say, 'You were brilliant!' but he was not there.

'I walked away recovering my composure,' explained Kerry, 'When it suddenly hit me – there was something strange about that rescue! Any ordinary man would have stopped to talk about the incident, and perhaps to offer some advice about the need to put on the pram wheel brake. Then another thing, how had he disappeared so suddenly and with no obvious place of cover? Then there was that tone of voice so peaceful, "Yes indeed!" in response to my exclamation "Praise the Lord!" '

Kerry described how she felt the blood rise up her neck and her cheeks flush as she came to realise that she'd had a divine encounter. She was thrilled and praised God from her heart.

I had a word with her husband Chris and he said, 'Did you know what name we had already given our baby girl? It was Ruhamah. It means God will have mercy.'

'Where did you get that from?' I asked.

'From Hosea chapter two verse one.'

So I looked up the reference and it said in the Living Bible translation: 'Name her Ruhamah [meaning 'to be pitied' i.e. shown compassion] for now God will have mercy upon her.'

The Welsh Mountain Angel

The next incident comes from one who gives her permission to use it but asks for her name to be omitted. She says:

> I am writing about angels as your tapes have interested us. As Scripture says, 'Are they not ministering spirits sent out for service to those who shall be heirs of salvation?' The following true story will bear this out.
>
> Mrs Prior was a godly soul who lived in a row of Welsh houses perched on the mountainside at the edge of Cilfynydd (pronounced kil-vunn-eth). Once a week Mrs Prior took the bus down to Cardiff where she would have tea with friends before proceeding to the Bible reading. One bitter winter night, she arrived back on the late bus to find it was snowing in Cilfynydd. She was elderly and frail and dreaded the walk uphill to her home. Naturally, she prayed, and when the bus arrived at the bottom of the treacherous slope, she was surprised to see a man whom she did not know waiting for her. As she stepped off the bus he took her arm and said, 'Come along old dear. I'm on my way to the club at the top.'
>
> He took her right up to her house and stopped outside as if he knew where it was, and then waited while she unlocked the door and switched on the light in the hall, then he departed.
>
> But who could he be? Mrs Prior had lived in Cilfynydd for over 80 years. She said she knew every soul in the town, yet she had never seen this man before and never saw him again.

A Voice in the Ear

Another listener's story:

> The following incident remains clearly in my memory after forty-four years. I was twenty-three years of age and very ill indeed. Doctors had been unable to diagnose my condition until I had a burst appendix and peritonitis. I was lying behind screens in Worthing hospital waiting to be taken to theatre. I was so ill that the surgeon had been fetched from the theatre to see me. He had given instructions that I was to be prepared for theatre and brought straight down to him at the finish of his afternoon list. So there I lay, wondering what could be ahead, and in considerable pain.
>
> Suddenly, I became aware of an exceedingly powerful being beside me at the head of the trolley. At the same moment a voice said distinctly in my ear, 'My God hath sent his angel.'
>
> All that I knew was that this being was very bright. I thought, 'If there is an angel there then everything is all right,' and then I went peacefully

to sleep until the porter fetched me.

You see I had been brought up from birth in a home where God was a gracious friend at all times, and a very present help in times of trouble.

I lived, but the surgeon told my mother later that I should be very grateful indeed for my life. As it was I spent thirteen weeks in hospital. Could I doubt that God had indeed sent his angel and spared me?

We will return to the subject of audible voices in a later chapter.

2   Visions

DEATHBED VISIONS

The Story of Ohn Maung of Burma

Ohn Maung was born in Kyaukpadaung, a town where there were no Christians. At the age of nine, while reading about the Buddhist version of hell he became very frightened. Eventually he went into a Buddhist monastery where for three years, in constant meditation, he denied himself sleep, hoping to find peace and enlightenment.

He then found comfort in studying indigenous medicine. This led him to visit a local hospital to offer help and there he found Christians who seemed to have found the secret of peace. He became convinced that he'd found the secret, and against strong opposition, he decided to become a Christian.

He married and settled in a Karen village. After a child was born to him and his wife, he arranged for himself to be baptised in eight months' time. Former friends severely criticised him, and then a few days before his baptism his first child died suddenly, and everybody said that it was punishment for changing his religion; but he was willing to suffer for Jesus, no matter what.

Following his baptism he seemed to have crisis after crisis. He was taken seriously ill and spent a year in hospital and felt so ill that he lost all hope of recovery. So he made a vow that if God would heal him he would become a full-time worker for him. Then a strange thing happened.

He had a night of extreme pain during which he repeated many short prayers. Suddenly, a bright light shone on his face. Where was it coming from? 'I looked around and found that it was coming from above the main door opposite my bed. I was startled to see the upper part of a man all radiant white. In his hand he held a bright staff which he waved at me. Then deep within me I seemed to hear him say: "Do not worry or be anxious!"

'Then he vanished, but at once I felt new life and vitality flowing through me. I was able to get up out of bed, so I began to pray and recite, "Come unto me all who are heavy laden and I will give you rest."

'I was thrilled and began to walk the hospital floor shouting, "I saw my Lord! I saw my Lord! I am now healed!" '

People sent for the doctor saying, 'He's delirious!' The doctor took Ohn Maung's temperature expecting it to be very high but to his amazement he found it to have fallen to normal. Two days later Ohn Maung left hospital completely well, and told his story around the streets of his home.

His father was furious, and came and scolded him and for two hours tried to entice him to give up his faith in Jesus. He even offered him great wealth if he would, but Ohn Maung had found a greater treasure. Eventually his father stopped worrying him and even asked for a copy of the Bible.

He then visited his own people in Kyaukpadaung and told them the Good News of how Jesus had given him peace inside and changed his life.

From Germany

Another letter has just come, this time from Germany.

'I have a little story which may be of interest to your collection,' says the writer.

> I've had an encounter with what one may call an angel, but naturally I'm not sure. I got saved and received the baptism of the Holy Spirit. I was going through a lot of spiritual attacks, so to say, maybe also due to my Nigerian heritage, and before I learned that bloodline curses had to be broken.
>
> One day I was lying down on my bed in broad daylight, being fully awake and not even sleepy.
>
> I saw a huge being. Now this is hard to describe. There was no fear. I was absolutely peaceful. I saw a being whose face was very bright. There was a strange light around it. His feet were bronzen and shiny, but they did not touch the ground. I do not know why. I was just looking at him and he was looking at me. He wasn't smiling or doing anything, neither did I see any wings. The light surrounding him was strange. His robe was white and bright. I just felt like asking him who he was but I didn't. Then he disappeared from my sight.

This reminds me of a similar description in the Bible. One day late in June, writes Ezekiel, when I was thirty years old, the heavens were suddenly opened to me and I saw visions from God . . . High in the sky was what looked like a throne made of beautiful blue sapphire stones and upon it there sat what appeared to be a man. From his waist up he appeared to be all glowing bronze, dazzling like fire, and from his waist down he seemed to be all glowing fire and there was a radiant halo like a rainbow all around him. That was the way the glory of the Lord appeared to me, and when I saw it I fell face down upon the ground. Then I heard the voice of someone speaking to me, and he said, 'Stand up son of dust and I will talk to you'.

The Spirit entered into me as he spoke and set me on my feet.

'Son of dust,' he said, 'I am sending you to a nation which is rebelling against me. They are a hard-hearted, stiff-necked people, but I am sending you to give them my messages – the messages of the Lord God, and whether they will listen or not, at least they will know that they have had a prophet among them.'

What God told Ezekiel is written down in the next forty-eight chapters of the book of Ezekiel. They are prophecies of happenings in the twenty-five centuries since Ezekiel down to our times and are still happening today. Among other things they tell how Israel will return to Palestine as the nation of Israel and how it will cause a lot of trouble in our times, but it also tells you what the solution will be. See my book *Evidence for Truth, Volume 3: Prophecy.*

VISION OF SISTER'S DEATH

Here is another letter that came to me during my broadcasting days with Hour of Revival on the subject of visions, this time in the form of a dream involving the death of a close relative.

> Before I walked down the line I thanked the Lord God for you. May God the Father, Maker of Heaven and Earth, be merciful towards you, your fellow workers of the Hour of Revival! May he strengthen you in love and peace where ever you go. Amen.
>
> Here, I'm one of your regular listeners of KTWR, and I listen to your explanation on the Scientific and Biblical points of view which keeps me wanting to learn more about the Bible. I want you to know that your voice is so dear in Papua New Guinea. All the way from England to PNG I don't know how, but Praise God! God can do it, on the air around the world. It's like climbing a ladder to see the wonder of the future.
>
> My mother did as she was told. My sister's last words to my mother were, 'Jesus is here, Mother, and I'm going with him.' She died then. My mother was hopeless standing there not knowing what to do. (She took five operations before she died.)
>
> My younger sister aged about twenty was dead at Easter in the hospital because of cancer. She was in a Bible College for three and a half years, just before her graduation. She was attacked by cancer right on her buttock. She really prepared her way to be with the Lord and before she shut her eyes she told my mother to move away from her bed because Lord Jesus is at her bed side to take her home.
>
> I didn't know that she had died. No one contacted me on the telephone or message through radio or by letter. But I dreamed that she came by a canoe to pick me up, after we got safely on the other side we both shook hands and then she left me standing there drifting away. I try to reach her but I found out that I couldn't move to her. I woke up from my dreams and

immediately realised that my sister must have died. I cried till the day break. After two weeks I received the letter from my parents about my dying sister.

The contents of the above letter show similarities with other experiences which portray God's intervention at death, a subject we shall return to in a later chapter.

STRANGEWAYS PRISON VISION

I was talking to a young man recently released from prison. He had led a really bad life. From the age of eight he destroyed things, at the age of eighteen he robbed 200 premises in a matter of weeks. Then his sixteen-year-old wife was pregnant for the second time. The prison chaplain saw him when he started his sentence. What he said left him cold; he was making no progress with him, so he said, 'Let me pray for you.'

'Oh, no!' groaned the young man. Then he changed his mind. 'This chaplain might not visit my expectant wife if I don't let him pray.'

The chaplain prayed earnestly and laid his hands upon the young man's head. The young man told me he was amazed at what then happened. 'Suddenly I knew that Jesus Christ was alive and real. There behind the chaplain I saw Christ. The blood was streaming from his wounds. He looked at me. It was for me, I knew. Me, a thief but not repentant. I stared, then the picture changed. I saw a door overgrown with weeds.'

He continued, 'And Jesus Christ was knocking on that door. I didn't know the scripture about it. I was totally irreligious but I knew it was the door of my heart. I said, "Jesus, please come in!" '

'What happened then?' I asked him.

He joined the prison Bible study group and witnessed to other prisoners all the time he served his sentence. That young man did have a chance to show Christ had changed his life but the dying repentant thief had no such opportunity, yet Christ saved him and his soul went to be with Christ. He was indeed a sinner saved by grace.

SHE SAW JESUS

I heard this young lady tell her experience to Keele University Christian Union and so interviewed her for more details afterwards. I had been invited to go there to speak on the subject 'Science versus the Bible'. It had drawn a large number of students who looked forward to some enjoyable arguing. They were surprised as usual to hear me say as a scientist that there was no conflict between science and the Bible. There was remarkable correlation, as we discovered in Volume 1 of *Evidence for Truth*.

It was very fitting that the young lady's story should accompany my science talk because it was her vision of Jesus which changed her from being an aggressive atheist into a believer. She was brought up from childhood as an atheist by parents who were atheists. As some of the details of her life are best kept confidential, she asked me not to reveal her name.

'At the age of seven,' she says, 'I was a fully fledged atheist. Although this may seem an extreme statement, it was nevertheless true. I had attended a dear little Church of England primary school in the days when there were still assemblies where we sang hymns – and I had always loved to sing these hymns and my heart was strangely warmed and certain special songs I knew word for word, although I could make no sense of them. However, love was absent from my life, and I grieved over this from a young age. It seemed that my mother's love came with the condition that I conformed to her values. As she was an atheist, I made an effort to win her love, and learnt to recite adult reasons for my atheism.'

Then she sang a tuneful little song of her own:

Could you know me completely, and tell me you'd forgive?
If you were wearing my shoes say – this is what you'd give!
I'm a message in a bottle, adrift upon the sea,
Surviving storms and sailing calms, my fate was mapped you see.
Friend, believe me when I say –
JESUS CHRIST!!! . . . I've lost my way.

'When I had written the words "JESUS CHRIST!!!" in the poem, I had intended them to be an offensive swear word – blasphemy.

'When you've got lost, you just don't care,' she reflected. 'You take the first hand offered because you dare to taste the nectar of their affection.'

Much of her thought life was looking for answers and reasons for living and for love. She thought that free sexual love would give it, but did not realise that the young men she was indulging would gratify themselves without any commitment and would not give the real love she was craving for. It was as she was sitting with a guy in front of her that she saw a vision of Christ. She knew very little about him but she knew it was him because he wore a crown of thorns. Here was Christ looking at her with real love in his eyes – yes, it was her he was looking at – and with real love, pure love, good love, honest love, redeeming love. She determined to find that source of real love. She found it six months later. She went to a gospel meeting where it was explained how she could find Jesus as her Saviour. She accepted his forgiveness for all her sins. She accepted Jesus into her heart, and accepted his full and free salvation, realising that it was free because he had paid for it by his suffering on the cross. This was the love she needed and which now satisfied her.

As the students realised what kind of lifestyle she had been leading, and how Christ had satisfied with true love and purpose, they stayed for further discussion at the end following my answers to scientific difficulties they'd raised. It was actually my title 'SCIENCE versus the BIBLE' that had brought them along and enabled them to hear the woman's testimony.

Is Science Contrary to the Bible?

The talk which followed was another surprise to many who were present. I was able to tell them that there was no conflict between science and the Bible.

We looked at the first chapter of Genesis. The order in which things were created were the same in the Bible as they were in science. I showed a picture on the overhead screen of the British Museum list of events and then ticked them off in the same order. There was a remarkable correlation:

Well, as you can imagine, the students were quite surprised to see that the science of the first chapter of the Bible was in harmony with the British Museum science book. They were in for a further surprise when I showed them that the archaeology of the next nine chapters was in harmony with archaeology, and that I as an archaeologist had worked with leading experts who found this so.

Of course, some of them asked how this got into the Bible. The first eleven chapters were about events which happened thousands of years before Moses so how did he know about these prehistoric events. I pointed out that God knew all about it and that these scriptures claimed that God was in the habit of talking with Moses 'face to face to face', and that Moses wrote it all down as he was trained to do in Egypt's royal palace. In fact on the tomb walls you find pictures of scribes writing everything down on scribing boards. Moses lived in a very bureaucratic age, and who could know better than God himself!

Farming comes next, in chapter 2. Archaeology and the Bible both agree that the next great step forward was agriculture and animal farming.

Farming started in the Garden of Eden and spread from there to the rest of the world. This was the next surprise when I showed them that not only was there harmony between science and the Bible about the origin of the universe and the order of creation, but also the next ten chapters revealed remarkable correlation in archaeological research. After creation the next big step was the introduction of farming. Where did it begin? Chapter 2 tells us. This chapter is not a second story of creation as some have thought, but the account of the next important cultural step forward. I went on to tell them that we archaeologists had found that the geographical description of Eden was correct. It was at the sources of four great rivers which arose in the mountain plateau near Lake Van. Sheep and cattle spread to all the world from here in western Turkey, and so did the first farming tools. These were flint tools and polished stone axes, and we are able to trace migration by these tools even to Papua New Guinea.

Then I was in for a surprise. A student said,

'I'm from Papua New Guinea! Yes, and we find those stone tools there – and the ground and polished stone axes – in fact we were still using them up to fifty years ago!'

'But what about the Flood! You don't really believe that happened do you?' Another said this with a laugh.

'Our archaeologists have excavated ten sites in Iraq,' I replied, 'where the ancient cities reveal a different culture before the flood from the one after it.'

'So it wasn't worldwide then?'

'Excavations all over the world show that it was worldwide. With other scholars I have found evidence in Egypt, Europe, the Black Sea, Australia, England and America!'

'Well, where did all the water come from?'

'The *New Scientist* reported recently that it was discovered that there was more water under the earth than even that contained in all the oceans of the world, and that is where Genesis chapter 6 says that most of the water came from.'

Of course it rained torrents of water as well, but the Bible does speak of most water coming from the great deep and the waters under the earth. We also have magnetic evidence that the axis of the earth changed at the time of the flood. For the earth to start turning at a different angle, that would release water from the great deep, and also cause the oceans to flood out of their beds by centrifugal force changing direction. The oceans are over twice as deep as our highest mountains. That why Noah's ark was carried up above Mt Ararat and why it took the waters over a year to recede.

The students had received many surprises, and split up for discussion. A large number were eager to ask more details from the atheist who said she'd seen Jesus and that it had changed her life.

NEAR DEATH EXPERIENCES

Glimpses of Glory

A neighbour was telling me of the passing of their daughter aged eleven. A short while before she died, she said, 'Jesus said let the little children come unto me.'

Her last words were, 'Mummy, I'm going to such a beautiful garden.'

People of all ages and nations have had a glimpse of heaven's glory.

So what is heaven like? Human language and the five senses are inadequate to describe it. 1 Corinthians 2 says, 'As it is written, eye has not seen nor ear heard, neither has it entered into the heart of man, the things which God has prepared for them who love him.'

So, because it is beyond human description, St John is shown the glory in symbols and figurative language. Revelation 21 reads: 'The city of gold . . . having the glory of God, and her light was like unto a stone most precious, even like a jasper stone, clear as crystal.'

The beauty of heaven has also been reported by others. The following near death experiences were sent in to me by listeners.

Saw Hell and Didn't Like It

What will you make of this I wonder? It's most extraordinary; I'm not sure what to make of it myself. The film studio of Howard Condor of the Christian Television Association were doing some films for me at the time featuring Sir Cliff Richard and an MP, Gary Streeter. Gary had left a very elite professional position because he felt God wanted him to become an MP. He believed his Christianity would help the country! By which he meant that commitment to honesty, self-sacrifice and forgiveness, motivated by faith in Christ, would restore our land to happiness.

I met a man there, Ian McCormick, who had a most amazing story to put onto celluloid. He was diving off the coral reef in NE Australia with some local divers, when a swarm of large box jellyfish floated among them. They were like Portuguese Men Of War but these were far more deadly – get stung by one of these and you are dead in twenty minutes. As the jellyfish floated among them, Ian felt the sharp pain of being stung.

In fact five stung him. His arm was swelling, his blood was pulsating, his right lung started restricting his breathing. In a few seconds all Ian's life passed before him.

There was a youth standing on the reef, 'Pull me out!' gasped Ian.

He did and beckoned for a boat. The boat got him onto the shore. By this time Ian felt the poison move into his kidneys. Then his right side became paralysed. The youth tried to pull him up to one of the bungalows but no one came out so Ian sat on the road.

At this stage the victim usually falls into a coma and never comes out. Ian's eyes began to close, but he heard a voice speak to him, 'Son, if you close your eyes you will never open them again.'

He fought to keep his eyes open, and heaved himself upon his right leg which was still good and hobbled towards a petrol station. Three Indians in a taxi drew up and got out.

'I'm dying!' gasped Ian, 'Get me to hospital!, I'll pay you!'

'How much money?'

'Anything, I'm dying. I've been stung by a jellyfish!'

All three walked away laughing. Ian then heard a voice which said, 'Son, are you willing to beg for your life?'

So Ian begged for his life before the three. One came in response and put him into the taxi, demanding a huge fare, but when he saw that he had no ready money with him he forced him out near a hotel.

The security guard of the hotel saw him and thought he must be drunk. Ian shouted, 'I'm dying, I'm dying!' but the guard saw how his arm was scarred and swelling and thought he was a drug addict.

Ian was desperate and as his body began to go into spasm, two Chinese men jumped on him to hold him down. He felt poison pouring into his bone marrow. He pleaded with the men to take him to the hospital.

'No,' they said, and carried him to the hotel.

To cut a long story short, unnatural strength enabled Ian to maintain consciousness until the ambulance arrived.

Inside the ambulance it was as if he saw his life surveyed on the wall opposite him. Then his mother's picture appeared. She was praying for him. God had told her back in England that her son was dying, and on the wall of the ambulance she said to him, 'Call on God to forgive you.'

Ian didn't know how to pray, or even whether there was a God to pray to. 'Help me to pray,' he said. Words appeared: 'Forgive us our trespasses.'

It was part of the Lord's prayer which his mother had taught him. 'But how can God forgive all those sins surveyed on the side of the ambulance? Yes, please, please forgive me.'

Words appeared again, 'As you forgive those who sin against you. Do you forgive?'

'Yes, yes, I do forgive.'

'Do you forgive those Indians who pushed you out of the taxi?'

'What! For all their heartless treatment when I was dying?'

'Yes.'

'Well if you are willing to forgive all my badness, I'll forgive those Indians.'

'And do you forgive those Chinese men?'

'If you can forgive me I will forgive them.'

Then appeared the words, 'Thine is the kingdom'.

Once at the hospital, things did not go well, and he felt the poison moving into his eye sockets. He could not keep his eyes open any longer; everything went black. He put his hand out to feel for the wall, but there was no wall there. He put his hand to his face, but it passed through his face. He felt he was standing outside his physical body. The darkness was intense and there was an evil presence and fear filled him. A voice screamed at him, 'You're in hell!'

His mind reached out, 'But Saviour, you forgave me.'

Then light appeared and drew him into a tunnel. He felt drawn to the light – it was living light. The light filled him, fear vanished and peace filled him. It was a wonderful peace and he saw a wonderful radiance that was drawing him onwards. He felt he was looking into the radiant centre of the universe. It was brilliant and glorious. There seemed to be a person there. Joy flooded his being. Was it a dream? Perhaps I'm dead!

A voice came from that radiant centre. It was the same voice he'd heard at the beginning.

'Ian! Do you wish to return to life? Ian if you wish to return you must see things in a new light.'

Then appeared the words, 'GOD IS LIGHT! (1 John 1:5)'

Light began to penetrate his life deeds and wash them clean. Ian wept, he felt love filling him – God's love and forgiveness, accepting him as he was. As he felt this love filling him and his being stepped into that light and shimmering radiance, from it came healing and peace, and in that light came the radiant feet of a man. Ian looked up to see a radiant face veiled behind that radiant intensity so that he could not see the actual facial features. Ian was flooded with joy. He felt God had washed him crystal clean.

The voice came again. 'Ian, do you wish to go back?'

'No, let me go in. Nobody's loved me as you do.'

'Your mother loved you and prayed for you!'

Ian thought, If I don't go back she won't know that I have not gone to hell. She won't know her prayers were answered, but she'll know if I go back.

'How do I return?'

'Son, you must see things in a new light – God's light. You must be born again. John chapter three.'

'Lord, how do I get back into that tunnel?'

The voice said, 'You must tell others as well. I love all those people down there. I want them to know I love them and died for them. Open your eyes!'

He opened his earthly eyes and saw the doctor cutting into his feet to drain out the poison. The nurse jumped up.

The voice spoke, 'I have just given you your life back. Go and tell others!'

'How can I, like this? Please heal me, God!'

Ian felt warmth and power filled his body, and he sat up. The nurse jumped back again in shock and knocked the other nurse over.

Ian walked out of the hospital fully healed. When the fishermen saw him they ran away.

The voice said, 'Son, in that ambulance you prayed that prayer (in Matthew 6:12): 'Forgive me my sins because I forgive those who sinned against me. When you prayed that prayer I saved you when I was on the cross (Acts 4:12). I took you through the darkness to show you what I'd saved you from. When you prayed, I became your Saviour. You are a reborn Christian. Read the Bible.'

It took Ian only six weeks to read from Genesis to Revelation, and he learnt hundreds of texts by heart. He could quote them as well as any Billy Graham, giving book, chapter and verse. He must have quoted at least thirty texts with full clarity. He always added the Bible reference: 'Christ died for our sins, the just for the unjust' (1 Peter 3:18); 'He bore our sins in his body on the tree-cross' (1 Peter 2:24); 'Believe on the Lord Jesus Christ and you will be saved' (Acts 16:31); 'It is appointed unto a person to die once and after this the judgement' (Hebrews 9:27); 'I implore you as if it were Christ imploring you, be reconciled to God' (2 Corinthians 5:25), and so on and on with an explanation each time. He was as clear as a gospel preacher with years of experience, and people couldn't resist listening. No one would have thought that he'd been an atheist.

Dave Cole's Testimony

Can I ask you for a moment to picture the scene: a perfect day in August 1976 in sunny Majorca, Spain. A beautiful blue sky – not a hint of a cloud, but a day that was to change the rest of my life.

My family (my wife Elle, daughter Lisa who was 11 years old and my mother recently widowed) and myself had gone off to Spain for our annual holiday. Elle and I had hired a scooter to get around on, as we did not enjoy organised coach tours.

On August 26th I had gone off on my own to get some petrol from the local village, as we were planning to go on a trip that day. It was a trip that I was never to return from. After filling up with petrol, I looked the wrong way coming out of the garage and had a head-on collision with a car that was travelling at 60 mph. I was only dressed in a pair of shorts, a T-shirt and flip flops, not the ideal dress for such a serious accident! As you can imagine, I was in a pretty bad state, so bad in fact that *I died at the scene of the accident.*

My out-of-body experience was that I felt I was looking down a tunnel at myself on the road all smashed up with a whole bunch of people staring down at me. I used to wear three gold chains (I was really into gold jewellery). A lady in the crowd had one of the chains and was going round to different people asking if it belonged to them. I knew it was mine and was trying to tell her to give it back to me but she just did not hear me or see me and continued to go around the crowd. It's funny but I never did get that chain back although the other two were still around my neck.

Call it what you like, with hindsight I know that God had his hand on me. At the precise time the accident occurred, a doctor 'just happened' to be passing on his way to work. He stopped and was able to resuscitate me. Also the guy who we had hired the scooter from was passing. He was able to identify his bike and also recognised me to a certain extent despite my face being badly smashed up. This enabled the police to get in touch with my wife who was waiting back at the hotel for me.

I was taken to the Poly Clinica Miramar in Palma which was over an hour's drive away but the best hospital on the island. I remained in a critical condition and unconscious for several days. I do not remember any of the details of the accident but my wife began to piece information together from eye witnesses.

When I eventually came round, the doctors came to tell me the extent of my injuries which were: both legs broken, one in 17 places the other in 7 places; both ankles smashed; my right hip was in my stomach, which had caused many internal injuries; a broken arm and lots and lots of cuts and bruises all over my body. I was in the clinic for many weeks undergoing various operations. When I was well enough to travel, I was flown back to England and spent the next two years in Guys Hospital, London, where they started to rebuild my legs. There was a time when I was told that I would not be able to walk again. I was devastated.

During this time a patient on my ward started to tell me about God. Much to my regret I used a barrage of four-letter words to get rid of him and his God. How could a God who was supposed to love allow this to happen to me? I'd led a life that was not too unsavoury. I loved my family and they meant the world to me, yet here I was a guy that lived life to the full, now being told I would spend the rest of my life in a wheelchair. I guess I began to think of all the things I would never be able to do. But that was not to be. After many more operations for plates, screws and bone grafts they were able to teach me to walk again. Eventually I was allowed home.

During this time our marriage was over, apart from the fact that we were still living under the same roof. My wife had made a mental decision to leave as soon as Lisa was old enough. I was not the same guy she had married. I had sunk into the depths of depression and there was nothing that I could do about it, or so I thought.

Our daughter Lisa was moving from being a little girl into a young woman and was going through her own problems with growing up and she had begun to rebel. She had had no father figure for almost two years, so our house was more like a battleground than a home. She was going to our local school where her teacher was a born-again Christian as was her daughter who was one of Lisa's best friends. She also went along to the youth club which met at our local church.

Then one evening Lisa attended a house-church. She came home and said she had given her heart to the Lord Jesus! We didn't know what on earth she was on about! A few weeks later she came home and told us that in the church she was going to, people were speaking in tongues! That was it! We thought she had got involved with some sort of fanatical cult.

We needed answers to the questions that were going on in our minds, but where could we go? We contacted David, the father of one of Lisa's friends, who was also a deacon at the local church. He said that he would like to come round and a have a chat with us about the house-church that she was going to. He told us that what Lisa was experiencing was all in the Bible and it was all OK. After that evening David started to visit us regularly. He also used to come into the hospital to visit me when I was having small operations on my legs. The evenings always ended with us talking about God, Jesus and the Holy Spirit. He would also pray for us on these occasions.

Troubles Traced to Ouija Board

After several visits David felt that a lot of our troubles could be due to our past experiences with the occult. We had had many dodgy experiences with ouija boards which David knew nothing about. When he prayed for my wife and I we felt a physical shiver run through the both of us. We were later led to renounce our connections with the occult and to destroy articles which had been used in seances.

One Sunday Lisa was going to be singing at the church and we had an invitation to go along to hear. We felt a bit like fish out of water when we arrived, but we did enjoy hearing our daughter sing. We were then invited to the evening service where there were to be a couple of full immersion baptisms. Along we went. The only time I had ever been to church was for weddings, funerals and the occasional christening, yet here I was going twice on a Sunday. Was I becoming a Holy Joe?!

There was a young lady being baptised and what she said made such an impact on me. She said that Jesus Christ was the most exciting man she had ever met! As she was baptised it was as though someone had punched me in the face – I just went all weak at the knees and I looked at my wife and she was the same – what on earth was going on?

This was the time we met pastor Paul Rigden Green. He was a little man with a big heart and had so much love – Jesus just radiated from him. It was this man who taught me the real meaning of love. He asked if he could come round and have a chat with my wife and I. We readily agreed.

After a few visits he asked us if we wanted to make a commitment to Jesus. We both shouted YES!! as though somebody had said it through us. We thought we were just going to say an Our Father type of prayer, but the pastor led us in a prayer to give our hearts to the Lord Jesus.

Lisa came home shortly after this and when the pastor told her, both she and the pastor began to cry. We thought what's the matter with them! The next morning my wife went off to work: remember up until now we had lost all love for each other and were in the pits, yet on this day both of us had such joy it was hard to describe. I was still in terrible pain unable to move more that a couple of steps yet it was as if a great weight had been lifted.

Since that day a great deal has happened to us but we have never looked back but gone on with Jesus. Today our marriage is fantastic! A precious, beautiful thing that only Jesus could repair.

Mrs Jang's Story

Mrs Jang lived in the city of Wand Kia Kwan Dswang. Her husband had accepted Christ and wished his wife to learn the truths of Christianity. In deference to her husband, she attended Miss Vaughan's class for women. So unintelligent was the pupil that it seemed impossible to teach her enough gospel truth to save her soul. Miss Vaughan's reliance was on God's power and faithfulness to fulfil his promise in John 14:13–14. After four days of simple instruction, Mrs Jang was gloriously converted and returned to her home, a new creature in Christ Jesus. About six months later she contracted tuberculosis; her pain was also spiritual because of the unbelief of her family, who persecuted her bitterly. But amidst her trials Mrs Jang maintained a bright testimony for Christ.

Miss Vaughan made what she fully thought was her last visit to the dying woman. The next morning Mrs Jang's father called in to see Miss Vaughan. He was very excited and exclaimed, 'The Lord has performed a wonderful miracle. She is alive again!'

Mrs Jang had died at 3 o'clock. They had immediately prepared her body for burial. At about sunset they heard a noise in the death chamber. When they opened the door they could hardly believe their eyes. Mrs Jang sat erect on the kang. She had removed her grave clothes and put on those she had been wearing before her death.

The story related afterwards by Mrs Jang to Miss Vaughan was all the more remarkable because the missionary had never taught the ignorant women anything about the book of Revelation and the glories of heaven. She had received only eight days instruction in her life. This was Mrs Jang's story:

I remember seeing all the family around me crying. Then the Lord Jesus came into my room and took me by the hand and said, 'Come with me.' In a short time we were before a gate of pearl. It was the gate of heaven. Angels opened it and we went in. I saw many beautiful houses, all of pretty colours. I walked beside the Lord on the golden streets and oh, Miss Vaughan, I was so glad you had told me to unbind my feet. I would have been so ashamed to walk beside my Saviour with little feet. Then we went on and I saw thousands of angels in a circle, singing and playing lovely music. In the midst was the throne of glory. The heavenly Father sat upon it and when I saw him I was afraid. I hardly dared to lift my eyes. 'You have come,' he said. I answered, 'Yes, Lord.' Then he said, 'You may go back for a while but you must return to me here on the twelfth of the month.' So, here I am and now they will have to accept my testimony, for I have walked on the golden streets and I have seen the Father.

And believe they did. People flocked in from miles around to see and hear Mrs Jang. Her testimony was irresistible. The power of the Holy Spirit was upon it and hundreds of people were converted. After her miraculous return from death, Mrs Jang waited peacefully for the twelfth of the following month when she said the Lord would take her back to heaven. When that day came the family tried to persuade her that she had made a mistake about the date. But her eager trusting heart was not to be deceived. Late in the afternoon she asked her mother for her grave clothes. Under strong protest they were folded and put on the bed. At sunset, while the family were at their evening meal in an adjoining room, she dressed herself quietly in her burial garment, then lay down and her beautiful soul went back to her God.

The influence of that miracle lived on. Even years afterwards, missionaries in that vicinity found an eager response to the gospel message. The people said, 'This is the Jesus doctrine believed by Mrs Jang who went to heaven and came back to tell what she saw.'

John Naylor, Aged Forty

God spoke to John in a vision while he was in hospital in 1971. Previously, John had been a heavy smoker and drinker with a violent temper, a blasphemer with a tongue like a whip. It is a miracle that such a man became soundly converted to Jesus Christ. His one desire was that others should know the gospel.

An angel seemed to escort him upwards out of the world to a realm of indescribable glory. In this passage he was aware of lost souls without hope. Afterwards the nurses could not help John to interpret the vision but words remained impressed upon his mind, 'See Les Morris, he will understand'.

At Christmas, John was allowed home for a few days. Within half an hour of arriving home, John was speaking to Les Morris, asking him to call. When Mr Morris answered John's request, they spent six hours together talking of Jesus Christ and the way of salvation. It was plainly visible that John was already a changed man. God had given him that new birth and faith to believe the gospel message.

John Naylor became a witnessing Christian, attending Bethesda Chapel in Widnes. At home, John's wife rejoiced in the greater happiness of their marriage. She and their children began to attend services with John. Later back at work, John was greeted with surprise and respect as workmates saw a changed man.

Don't Weep for Me

Then there is the story of a Christian woman who lay dying on a rush mat on a hard beaten earth floor in a miserable mud and wattle hut. As was the custom, she was surrounded by mourning friends expressing their grief with tears and exclamation of sorrow. The dying women opened her eyes and seeing her sorrowing friends said, 'Don't weep for me. Jesus has taken my hand.'

With that, she 'was not', for Jesus had taken her to be with him.

Death at Birth

About thirty years ago, I had my first baby. It was stillborn. I was in labour from Thursday to Monday. When all was over, I was in a side ward. I had this feeling of being on the edge of something, I don't know what but, while I was on that edge, it was beautiful. I can still see the picture and smell the fresh clean air but not as real as I did then. I feel if I had gone over the edge I would have been dead.

My appendix had ruptured and then my body functions had stopped. My father was met at the door by a nurse's aide attending my body which was covered with a sheet. Meanwhile I was walking up a beautiful green hill following a radiant yellow light, a tall angelic presence by my side. We stopped outside a walled city. The gates dissolved and I saw a Presence, whose light flowed through me with cleansing, healing powers. Standing there I saw shafts of light ascending from earth to heaven, powerful direct rays beamed directly to the throne room where I felt the great light, the source of all energy and creative power. I saw prayers. I heard prayers. Then I observed one shaft of ascending prayer in the form of light and recognised the voice of my earthly father as he prayed a one word prayer, 'Jesus'. I turned back, feeling as though I was descending on an elevator. When the hospital appeared I felt myself drifting down to it and into room 336.

Then sunbeams were streaming into the room across my bed. In the centre of one sunbeam were ivory letters saying, 'I am the resurrection and the life. He that believeth in me though he were dead, yet shall he live' (John 11:25).

When I reached up to touch these words of Jesus, the sheet fell off my face and life flowed into my fingers and down my arms into my body. I sat up before my weeping father. Two days later I returned back home.'

We Held a Women's Meeting

'The mother of a large family lived in the flat above. She joined our gathering. She heard us singing and said that the hymn that appealed to her was 'Precious blood of Jesus'. She loved coming to the simple meeting each week and was happy to be allowed to help by taking up the collection. It was all so new to her.

One day her daughter came to us after the usual meeting. Could we, that is my co-worker and myself, come up as mother had had a heart attack and the doctor had just left and given them no hope. We knelt and prayed. The next day mother was sitting up in bed. This is what she said to me and I shall never forget it.

'I have seen the Lord Jesus. He has forgiven me my sin and he stood by a half-open gate and it was all surrounded by flowers. It was beautiful and you and Mrs B were praying and he was looking at you and I would have loved to have gone with him through the gate. It was beautiful. I have no fear, I have seen the Lord.'

She lived a further four years. Her family said she was now 'religious'.

A Twin Experience

A lady sent the following to me:

My friends, Eve and Elmer, were twin sisters in their fifties. Eve was ill in her bed at home. One morning Eve called Elmer in a most excited shout. Elmer rushed into her room and saw her with her arms stretched to the glory of her Saviour. The radiance of her face was ethereal. Then she had passed away. Thank God for such assurance. Elmer died a few months later in the same glorious way.

Kathleen

Kathleen had been brought up to go to chapel, Sunday School and Bible Class but had never felt sorrow for sin. After her marriage, a daughter was born. Shortly afterwards she had a dream in which she was shown how dreadful it was to die without hope and what a dreadful sinner she was. She also saw a most beautiful garden where peace and happiness reigned but only those could enter whose sins were forgiven and who esteemed Christ more than their dearest ones on earth. She knew she was unwilling to part with her husband and little daughter. She felt that if she were to die she would be 'eternally lost'.

By early evening she realised she was about to die and asked her sister-in-law to pray for her that she would be 'taken home'. She said that at last she was willing to go. Later in the evening, more relatives arrived and Luke 23:39–45 was read to her. She called each member of her family to her bedside and gave them good counsel exhorting them to pray for forgiveness of their sins and hoped that when they came to die they would each realise the sweet blessing she then experienced. She told them not to weep for her and that it was the Lord's appointed time to take her to heaven and they were not to look for causes.

After the relatives had left and she was alone with her husband, she continued to speak of the peace she felt, closed her eyes, sat up in bed, and with outstretched hands exclaimed, 'Coming, coming, coming.'

A sweet smile lit up her face. She held her arms high in the air and said, 'Beautiful, wonderful, praise the Lord, to think it is me, unworthy as I am.'

Then in a loud clear voice she said, 'Bless the Lord, oh my soul and all that is within me bless his holy name. Goodbye, goodbye, everybody, I must go.'

After a short time she said, 'I am not going yet. The Lord is not ready for me yet, we must wait the Lord's time, my lovely Lord Jesus.'

Then she saw people weeping around her bed, and she said that they should sing rather than weep because the mercy of the Lord had been shown to her.

She continued to say, 'Jesus has washed me as white as a lamb.' Then she pulled a sheet over her husband's shoulder and said, 'They are all arrayed in white robes. I am going to a land where there is neither heat nor cold. This bed is just like down.'

The rest of the night was passed in praising, blessing and adoring the Lord.

The next day she said, 'When I feel I am sinking, he puts his kind hands underneath me.'

On the evening of the next day, she spoke of John 4:29, also the story of the wedding feast where those that were ready went in to the celebration and the door was shut. She eventually slipped peacefully into unconsciousness and passed away.

The following Sunday the pastor spoke from Matthew 23:10, the account of the marriage feast. Later a friend told him that the text he had chosen had been the means of awakening concern in Kathleen's soul when she was quite young.

Other Women

I quote two more accounts:

'My mother-in-law was taken ill. They found it to be inoperable cancer, very far gone. Dad was singing with her one afternoon. All of a sudden she sat up, arms out, face shining. She could see the Lord. She fell back on her pillow, gone to be with him.' Such experiences remind us of Stephen in Acts 7:55–60.

'Mother suffered a major heart attack and while being taken to hospital in the ambulance in dreadful pain and agony, she just kept telling her Lord how much she loved him. That is how she slipped away saying "I love you".'

Men and Death

My husband, Peter, died of cancer in April, aged forty. Peter appeared to be asleep or in a coma for most of the time before he died, then suddenly he said, 'Lord, I've done everything; there's only one thing left for me to do.' And I knew he meant to die.

During those nights he prayed the most beautiful prayers in his own normal voice. A little while before he died he reassured us by mouthing, 'Don't be afraid, I'll be all right.'

Since Peter died, I have felt the presence of the Holy Spirit in a way I've never felt it before. I pray that God will continue to use Peter's testimony to convert people. Many are going to church who never have been before. Some have heard from others about Peter, a quiet man. Our God is great and to him nothing is impossible.

John Had a Vision

A listener's brother-in-law, John, aged fifty-eight, had a vision in October 1977.

He said, 'I was in heaven with Jesus and the angels and I was looking down on earth and saw an open grave with my friends and loved ones all around bathed in lovely sunshine. As I watched they were all praising God with arms raised to heaven.'

After he shared this vision with us, it was removed from all our memories. Two weeks later, John suffered a heart attack and the Lord took him suddenly. We discussed the funeral with the pastor.

'Shall it be a burial service or a cremation?' My sister said, 'Don't answer that, the Lord has just reminded me of John's vision.'

The Lord took control of every detail of the arrangements. The church was crowded to the porch and as the hearse arrived we heard clapping and they were singing 'Thy loving kindness is better than life'.

The Lord guided my sister and I independently to choose the same hymns, so we knew they were right.

The soloist had a vision. She saw John standing in sunshine on a seashore. Out at sea in a tiny boat tossed by waves was my sister Hilda. John said to Jesus, 'Is that Hilda. Is she coming too?'

Jesus said, 'That is Hilda. She is coming but there are many drowning out there and she is going to get more in the boat before she comes.'

Each time since, when one is saved we say, 'Another one in the boat.'

At the grave in sunshine as John said, we sang 'How great thou art', (and raised our hands in praise). My sister then told everyone of John's vision. The undertaker said to his wife, 'There must be something in this Christianity.'

John's sister-in-law and my sister were both saved as a result of that thanksgiving service. We had requested a gospel address as John was a lay-preacher.

Family Experiences in Old Age

Here is a collection of accounts from various letters I have received.

'I was with my mother as she lay on her back. All at once she half lifted herself up, stretched out her arms and shouted, "Wait for me, Ted [my father], I'm coming," and fell back dead to the world but alive in Him.'

Dr Shewell Cooper told me about the death of his mother. She was a very wonderful Christian. The family were gathered around her bed. She was lying there very quietly and very composed, very peaceful and then suddenly her eyes opened and then it seemed as if a door in heaven was opened and the glory of the Lord was reflected in her face. With an audible voice she said, 'I can see Jesus and he's brought Daddy too.'

'My elder sister had been in a home for a year and was desperately unhappy. She could not manage to smile at me, but said, "No, it is not possible," which distressed me. But as she died, though unconscious, she was smiling. My other sister was conscious when she died. She was no longer with me. Her eyes were wandering from side to side, everywhere, full of interest. Obviously she was watching the next world building up around her. It was very wonderful.'

'My grandmother passed away. After she died, my mother, her sister and aunt had occasion to go out into the garden into the midnight air. All three heard the most beautiful singing in the sky, they said it was past human voices.'

'My father's father lived with us and sought through life to serve the Lord in so many ways. When he was dying he would not keep the bedclothes on. My mother said to him, "Granddad, do keep wrapped up, you will get cold." His reply, "No, I don't want anything between me and the Lord, can't you see him? Oh, he's beautiful, he's beckoning for me." With that remark Granddad passed into his presence.'

'When my father's oldest brother was dying, he said to his wife, "I am in a most wonderful garden. I have never seen anything so beautiful, the Lord is there. He is picking the flowers. He is coming nearer and nearer, soon to pick my flower." With those words, he had gone to be with the Lord.'

'My father had a very unusual passing. Four years prior to his home-call, he had been desperately ill. He possibly would go within a week. During that week, he had a dream or vision at night that he was in heaven and he was looking for St Paul and he just couldn't find him. The following morning he was better and he picked up his Bible from the locker and opened it at Philippians 1:23–24. 'I am hard-pressed from two directions – to stay here, or to depart this life and to be with Christ which is very much better, but to remain in the body is more necessary for your sake.' When I saw Dad he said, "I shall be coming home." And he did. Four years later when he was again in hospital, we knew then there was no hope as he was in a coma. The sister of the ward said, "We just cannot understand why he just keeps smiling." But I knew he was meeting with those he knew and recognising them. About six hours later he went home to be with the Lord.'

'Three days before my mother passed away, she asked all the neighbours to come in together. They all stood around the bed. She told them she was going to glory to be with the Lord. She shook hands with each one and hoped she would meet them again in the glory. It was a very moving experience.'

'I was with my Christian friend before she passed away. She turned to her daughter and said, "Oh it's lovely, the pearly gates are opening." She peacefully fell asleep in Jesus.'

'Another friend saw her grandmother when she was dying. She said, "There's Granny, she's lovely, she's no longer old, but young." '

'In the Launceston General Hospital, Tasmania, the old city missionary lay dying. I bent over him and whispered, "Think of Jesus."

'He replied ever so softly, but confidently, "He will carry me through."

'I thought of the chorus:

Ask the Saviour to help you
Comfort strengthen and keep you;
He is able to aid you
He will carry you through.'

'A very old and gracious Baptist minister yearned to depart and be with Christ and often he repeated the hymn:

Weary of earth and laden with my sin
I looked at heaven and longed to enter in,
But there no evil thing may find a home
And yet I find a voice that bids me come.'

'During the Simba rebellion in Congo, Zaire, hundreds of Christians met their death hiding in the forest. One old man died surrounded by his pagan relatives.

As he passed away, their testimony was, 'We have never seen anything like it!' His eyes brightened up with joy as he passed away.'

'Old Fulani lay dying. It was clear to his Christian friends that he had only a short time to remain on this earth. The pastor called a few of the church leaders together and suggested that they went and had a time of prayer with him. They entered his hut and greeted him and explained why they had come. "That is good," said the dying man. "But before you pray, I have something to say to you. Have your prayer meeting but be careful how you pray. Don't ask the Lord to heal me. I have had a foretaste of glory and I want to go to be with the Lord."

'The prayer meeting was held and Fulani was soon with his Lord.'

'An old man was brought to Dr Moore who saw that he could not live much longer. He asked the doctor if he was going to die. The doctor evaded the question but, in an aside, he told the pastor who was present that the patient had not long to live.

'The dying man noticed and asked the pastor what the doctor had said. "As you are a Christian," replied the pastor, "I will tell you. You are near death."

'The old man let out a shout of triumph. "That's what I want," said he.

'He was taken back to his village and died triumphantly.'

An old man was dying in the village of Bopepe. He called for a hymn book and asked for the song 'My home is Canaan'. He tried to sing it and then prayed. As he said 'Amen' he entered heaven.

An old gentleman who had no faith but a guilty conscience, required constant attention and difficult nursing. He bitterly complained of his miserable state and the frustration in his home. Through the caring and help of a friend, he found peace, faith and forgiveness, making restitution for dishonest acts and his complaining attitude. Just before he died, he said, 'I thank God for my illness, without it I would never have had this peace.'

'When the time came for the father of my sister's friend to pass to his reward, a light illuminated his pillow, his face shone and he said, "Oh the light." '

'When grandmother was on her death bed, my father was there and told me many times that she said as her last words, "Thousands upon thousands made perfect." '

'My aunt wrote to my father to inform him of his mother's death. She had been present at her mother's passing who said that Jesus had come for her with a lantern in his hand.'

An Historical Account

Finally, we have a historical account from 1631 concerning the Moderator of the Church of Scotland.

He came down to breakfast and, having as usual an egg, said to his daughter, 'I think I am yet hungry. Ye may bring me another egg.'

But instantly after falling into a deep meditation and after having mused a little, he said, 'Hold daughter, my master calls me.'

Upon this, sight failed him: asking for his family Bible, but finding he could not see, he said, 'Cast up to me the eighth chapter of the Epistle to the Romans and set my finger on these words, "I am persuaded that neither death nor life shall be able to separate me from the love of God which is in Christ Jesus my Lord."

'Now,' he said, 'is my finger upon it?' and being told it was, he said, 'Now God be with you my children, I have breakfast with you and shall sup with my Lord Jesus Christ this night.'

CHILDREN AT DEATH

Out of the Mouth of Babes

On Palm Sunday Jesus was so glad at the praises of children. He said, 'Out of the mouth of babes and sucklings thou hast ordained strength.'

This reminds me of a letter we have received from a mother. She writes, 'I was interested in your answers to the death of a child as, when I lost my daughter of three and half weeks, I had great peace that I would see her again, but it never occurred to me that she would be any different to how I remember her. Can you tell me why you say she will be grown up?'

I did not intend to say that a baby would be grown up; that we don't know from Scripture. All that was indicated was that there was a higher degree of recognition than was humanly possible. It arose from the remarkable experiences of Rachel, a girl of eight years old. When she was dying she recognised her baby brother who had died soon after birth and whom she had never seen. It was her father, a vicar, who told me.

Rachel was dying of cystic fibrosis. She was a lovely radiant Christian who had taken Jesus as her Saviour a year before. Cystic fibrosis gradually makes it impossible to breath as the chest fills up with liquid. Rachel had breathed her last. The doctors withdrew the life support machines and sadly diagnosed her death. Her chest was flat and still.

As the parents stood sorrowing, Rachel started to breath again. She sat up, her face radiant. She was looking past her mum and dad and said, 'It's beautiful! Can you hear them singing!'

She then got out of bed and hugged her parents. For two whole hours Rachel described heaven and rejoiced. Her father said it was the happiest time of her life.

'What can you see, darling?' asked her father. 'I see Jesus,' she said. 'And there is my little brother.'

This went on for two hours. Then she hugged her parents, said goodbye, got back into bed and lay dead.

For Rachel to have recognised her brother whom she had never seen and who died at birth, seemed to indicate some maturity in the baby. At any rate, there was a recognition of personality which was beyond human experience. Jesus said in Matthew 18:10:

'Take heed that you despise not one of these little ones, for I say to you, that in heaven their angels do always behold the face of my Father who is in heaven. For the Son of Man is come to save that which was lost.'

Recognition in Heaven

Will you recognise your loved ones in heaven if they are saved? We ask because the disciples recognised Moses and Elijah when the Lord Jesus was transfigured. Just like the little girl aged eight who was dying and recognised her brother who died before she was born, and who had been only three hours old when he died!

You know there are things more wonderful in heaven then we ever dreamed of! Truly the Bible says, 'Eye has not seen and ear has not heard the wonderful things which God has prepared for those who love him.'

Let me repeat the details of that girl's death.

She was pronounced clinically dead by the doctor. All the life support machines were switched off. Her heart had stopped; there was no breathing. Her chest was still. Her mum and dad stood weeping. Suddenly she sat up in her bed. She started breathing. Colour flooded her cheeks. Her face glowed. Her eyes opened wide in wonderment at what she was seeing. She was seeing heaven, its joy, its light. She described the music and the singing. She saw Jesus and then she saw her newborn baby brother who died before she was born. Now for her to recognise him and for him to recognise her, must mean that there are ways and means of recognition in heaven beyond our five senses. This raises other questions which we will look at later. Will there be male and female in heaven? Will there be marriage in heaven? All these questions we will look at in the light of Holy Scripture.

But to return to the subject of that baby. There is a passage in the Old Testament in which King David said something strange about his baby who had died. It is in 2 Samuel 12. David urged God to spare the child's life. He fasted and refused food. He prayed. He lay face down on the cold ground and cried to the Lord. His servants tried to lift him off the ground in vain. Seven days like this and the child died in spite of it all. The servants were alarmed and whispered to each other, 'David will harm himself in his bereavement.'

'Is the child dead?' asked King David.

'Yes,' they whispered.

To their astonishment, David got up off the floor, washed himself, put hair cream on his head, changed his clothes and went into church and worshipped God. Some stay away from church when tragedy hits them. Why this, they asked. Note David's reply.

'Now he is dead, there is no purpose in fasting. Can I bring him back again? One day I will go to him, but he will not return to me.'

To David, heaven was so real that earth's sorrows vanished into glory.

3 **D**IVINE GUIDANCE

GUIDED TO AN ATOMIC TIME

As I walked through my home town of Kidsgrove, I was thinking about the word 'atom' which occurred in Paul's words about the resurrection. Why should the Holy Spirit have guided Paul to use that particular word? He had been writing that spectacular chapter about the resurrection of the believers which would happen at the second coming of Christ. He says in 1 Corinthians 15:52 that it would happen 'in an atom' of time. The word 'atom' actually occurs in his Greek which was the language he wrote in, but it is translated into English as 'in a moment'.

I said to the Lord, 'Lord, show me something about it.'

I felt the Lord say gently, 'Look across the road.'

I looked across and there was a library, so I said, 'But Lord, that is only a small local library with mostly romantic novels. They are not likely to have anything about such a technical subject.'

The Lord seemed to say, 'Go across.'

I crossed the road and entered the library foyer. The Lord said, 'Turn left.'

I turned left. The Lord said, 'Walk between those book stacks.'

I did so. The Lord said, 'Stop.'

I stopped. He said, 'Put out your left hand and touch a book.'

Without looking, I did just that and pulled out the book. I looked at the title and saw that it said *Greenwich Mean Time* by Derek Howse. The Lord said, 'Open the book.'

I did and it opened at Chapter 5 and the heading seemed to jump out at me. It was 'Atomic Time'. I was thrilled and said, 'Lord you are wonderful. Why, St Paul was right up-to-date!'

I proceeded to read the chapter. I had only a piece of card about three inches square so I wrote down a summary of information on that. I have the card before me now on which I wrote:

In 1972 UTC (Universal Time Clock) was tied to atomic time TAI (International Atomic Time). Clocks [are] operated by the Caesium Atom (133). World has adopted Atomic Time. Leap seconds – one to add in 100 years? From Greenwich Mean Time by Derek Howse, OUP, 1980.

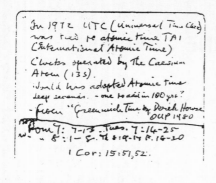

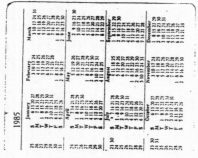

Figure 3.1. Author's notes on 'atomic time'
in answer to his prayer for understanding of
Paul's use of the phrase in 1 Corinthians
15:52.

So, since 1972 the world has been measured by atomic time. This is more accurate than Greenwich Mean Time and so has to have a leap second added only every hundred years. Atomic time is measured by the caesium atom by the revolution of atomic particles whizzing around almost at the speed of light. The time measured is called the Universal Time Clock.

You can imagine how elated I was at the Lord speaking to me in this way. So 1 Corinthians 15:52 literally says, 'Behold I show you a mystery. We Christians will all be changed in an atom [of time], in the twinkling of an eye, at the last trumpet.'

That shows the precision and suddenness by which our earthly bodies will be changed into resurrection bodies. God will implement this miraculous change so suddenly that it can only be measured by the Universal Time Clock in atomic time. And think of it! God has that atomic moment already fixed. Jesus said so just before he ascended into heaven (Acts 1:7). Wouldn't you like to know when it is? But Jesus said only the Heavenly Father knows (Matthew 24:36). Angels will come into it again. Jesus said that when he returns by descending from heaven, 'He will send out his angels again with a loud trumpet call, and they will gather the saved, from one end of heaven to the other' (Matthew 24:31). This sudden coming of Christ could be any time now according to prophecy that is being fulfilled in the world today. So why not tell the Lord you are giving him your life right now, to do an urgent job for him?

WHY I RETURNED TO UNIVERSITY

I've been asked to tell you, for your encouragement, about another wonderful way of God's guidance to me. People sometimes ask me why I went back to university to study the science of anthropology. It was because non-churchgoers were always asking questions about the science of man and the Bible.

Earlier, I'd had a terrific debate with a professor of geology through the local paper. This widely-read paper had given a whole page to it each time we corresponded and it ran into several weeks. Everybody agreed that the professor had been defeated.

I felt that I would like to look into the whole matter of man's origins and earth's history by taking degrees in these subjects. That was because a lot of well-meaning Christians had been making pronouncements upon matters in which they had had no training. I had no fear about it because I knew that the God of the Bible was the same as the God of creation. I had full faith in the divine inspiration of the Bible and that there was no need to be afraid of science, provided it was factual rather than theoretical. One had only to be careful to discern what was true evidence and what were theories arising out of prejudice or which were twisted.

I knew that as I was anchored to the rock of God's infallible Word, the Bible, all else would fall into its proper place. For the Bible itself states, 'Your Word is true from the beginning' (Psalm 119:160). It was *the beginnings* that I was to do research on. I felt called by God to do this and report back to the Christian public. There were very few Christians who had become qualified in anthropology and there were fewer still who could examine the connection between what the Bible said and what interpretation some scientists had put upon the skulls of primitive man. I knew there would be no conflict between facts and faith in God's Word.

This is indeed what I found. Science, and especially anthropology, had undergone major changes in their theories in the second half of this century. Changes which the general public seemed unaware of. Changes which were towards a more biblical picture. At the same time, there were some very intolerant Christians who insisted on certain interpretations, interpretations which the Bible text did not support. I suppose that an early example of this was Calvin, when he strayed into science. He insisted that the Bible said that the earth was flat. Well, Calvin's teaching on salvation was good but he was no scientist. Apparently, he ignored statements in the Bible about the round world; it was such statements which made Columbus sail west to get to the east. As St Paul said, we must 'rightly divide the word of truth' or again, 'Let God be true and every man a liar'.

It is important to be anchored to the rock of God's Word in order to ride the storm of man's shifting opinions, otherwise one would be blown about by 'every wind of doctrine'. So as I was sure of my Bible and was sure of my Saviour I knew that the storms of unbelief would blow themselves out.

First Impressions – Brachiators

As I studied science, first at London University College and then at Oxford, I was surprised at the changes which discoveries had made and how out-of-date popular statements were. How often have I heard on the popular nature programmes such a statement as the following: 'When our ancestors stopped swinging in the trees and took to walking on their hind legs, the first step between ape and man was taken.'

I was surprised to find that for thirty years anthropologists had no longer believed this. The evidence was that our ancestors had never swung in the trees. The evidence was from two sources – biological and fossil.

Take the biological. Scientists had realised that if we had ancestors which swung in the trees (this is called brachiation), our arms would have vestigial evidence. We would have long arms and long curving fingers to grasp the branches – that is like the apes. But there is no such structure in the human frame. For this reason, anthropologists hoped to find man's antecedents by looking for skeletons with arms and legs of equal length.

Then there was the fossil evidence. It was seen that all specimens of early man walked upright. There were no such creatures as stooping ape-men. All the models in the museums had to be changed. In spite of this, books and TV programmes have shown drawings of a series of stooping ape-men. This is how the public get deceived. More recently, an article appeared in the *New Scientist* by Dr M. Pickford. He lamented the fact that increasing finds had not brought the much hoped-for ape-man links between ape and man. He said that just in that long period where we would expect to find ape-men fossils learning to walk upright, there was a complete absence of them. Consequently, most specimens of early man have been renamed by anthropologists as 'Homos'. That means, man. For example, what was once called Java ape-man is now renamed Homo-erectus. That means upright walking man. This specimen had been exhibited in museums for years as a half-stooping ape-man. When other specimens were found which showed they walked upright, Dubois, the man who found the specimen, admitted that he had kept hidden four leg bones which showed that this specimen did walk upright. He had kept them secret because they did not fit in with the theories of the time.

The lesson to me was that, although we should always be open to correction by facts, we should not abandon truth at the first challenge, as some have done. I remembered that God created me to walk upright in another sense – to walk upright in his ways. Isaiah 2:5 says, 'Come, let us walk in the light of the Lord'.

Flatheads

In the anthropological department of University College, London, there were cabinets displaying primitive skulls. Some of them had very flat heads with prominent eyebrow ridges. I knew that a few had been pieced together according to prevailing theory and were misleading but there were others in those cases which were whole and had not been pieced together. Where was I to fit them into the biblical picture?

There were a number of possibilities which you can see in my book entitled, *Who Was Adam?* One was that God had created earlier types which had disappeared from the earth. Had they disappeared in the same way that the dinosaurs had? They may have been wiped out by some calamity. There are several places in the early chapters of Genesis where this could find support and the archaeological evidence in the cave diggings would further support this possibility.

Another possibility was that in the Bible, God had only told us about our present human race which was descended from Adam. Why? Because *our* race had rebelled against God and the Bible is the story of how God planned to save it through Jesus Christ. It is not our business to be nosy about former creations God might have made. On essentials, however, it is sufficient that the scientific evidence shows that *all people and tribes on the earth today are descended from one origin.* Did you know that that is what science has found? That everyone on the earth today is descended from one origin? It is tragic that people are not told these things. The Bible has said that all along and even tells you their names – Adam and Eve. A genetic experiment has shown that all the races were descended from one woman, sometimes referred to as Big Mamma. Here is a report recorded in *Newsweek* in 1992:

> Genetic scientists are still reeling from their latest discovery . . . that every human being that ever lived is descended from the same woman [because only the mother's DNA is passed on which creates the machinery to supply the fuel which drives the body's cell mechanism]. The find that sent the evolutionists back to the drawing board follows state-of-the-art research on the placenta of newborn babies. Harvard palaeontologist, Stephen Gould, says that, however different we all look, all of us come from the same ancestor – there is a kind of biological brotherhood that is much more profound than we ever realised.

Genesis 3:20 agrees with that. It says, 'Adam called his wife Eve, because she would become the mother of all living' (NIV). See how accurate is the Bible account!

The Royal Anthropological Institute also reported two separate experiments. Two independent scientists had taken sample people from different tribes and nations representing the world. From their genetic fingerprints, it was found that everyone on earth today descended from one origin.

One thing science does not tell you is that sin also started with Adam and Eve. That is when they hid themselves from God. That trend has been passed on to you and me. We run from God until the love of Christ's sacrifice draws us to him. 'If I be lifted up,' said Jesus, 'I will draw all men unto me.'

Oxford and Evans-Pritchard

When I went to Oxford, I found there was a gracious humility in its profound learning. I still find it when I visit it for research purposes. Evans-Pritchard is acknowledged as one of the greatest anthropologists. He corrected the trend among many of forming an idea which looked plausible and then going out to prove that it was correct. This left the theorist open to twisting the evidence to suit the theory. He insisted on the empirical method which is to collect all the details from actual research and then form a conclusion, while still being open to correction by more discoveries. Improved scientific instruments have forced scientists to do this which has led them back to a more biblical conclusion. Many have not realised this.

As I am telling you about divine guidance, I'd better tell you how I got admitted to Oxford's Anthropological Department. It was 'by chance' that I was in army officer's uniform passing through Oxford when I parked beside the Anthropological Department. I felt the Lord nudging me to go in and chat with the professors. They said something to the effect that all postgraduate places were full, but they had a vacancy for an army officer which they were allowed to use in the physical anthropological section.

'We could squeeze you in, especially if you are a sports colour man, and especially if you are a rowing blue.'

I had to reveal that I was only a hockey blue, but that seemed to help!

Piltdown Fraud

The newspaper debate referred to above (which indirectly led me to Oxford) had been sparked off by the exposure of the Piltdown Fraud. Many today have not heard of this and so here are the details briefly.

The Piltdown skull had been discovered in 1912 at Piltdown in Sussex. It was widely proclaimed as an important missing link between apes and man. For forty years, plaster casts of the skull had been sent around the world as evidence of ape–man evolution. Any objections to its suspicious nature had been dismissed as irrelevant. Then in 1952, leading anthropologists re-examined the specimen. Why did they do it? It was because it no longer fitted in with the revised pattern of evolution theory.

Radio-carbon tests revealed that the skull top was only 400 years old and not the very great age originally claimed. Further investigation suggested that it had come from a Saxon grave, but the shattering revelation was that the jaw was that of an ape. So no wonder it was presented as a link between ape and man! The jaw had been filed to fit the human skull and the teeth had been filed and stained with chromate to make them look ancient and ape like.

A leading anthropologist, Professor W. E. Gros Clark says it was 'a most skilful forgery'. Intensive studies (initiated by the Department of Anatomy at Oxford University in collaboration with the Department of Geology at The British Museum) demonstrated quite clearly that the mandible and canine teeth are those of a modern large ape which had been faked with the most remarkable skill to simulate fossilised material. So it must have been done by a trained anthropologist. 'It had been deliberately faked to give it a fossilised appearance' *(History of the Primates*, W. E. Gros Clark, British Museum) and (*The Scientist's Library*, W E Gros Clark, University of Chicago Press).

This was not the only fraud by a long way. Manchip-White in the *Universities Library* refers to the leg bones which Dubois, a Dutch anthropologist, hid under the floorboards of his house for 20 years because he wanted to present the Java Man as an ape-man walking with a bent stoop. Manchip-White said that anthropology is characterised by a long suspension list of skulls ignored because at the moment they don't fit in with the latest theory of succession.

Experts on Archaeology

At both London and Oxford universities, I was fortunate to be tutored by the world's leading archaeologists, especially on Middle East archaeology. Professor John Evans gave me all the facts about the first farmers and how the development of the barley, rye and wheat began and how the domestication of sheep, goats and cattle began in the Middle East and spread to Mesopotamia, then to Egypt and India. I quickly saw the relation of this to Genesis chapter 2 where God introduced Adam to farming, which was not realised until then.

Professor James Mellart personally told me how he had found the next big advance in culture. It was the first Stone Age city on the Konya plateau, 3,000 feet up in central Turkey. This was dated about 6,000 BC and was a city of 8,000 people with specialised trades all carried out with flint and obsidian tools. I went to Turkey to investigate and quickly associated Genesis chapter 4 with this when Cain left Eden and built a new Stone Age city.

Professor Seton Lloyd told me how he had visited the remains of the tower of Babel. He rode to it on horseback. It was a dramatic sight. The great mass of solid brickwork cemented together with bitumen looked as if it had been struck by lightning and fireballs repeatedly until it was fused, melted and split into two. It looked like a tremendous iceberg. I read with greater understanding the account in Genesis chapter 11:1–9. Here it is:

> And the whole earth was of one language and of one speech. And it came to pass, as they journeyed from the east that they found a plain in the land of Shinar [now called 'Sumar' in Mesopotamia]; and they dwelt there. And they said to one another, go, let us make brick and burn them thoroughly. And they said, let us build us a city and a tower whose top is unto heaven and let us make us a name lest we be scattered abroad upon the face of the whole earth. And the Lord came down to see the city and the tower which the children of men had built. And the Lord said, 'Behold the people are one and they have all one language . . . Let us go down and confound their language that they may not understand one another's speech'. So the Lord scattered them abroad from thence upon the face of the earth and they left off building the city.

Every detail of that account has been confirmed at the many archaeological sites in Mesopotamia. There are thousands of bricks and the tower was built of baked brick and bitumen as described. There was also the mysterious sudden appearance of new languages – Accadian and Sumerian. It was Nimrod who built Babel and a hunter's tablet of Nimrod has been found. 'Nimrod was a mighty hunter before the LORD' (Genesis 10:9). Also, the dispersions described in chapter 10 from Mesopotamia to Europe, Egypt and India have been traced.

Yes, I soon found at university that you could always trust every detail of the Bible's ancient history and this has been recorded in my works on archaeology and the Bible.

The Devil Was not Pleased

During one lecture in the Anthropological Department of University College, I had an extraordinary experience. I have kept quiet about it for obvious reasons and I will not mention the name of the Professor involved except to call him Professor B.

In the lecture room there were about a dozen anthropologists with myself. It was not a discussion session and I was not saying a word. Suddenly Professor B went into a trance. He was obviously not conscious and out of his mouth a voice spoke. It addressed itself to me by name. It said, 'I will see that you suffer for this Pearce. I will see that a lot of trouble comes your way!' I sensed that it was the voice of an evil spirit from this atheist. All those present looked around in astonishment. They looked at me and they looked at the Professor who shook himself out of his stupor and continued with his lecture. Obviously the devil was not pleased. He was angry that I was getting information which I would use in the interest of factual faith – information to unmask the unbelief which Satan was spreading through the world. Satan's main objective was to propagate that strong delusion which would deceive many as the New Testament says. I am afraid trouble did come my way.

It also told me that Satan was blocking information which revealed that the Bible was accurate, even its ancient prehistory.

GUIDANCE TO A DYING MAN

Guidance stories are popular, but I rather like this one especially as it happened to me!

Have you noticed how some folk who have no contact with religion, suddenly cry for help? I was walking along a road in Peckham, London, when I felt a strong urge to turn off to a side road. It contained terraced houses probably built over a hundred years earlier, unpretentious working-class buildings of London clay brick, but in good repair and practical for those who preferred not to worry about gardening. A low wall a few feet in front of each house would hide a dusty privet hedge, sometimes clipped. Behind this would struggle a few flowers such as 'flags', as they were called, or irises.

Around this area lived a man whom I could always visit if my hunch did not materialise. He was a road sweeper who was a delight to call upon. He was proud of his job, too, because he always aimed to do it well.

'You can look around any of my roads,' he would say, 'and they're the cleanest in Peckham, because I do 'em fer Gawd!'

He'd wheel his trolley along with its brooms and shovels with a song on his lips as he shovelled up the dead cat and a few empty cans and, with a professional sweep of his curved shovel, would land them accurately into the deep trolley. He enjoyed nature too with all 'the good Gawd's sparrers an 'oppin in the gu'ers'. His cockney accent was rich. I felt he was a grand example of the dignity of dedicated human labour.

Whenever my wife and I went to tea with him and his wife, we would be treated to homely refreshments on plates brought out from the deep recesses of an old veneered cabinet, and placed upon a beautiful freshly-ironed white tablecloth. The white bread sandwiches too would be neatly and precisely cut. The repast would not be without music. Ted, as his name was, would seat himself at his old Victorian piano and strum out some delightful tunes with vigour. The two loose empty brass candle-holders would swing on their hinges and add a slight percussion effect embellishing his enthusiastic songs: 'Sally in our alley', 'Come into the garden, Maude!' and 'We'll hang out the washing on the Seigfried Line' would be interspersed with, 'There's an old rugged cross'. The piano gave a Winifred Atwell off-tune effect as it had not been tuned for years. This all added to the richness of the music. We would come away feeling uplifted by his cockney godliness.

The side road into which I had turned was near Ted's house. So, I thought, if my hunch didn't lead to anything, I could always visit him.

I continued down the road on the left side pavement for about a hundred yards. The road began to bend around to the right, then the Lord seemed to say, 'Stop!'

I stopped.

'Look across the road!'

I looked across the road and saw that one of the terraced houses had an old heavy panelled wooden door with a heavy cast-iron knocker in the middle.

'Go across!'

I went across and put my hand on the knocker and tried to knock softly, but the sound echoed down the hall inside. The door was opened by a slightly-built woman of average height. She looked at me, saw my dog-collar, and stood for a moment. I expected her to say, 'No, not today thank you,' but to my surprise she burst into tears and said, 'Thank Gaud yer've come. Me 'usband's in 'orspital dying of a cancer. 'E said "Send for a parson! I'm not ready to die!" 'E kep on urgin' me. Kep on, 'e did. Well I said I don't know no parson. I didn't know what to do. I came 'ome and screamed "Gaud 'elp us!" '

I asked what hospital he was in and what ward. It didn't occur to her to ask me in, so I wrote down his name and ward there and then. She then interrupted, ''E won't be able to talk – cancer's in 'is throat. They've put a tube in it, so 'e can breave.'

I quickly went to the hospital, and walked down the ward. His face lit up when he saw me. He pointed to his throat and in a harsh whisper he rasped, 'I'm not ready to die.'

I told him about the man hanging on the cross next to Jesus. How he turned to Jesus for help and forgiveness at the last minute, and how Jesus said, 'Today, you will be with me in paradise.'

I continued, 'So you see that man was forgiven and promised eternal life even though he believed in Jesus only at the last minute.'

To encourage his faith I told him how God had sent me to him, and that proved that Jesus was seeking him. You should have seen the peace which came over the man's face as he responded. At his funeral later, the story was told to those present, and many were moved to tears as they were urged not to leave things to the last minute but to enjoy salvation now.

GUIDANCE TO LAND FOR A HALL

Another occasion when I was guided by being told to look across the road was when we needed some ground upon which to build a church hall. The problem was that there were no open spaces available. All had been either built on or purchased for use. I was walking along the main road thinking about the problem when I said in my mind, 'Lord, show me where to enquire.'

Instantly I felt the Lord nudge me to look across the road. I did, and there directly opposite me was a large garage. I said, 'But Lord, I'm not likely to get any information from that garage.'

The Lord nudged me again, 'Go across!'

I went across and to the enquiries office. Behind the window was a very pleasant young lady. I said to her, 'This doesn't seem to be the right place for me to ask this question, but do you know of an empty plot where I can build a hall for Christian use. Everything around here seems either built on or booked!'

'Oh! Its funny you should come here and ask that,' she said. 'The manager of this garage was only saying to me yesterday that he didn't know what to do about a small field he owns farther along this main road. He's disappointed with the borough council. He gave that land to them two years ago to use for the municipality, but they've done nothing with it! I wonder whether he could take it back and give it to you.'

Well, as you can imagine, I held my breath, first of all at the wonderful guidance through what looked like a very unlikely place, and then at the remoteness of the possibility that a borough council was likely to give back land to a private concern. But as the Lord had guided in this way I felt confident that he would overcome the other seeming impossibility.

That pleasant lady arranged a meeting for me with her boss. He was very supportive and wrote to the council. When they replied he called me and said, 'I'm afraid I've a disappointment for you. The council say that they're not allowed to give the taxpayers' property away. Even if they agreed to dispose of the field they would have to sell it. So I suppose they would demand its full value, and I don't suppose that would be cheap because its in a prime position on a main road into the city. Moreover, its a four-acre field which could be used as a sports ground.' (Just what I want, I thought.)

The receptionist who was also with us said, 'The boss will go up and see them. He can argue the hind leg off a donkey.'

He looked as if he could, too. This he did and came back to me and said, 'They've agreed to sell it to you!'

He laughed, 'I threatened them with all sorts of repercussions bar an earthquake!'

'Oh! Jolly good!' I grimaced, 'But what sort of price do they want?'

He looked apologetic. 'They have to charge to make it a legal trans-action.'

'Yes, yes, of course, but how much?'

A big smile came over his face, and he said slowly, 'They say that you must pay one pound!'

Later, I began to build a two-storeyed hall, with a capacity on the main floor for 300 people. The work was done mainly by voluntary labour. A flourishing youth work was set up, and Christian films were shown which included Billy Graham and Cliff Richard films that were attended by capacity audiences.

Figure 3.2. Picture of author holding plans he designed for Bucknall church hall which was built using voluntary labour. God's choice site cost £1!

WOMEN MESSENGERS

There are a few cases in the Bible where God used a woman to take his instructions to someone. One such woman named Huldah sent God's message to King Josiah.

I have one other case where a godly lady was sent to me with a message. It had direct relevance to a special project that I was on, about which she could not possibly have had any knowledge. She came to me and gave me this note written on a piece of paper: 'The Lord told me to tell you to read Ezekiel chapter 9 verse 3 and chapter

10, and to go ahead with what you are doing.'

I read it when she had gone and I could see its relevance immediately. Also, I knew that she herself would not know how the passage applied or what it was that I was doing. Without that knowledge the message would have no meaning. So what did this strange scripture say?

It said: 'One man among them was clothed in white linen, and had a writer's inkhorn by his side, and they stood by the altar.'

The statement then said that the man clothed in white linen with the writing materials in his hand was then to take the burning coals from under the altar and scatter them over the city. What did this convey to me, and to what I was doing?

I was at that time changing the Old English of the Prayer Book Holy Communion Service into modern English. Why? Because congregations had repeated the prayers in medieval words ever since Archbishop Thomas Cranmer had compiled them nearly 450 years ago in 1552. They were even older than Shakespeare! They were in beautiful grammar, but many of the words were not now in general use, and some had even changed meaning; for example the word 'prevent' now meant stop something, but its original meaning was 'open up the way'. Also for the modern generation the word 'manifold' meant a heavy cast metal distribution pipe under the car bonnet!

In that Bible passage there were three items which for me correlated with what I was doing. The first was the writing implement called the 'inkhorn' so it was to do with what I was writing. The second was the reference to one wearing a white linen garment beside the altar. I was an Anglican minister who always wore a white surplice when celebrating Holy Communion. Thirdly, the altar of sacrifice in the old temple depicted prophetically the death of the Messiah for our sins, and this was what we thankfully remember during Holy Communion.

What was it that had urged me to undertake this task? It was that the Church of England had formed a liturgical committee, as it was called, to revise the Prayer Book services, but to my surprise they were merely revising it again into Old English!

So I wrote to them and asked why they were putting it into Old English again, instead of into present-day language?

They replied that many people thought it was respectable to pray to God in Old English, and that there was no hope of liturgy in modern English for years to come. The surprising thing is that this was true. Even most of the Free Churches prayed in Old English all around the world. I informed them that I was writing the Communion service in today's English and that there were about a hundred churches willing to try it out with me.

The Alarm Bells Ring

This rang the alarm bells. We were told that no unauthorised service could be tried out in a consecrated church. One vicar told his bishop that he was intending to try out our modern English service, but was told that he would be disciplined if he did. That was thirty years ago, of course. The Anglican Church is more relaxed now.

We noted that the service could not be tested in a consecrated church. Now only the two older churches in my parish were consecrated. The two new ones I'd built were 'only dedicated' churches. So we went ahead and tried out the services in the 'only dedicated' churches. These were attended by Methodist ministers and some Baptists, as well of course by Anglicans, and also by the ordinary lay worshippers. These latter folk were important because we wanted to check with them that they were comfortable with the everyday language. The enthusiasm grew until about a hundred churches were trying out the modern English including many Methodists and others. Then the *Church of England Newspaper* published the whole service.

There were some protests of course. Some thought that God should always be addressed in medieval English. Even in group prayer meetings it was customary to do so. Consequently it was very confusing. A young man who'd become a believer would be astonished to find he had to learn a new language, and his attempts would be something like this: 'O Lord, cantest thou not 'elp me right speedily t'morrer I beseechest Thee, for verily without Thy succour I cantest not do Thee laudable service.'

It is surprising to see that even the first edition of the Revised Standard Version of the Bible in modern English switched back to old English when it translated a prayer of one of the characters in the story (Hezekiah). This was quite unjustifiable as there is no change in the original language (2 Kings 20).

Within two years of saying that there was no hope of a service in modern English, the Commission were trying their first experiments in it, and they were graciously using some of our ideas. For example:

- The parts spoken by the congregation were put in bold type.
- That a member of the congregation could take the prayers.
- That a response could be made after each main subject.
- That a lay person could read the lessons.

This participation by people in the congregation is important and scriptural and has now become a feature of the new services.

I was told that our service was the first to appear in modern English in the Anglican Church, and even churches which did not use printed services began to realise that God could understand those who talked to him in their contemporary tongue. We felt that it was important to be pioneers so that only the biblical teaching should feature in it, such as the fully complete atonement by Christ which would assure the believer that he was completely saved.

When the first efforts of the Commission were printed, we found that reference to Christ's second coming was omitted. We pointed this out and so the words 'Christ shall come again' were added.

One of the few evangelicals who were on the Commission was Colin Buchanan whose worthy guidance was acknowledged by making him a bishop.

As I write, another Commission is making a further revision. We pray that they will be entirely guided by biblical doctrine.

Messenger Unknown

I've had second thoughts about that lady messenger – the one who brought me the passage of Scripture which encouraged me to go ahead with putting the Holy Communion service into modern English.

So what was my second thought? Well, she was quite unknown to me. Where did she come from? I assumed that she'd come from one of my daughter churches. There were very earnest groups of praying people among them who waited very sensitively on the guidance of the Holy Spirit.

It turned out to be an important stage in the history of the Church and that would justify special guidance. The Liturgical Commissioners were still putting their revision into Old English, and some were trying to re-introduce some of the unscriptural errors which had been removed at the Reformation. It was important that not only should an out-of-date archaic appearance be removed from worship, but also that the modern English should express all the glorious truth of joy in the full salvation of the cross for every one who believed.

So who could that messenger have been? Perhaps we're overstepping our curiosity.

The following chapter deals with miracles involving divine guidance other than through angels and visions.

4   GUIDANCE BY AN GAUDIBLE VOICE

Sometimes we hear of people being guided by a voice. Several people have written to me telling me of their experience when they heard that I was making broadcasts and writing another book. Most of them had not shared their story with anyone else, perhaps because they thought they would not be believed.

The stories vary. Some we'd feel could happen to anybody – which is comforting. Others? Well they're out of this world as you'll see.

VOICE AVOIDS ACCIDENT

A gentleman who did not know that I was writing on the subject must have been guided to send me his little experience. Incidentally he was not usually given to such experiences. Here is his story:

> I retired almost seventeen years ago from the British Ceramic Research Association, a Fellow of both the Institute of Ceramics and the Institute of Energy.
>
> This experience occurred about 1970 when I was assessing the change from coal to liquid petroleum gas in the firing of building bricks on a plant near Birmingham airport. My friend and I had finished for the day and were travelling home in my car on the A446. We were on a long straight stretch of road approaching a roundabout when a voice inside myself (!) told me very distinctly to hug the roundabout. I thought, 'What is happening? Am I going a bit loopy? Who is telling me how to drive my car?'
>
> I looked immediately in my mirror to detect some reason why I should obey, but there was no evidence of any vehicle anywhere behind. Nothing could be seen through the rear side window. There was no traffic visible in the side roads at the roundabout which I was told to hug. Should I take notice of the interior voice? It had been as clear as though someone was behind me in the car. I had to decide quickly. I remember thinking, 'Well, I don't understand, but perhaps I ought to obey the voice!'
>
> Thank God I did! For as we passed the roundabout a motor cyclist shot past my left side at great speed and away up the road I was due to follow. Why could I not see him? It was because he was crouched low over his machine below my visibility level.
>
> 'My word!' I thought, 'You will never know how near you were to death, or at least to a very serious accident.'
>
> My companion said, 'Well Albert, I never saw that chap. He must have almost brushed your car and he was bending so low that we could not see him!'

Urge to Go Back Home

A case of how calamity was avoided by hearing a voice was sent to me by a lady.

Eight years ago she lived in a suburban area of a large English city in a small building of six flats. One mid-morning she went out to post a letter. It was a beautiful sunny October day. The air was fresh and clean, so after mailing the letter she thought of walking into town. It would have been a lovely half-hour walk along a beautiful road. The autumn leaves of the trees on both sides were beckoning her on to see the changing colours. So she began to walk, but it was then that she got the impression in her mind that she must return to the flats.

'What for?' she asked herself. 'Everything was all right when I left.'

She was reluctant to forsake the pleasure of enjoying nature's beauty. The morning was so pleasant and the air so pure. It was tempting to stay outside. She paced to and fro for a bit, all undecided. But the voice became more compelling, so reluctantly she went back to the flats. She put her key into the door, pushed the door open, and then in a moment she knew why she had had to return. She could smell gas!

'Having been in the fresh air,' she wrote, 'I sensed that something was wrong the moment I opened the front door. Gas was coming from one of the rooms and was leaking into the corridors. Which flat was it coming from?'

The smell of gas got stronger as she approached the flat of two elderly ladies. She hurried to their door and thrust it open. The two ladies were there, already drowsy in their armchairs. She rushed to open the windows, turned off the gas tap and began reviving the ladies.

Why had the other residents not noticed that something was wrong? She found that they were out for the day and did not return until the evening. If she had not gone back those elderly ladies would have died.

She concludes: 'How I thank God for that compelling voice and his wonderful deliverance. God only knows what further dreadful consequences there would have been if I had not returned to the flats.'

Nearly Ashes to Ashes, But For the Voice

Another 'home experience' incident sent to me concerns a near escape from burns.

I lived in an old two-storey institutional building, In the basement of that building were two coal furnaces, the large one for the central heating and the smaller boiler for hot water. It was summertime. The central heating was off. When this large furnace was not used the person responsible for both furnaces did not come regularly, so one afternoon it was my turn to fill up the other boiler with coal and dross.

The boiler had a large heavy iron lid on hinges which could only be lifted with a special tool to enable you to pour in the coal. As I lifted the iron lid I did not see any glow. Had the fire gone out? No, there was still a glow underneath the ashes, so I took the shovel and with it I poured small pieces of coal onto the ashes and topped up with dross.

The moment I took the poker to rake out the ashes underneath I felt that someone was beside me. It was a strange feeling for I didn't hear anybody come into the basement. I looked around but there was no one. Stranger still I felt that this unseen being was going between me and the boiler.

Automatically I pulled myself away further from the boiler which was still very hot. I usually bent my back to rake out the boiler but this time I felt as if some force pushed my head down as well and also a voice was saying in my head, 'Bend down lower still.'

I did, until my head almost touched my knees, and instead of looking up when raking the ashes as I usually did I still kept my head low. I started to rake. After a few seconds I was startled by an explosion.

It shook the whole boiler. The force of the explosion lifted the heavy cast iron lid which fell back with a resounding loud 'Wham!' Startled and shocked and very frightened I jumped back. I stood for a second and was amazed to see the whole basement fill up with smoke, dust and ashes, so I fled from the boiler but was amazed to see that something within the boiler was burning furiously. Then another explosion lifted the lid. Again flames burst out.

It was a close escape for me. Had I not bent really low, or had I looked when raking, the hot ashes and burning dross would have been thrown into my face and eyes. I shuddered to think how I'd have been badly scarred. When I think of my remarkable escape and of how the Lord delivered me, I thank my God for his marvellous protection.

A STRONG AUTHORITARIAN VOICE

A Madras Indian whose name must remain confidential tells of his remarkable experience which changed his whole life. At the age of twenty he joined the Madras worshippers of the Kali goddess. On the day he joined, the priest made him a devotee of Madreveran, and he was shown a big image of him. One day a year was dedicated to him and when that day came this young Indian would have the honour of leading the service of worship.

The young man was thrilled at the prospect, and he could scarcely wait for the great day to come. His parents were excited too, because they thought that it would win special favour for the family if he did well in his worship. So they took great care in making his fancy clothes which had to be exactly right for the occasion. Relatives also brought beautiful oleander flowers and made the garland he was to wear around his neck.

The great day arrived. The idol was moved out to stand under a big tree near the temple. The young man's gifts were all ready and he carefully took them in the correct order to the idol. First was a basket of assorted fruits as perfect as could be found, beautifully arranged. Next was a bottle of rum, then some cigarettes, a bit of incense camphor to produce sweet fragrance and lastly a large cock fowl.

'I presented my gifts one by one,' he said. 'And repeated the proper prayer appointed to be said with each gift.'

He could see his parents watching anxiously, hoping that his gifts would be accepted. The priests and people were watching too, for they had also gathered round for this initiation. What were they watching for?

They were watching for an ecstatic rapture which would possess the novice if the god accepted his offerings and the idol's spirit entered the initiate. So his parents and all the others waited anxiously, all eager for his first offerings to be accepted, and the sign of spirit possession to take place.

The young man had gone through all the preparations very carefully, trained by the priest to chant the right words with the correct inflection of voice; to bow at the right time. The young man said: 'I wanted to be accepted by the idol even more than my parents wanted it. I presented each gift exactly as I had been taught. I repeated the prayers with exactly the precise incantation. I bowed low, as low as I could, repeatedly before the idol. Would the sign never be given to me! I strained every ounce of energy in intense concentration, yearning for the ecstasy that the idol spirit would give. My eyes blurred as I gazed unblinkingly into the face of the great idol above me. Suddenly a strange wave of excitement swept over me. I seized the cock, cut off his head with a swift blow of my weapon and sucked his warm blood.'

An awed 'Ah-h-h-h,' swept over the onlookers. The sign had come!

The Ecstatic Dance

The initiate dropped the fowl and began an ecstatic dance around the idol. He whirled and bowed repeatedly and the more he did it the more ecstatic he became. He whirled on for hours, forgetting everybody – the priests, the people and relatives – everything except a strange wild, abandoned feeling. Then the ecstasy left him and he dropped exhausted before the idol.

The people cheered heartily. The sign had come, good fortune was certain for the young man.

He continued devotedly in his worship, and every year he celebrated his idol's day with the special ceremonies. When ecstasy was high he was especially happy and felt that he was very religious, and everyone admired him for it. Yet although he was so religious he said: 'I was a notorious drunkard, a gambler, a thief, liar, deceiver and fighter. I smoked constantly. Should such characteristics exist in a religious person? I wondered, yet I'd never seen anyone in our faith who did any different.'

He continued in his devotions and read as many of the idol's holy writings as he could. One Sunday morning he was in the middle of reading when suddenly he heard a voice. It was loud and clear and said: 'You must not worship this way, or read these books. You should give up your evil ways and live an honourable life.'

It was not the voice of anyone he knew and it was so strong and authoritative that he put down his book immediately. 'If I shouldn't read these books then what (one) should I read?' he thought.

The Little Book

Then he remembered a little book which someone had given him long ago. It was called The New Testament. But he'd put it aside. He had no use for it, because he hated Christianity with all his heart. Yet he couldn't destroy it. Something seemed to stop him. Now where had he put it? He searched around and there it was. He picked it up, blew off the dust and in confusion opened at the back instead of the front, and read:

> He who sat on the throne said, look! I make all things new, and *he said to me, write, for these words are true and faithful* . . . But the cowardly, unbelieving, sexually immoral, sorcerers, idol worshippers, and all liars will have their end in the lake of fire and sulphur . . . There shall by no means enter the heavenly city anything that defiles, or talks filth, or a lie, but only those whose name is written in the Lamb's book of life.

Then on the very last page he read: 'I, Jesus, have sent my angel to testify to you these things . . . Come, let him who thirsts come. Whoever desires, let him take the water of life freely!'

The young Indian's heart was touched by the forgiving hand of almighty God, and immediately there was a change in his whole life. He says, 'I was saved, praise God! Right then and there, I saw a new heaven and a new earth.'

Guess Who!

Somebody else also heard a strong authoritarian voice. You'll guess his name as I tell the story. He also hated Christians and was carrying them off in truckloads for execution. On one journey to round up some more he heard a voice from the sky. It called his name and asked, 'Why are you persecuting me? It's hard for you to kick against your conscience!'

I was on the road recently where the incident happened. It not only changed a man, it also helped to change history, for he dared to tell his story not only to many a fanatical crowd, but also to kings and even the most powerful world emperor – Nero the tyrant – who said 'Off with his head!'

This persecutor-turned-preacher had a story so powerful that he and his colleague wrote a third of the New Testament which was about another all-powerful man, a Man whose voice had spoken to the persecutor – from the sky.

Well, in more modern times there were two sceptical lawyers who did not want to believe that story of the voice from heaven, so one undertook to discredit the one who heard the voice from the sky, and the other set out to discredit the claims of the One who actually spoke from the sky.

They decided to be fair, though. Their investigation was to be conducted along proper legal lines using evidence and detective work. They agreed to meet a year later to share their findings researched from the Bible accounts and from history. Their names were Gilbert West and Lord Littleton; both were rationalists.

They met as arranged and shared their findings. Gilbert West said, 'I'm afraid things have turned out differently from what I expected. All the evidence fully supports all that the persecutor-turned-preacher claims.'

Lord Littleton replied, 'There's no need to be embarrassed, because my findings lead me to a similar conclusion. The voice that spoke from heaven was that of the risen Jesus, as the man who heard the voice claims. For a zealous Pharisee steeped in prejudice to suddenly change and join the ranks of those he persecuted, there must have been an adequate cause, which is that the risen Christ did actually speak to him. Moreover, he thoroughly investigated the eyewitness testimony of over five hundred witnesses as he said in a letter to the Corinthians (1 Corinthians 15:3–8):

The Messiah died for our sins as prophesied centuries earlier in the Old Testament Scriptures saying: That he would be buried, that he would rise again the third day afterwards as prophesied. That he was seen by Peter (Cephas), then by the twelve apostles; after that he was seen by as many as five hundred people at one time, most of whom are still alive as I write . . . Then he was seen by James. Last of all he was seen by me.

So who was it? Yes of course it was St Paul.

Those two lawyers put their findings into a book which is now stored in the Bodleian Library, Oxford.

THE VOICE IN THE NIGHT

The next story used to be known by everyone. Can you guess where it's from?

It's about a boy who heard his name being called in the dark night when all the lights had gone out. Actually some lights should still have been on. They were seven oil lamps which were supposed to have been on night and day, but someone had been careless and forgotten to keep them filled with oil; and now it was night. One by one wicks sucked up the remnants of oil, became dry, and flickered out leaving an acrid smell as the smoking wick gasped its protest into the air of the screened compartment.

The last wick had just flickered out, when this boy heard his name called. The voice spoke his name quite clearly but softly: 'Samuel! Samuel!'

Sam was in bed, but he sat up puzzled. He was not usually called once he'd gone to bed. In fact they were rather glad that he'd got tucked up, because he was a lively character full of ideas, and the elderly man looking after him, whose name was Eli, would sink back thankfully when he was left quiet at last.

You can imagine his impatience when he heard the boy call, 'Yes, I'm here!'

Oh! Don't tell me those are his feet I can hear out of bed and running towards me! 'What is it lad?'

'You called me!'

'No I didn't, go back to bed!'

So Sam went back and lay down again, but not for long, because before he could doze off, he heard the voice again, 'Samuel!'

He ran again to Eli, 'This time you must have called me! I heard you distinctly!'

Eli was feeling his age and his eyesight was poor and so he could only blink at the boy in the dim light, and he said impatiently, 'My dear lad, I didn't call you. What's the matter – for goodness sake go back to bed – and tuck in nicely!'

We're then given an interesting piece of information: 'Now Samuel did not yet know the Lord.' What did this mean? Was it that had he known God he would have recognised his voice? Anyway, he tried to go to sleep again. Then, would you believe it, there was that voice again! For the third time, he heard his name called. He jumped out of bed thoroughly aroused. What was going on! Who was playing tricks on him! Was Eli going barmy in his old age?

Sam ran speedily to Eli, 'I'm coming! I'm coming!'

He got to Eli's side: 'You did call me! I distinctly heard you – or somebody's voice!'

'Somebody's voice . . . Oh, I see.' It was dawning on Eli, the chief priest in Israel, just whose voice that might be, so he said slowly, in a low voice in laboured meaningful syllables, 'Go back to bed, son, and if he calls you again, say very reverently: "Speak, Lord, for your servant is listening".'

The mysterious voice came again. Samuel was awestruck and trembled as he responded. It was a sad, resonant voice which replied. It had some very bad news for Eli. Eli himself was a good living priest, but his sons were an utter disgrace. They had been made priests automatically because of the status of their father, but they misused God's sacred services for immoral purposes. God could not tolerate such a complete reversal of holy worship. Eli's sons were blaspheming God.

Eli had been warned several times but had done nothing about it. One message had been from a prophet telling the father to give his sons the sack, but he had not acted, so perhaps a message through this lovable boy would move his heart.

'Look!' said God, 'I am about to do a thing which will shock Israel. Both ears of everyone of them who hears about it will tingle.'

Samuel was horrified. He fell into a deep sleep until morning, and when he got up he went about his duties in an automatic, detached manner as if nothing had happened for he was afraid to tell Eli.

But Eli called him over and said, 'What did God say to you last night?'

Samuel looked down at the ground.

'Now tell me everything! Don't hide a thing! I want to know every detail!'

So Samuel passed on the terrible news, but Eli's reaction was not to sack his sons. He just resigned himself to fate and said, 'Let the Lord's will be done. Let him do what he thinks best.'

Soon after, the Philistines invaded. They captured the sacred ark and killed the two blasphemous immoral priests.

Eli was old and heavy being 98 years old, so when he heard the news he fell back off his stool and broke his neck and died.

That story is in the first three chapters of Samuel's book in the Bible and is over three thousand years old.

A Voice in China

While we're on the subject of hearing a voice, there was a case in China of a man who was ill on his bed. He prayed that his life might be spared. He was then startled by a voice which said, 'You will be restored if you go to such and such a city where you will hear of a new religion.'

Immediately he felt better, and set out for the city twenty miles away. He walked around and asked people, but nobody gave him an answer, not even a clue.

At last, tired out, he went to an eating shop and sat down at a table. Opposite him was a white man waiting for his food. When the food arrived, the Chinaman was surprised to see the man bow his head and say a prayer of thanks for his food.

'The man must be religious,' the Chinaman thought, and he bent over towards him and said, 'Can you tell me about a new religion?'

'I certainly can. It's all about Jesus Christ. He was a perfectly good and kind man who died for our sins so that God could forgive us and make us happy. God sent him down from heaven . . .'

'I've never heard about him,' said the Chinaman, 'so was that recent . . . when he came down from heaven I mean?'

'Oh no! That was over nineteen centuries ago.'

'Then why has it taken you all this time to tell us such good news?'

GUIDANCE TO AN UNKNOWN DESTINATION

How do you get to an unknown building in a strange town? (I met another man who had a similar experience to mine, so it's encouraging to see that we can all get help.)

I had been invited to speak in a hall in Colchester. The letter had the organiser's address, and as there was no instruction on how to get to the hall, I thought that it might be near this man's home. I drove to the outskirts of the city and found that the address was in a new private housing estate. I drew up outside the house and rang the bell. No answer. I rang again. Still no answer.

So I went next door and said to the neighbour, 'Do you know where Mr So-and-so is? I'm supposed to be at your neighbour's meeting hall, but he has forgotten to put directions in his letter, so I thought he'd be here ready to take me to the engagement, but he doesn't seem to be in.'

The neighbour looked surprised. 'Oh,' he said 'he left half an hour ago!'

'Did he! Well I'm here in plenty of time. Did he not leave a message? He must have thought that he had told me where the hall was.' I was dismayed. 'Well do you know whether it's in town or out in the suburbs?'

'I'm sorry, I haven't the faintest idea.'

There seemed to be nobody else around, so I said within myself, 'Lord, as you know where it is you'll have to direct me please. Help me to be sensitive to your leading.'

I became very quiet within myself, trying to be sensitive to God's leading. As I drove, I wondered whether he would speak audibly. The first turnings were in the estate itself, and I knew from experience how many turnings one could take on an estate, sometimes going around in circles and finding oneself in a cul-de-sac.

So I came to the first turning driving very cautiously. There wasn't a soul about to ask. What was it to be? Left or right? I felt a mental nudge and turned left.

There were various turns after that. It was the mental nudges I found I was relying on. Then I came to a main road where it was either into the city or out to the suburbs. I realised that I could make a major mistake here.

The nudge came – city centre! Then a T-junction. After that another turning – left or right? Then how far into the city must I go now? Not very far! Turn off into this side road! I turned off into the side road. 'That doesn't look very likely.' Stop, turn left! 'But that's only a side road.'

Nevertheless I turned. My heart gave a leap, I could hardly believe my eyes – there right in front was the building. The organiser met me at the door showing no surprise.

'Welcome! You're just in time! We're looking forward to great things!'

'Do you realise that you gave me no directions?'

'Oh didn't I? The leaflet must have fallen out of the letter. Anyway you're here – that's all that matters!'

PRAYING FOR HEALING

Of course many of you can tell of various ways that your prayers have been answered. Others have wondered why an earnest prayer has not been answered. You may be surprised to know that St Paul had that problem. Many of his prayers had been answered, but there was one to which God seemed to turn a deaf ear. It was about his illness. He doesn't say what that illness was. He just calls it his 'thorn in the flesh'. It appeared to come upon him suddenly at various times, sometimes in front of his audience, which was very humiliating. Some have suggested that it was a form of malaria. He could have been infected by the mosquitoes on his journeys past various lakes in Asia Minor.

God never told him why he did not cure him. He only told him that he would be given grace to bear it. 'My grace is sufficient for you, because my power is made perfect in weakness.'

Paul had pleaded with all his might for his healing. It was so ironic that God had used Paul to heal thousands of people, yet healing was denied to him.

The only explanation he could think of was that the illness was to keep him from getting too proud because God had given him so many outstanding revelations. When his pleading for the third time was in vain, he accepted what God said and rested in his grace.

I wonder what reason you might have thought of why God did not heal such a wonderful man so full of faith? And why God did not even tell him the reason?

To me this seems to be the answer: because of his affliction, Paul needed to have a doctor most of the time. That would be why Dr Luke joined him on his evangelistic journeys. Because he was Paul's constant companion, Luke was able to write a history of the first thirty years of the newborn church, called the Acts of the Apostles. Without that in the New Testament, we would have very little idea of what happened after Christ ascended into heaven. In this way also the task was given to a scholar who became renowned for his accurate history and meticulous detail, both in the Gospel, which he wrote mostly from eyewitnesses, and his scholarly method of naming the political figures in office at the time of the various events he was recording.

When Sir William Ramsay checked Roman and Mediterranean history, he found St Luke's notes accurate to the finest detail.

An Illness for a Purpose

This leads me to tell you about an illness that seemed for a purpose, and a prayer which was answered by wonderful guidance.

I was Rector of a very large parish of four churches, two of which we had built. All this made for a lot of secretarial work, but in those days parishes did not employ secretaries as they do now. The need had become critical and we could not afford to pay anyone full-time, so I felt guided to spend half a day in prayer.

I laid the whole situation before the Lord. To sum up I said that we needed a full-time male secretary who was able to do shorthand. Then I said: 'And who does not need a wage or payment.' I then added: 'Of course that last item – no pay – seems impossible.'

The answer came back 'Well, Victor, if that's impossible, why bother me!'

'Sorry Lord,' I said. 'I trust you'll do it.'

Next Sunday I had to take an 8 o'clock service at a church ten miles away, and then stay for breakfast with the church warden so that I could take the next service at 11 am.

At breakfast I found that the warden was very worried about his son. He said that he had become ill while he was at Cambridge. The months had dragged on and he was getting no better, and that was in spite of constant earnest prayer. He said that it was worse because he has nothing to put his mind to.

His next words made me sit up! 'Do you think you could engage him as your secretary? He types rapidly and can do shorthand, which is unusual for a man, but that's because he's trained as a lawyer and he has a Cambridge Bachelor of Law degree.'

A smile burst all over my face. 'Why that's just what I was praying for only two days ago!'

And then I stopped. 'Oh, but I'm afraid we have no money to pay his wages.'

The warden looked at me and said, 'Of course you haven't. I'll pay his wages full-time.'

He came the very next week. He was very thorough. All the files got put in order and letters got answered and business enacted. Because of this I was able to reply to the many people who wrote to me about their difficulties and problems, some asking about the way of salvation.

The letters about salvation were a big help to my secretary, and within three months he said to me, 'Those letters have helped me to find Jesus as my own Saviour.'

Soon he was the picture of health, and he said, 'God has completely healed me.' He certainly had. It was a wonderful miracle, and wasn't his father delighted! He felt he'd made the best investment ever!

5   PEOPLE WE WOULD BE SURPRISED TO SEE IN HEAVEN

Would you be surprised to see Nazi war criminals and Japanese war camp tyrants in heaven?

It is a hard lesson to learn that God's purposes are sometimes served through the destructive course of worldwide wars, as we shall see in the next chapter. Meanwhile, we consider the miracle of God's mercy towards some of those who were wartime tyrants.

SEVEN NAZI WAR CRIMINALS

After World War II had ended, twenty-two Nazi leaders were tried and sentenced in October, 1946. Twelve of them were sentenced to death by hanging, seven to imprisonment, and three were discharged as not guilty. I still have the newspaper reports and pictures which I have preserved all this time, some of which are shown here.

Figure 5.1. Nazi chiefs in the dock.
Source: Daily Graphic, *October 1st, 1946*

Figure 5.2 Twelve Nazis to hang.
Source: Daily Graphic, *October 2nd, 1946*

Also shown here is part of the report which I sent to one newspaper soon after the executions, telling of an amazing event. It describes how the prison chaplain to the Nazis witnessed Goering break down in tears when told of his daughter's reaction to his death sentence: 'I hope to meet Daddy in heaven.' Despite this, Goering ridiculed the Bible and said, 'Death is death. She believes in her manner, and I in mine.' Later he committed suicide with poison.

One Who Saw Jesus

However, this ultimate rejection of God's mercy was not the fate of all of the Nazi prisoners. One of them told the chaplain that Jesus had appeared to him. *He was one of seven who claimed that they had been converted.*

Such a report would be viewed with much scepticism of course.

Was this their final trick? Their final escape? A clever trump card to cheat divine justice? They were all well-known names linked with war crimes, cruel concentration camps, and invasions killing millions of people. Did they think it right that they should think to escape divine justice by claiming repentance and conversion?

The one who said he had seen Jesus was Wilhelm Crick, aged sixty-nine. He helped Hitler impose a reign of terror over Czechoslovakia, a ruthless killer who suppressed the Jews. Yet in the last minutes when the chaplain visited his cell to pray for him and then lead him to the gallows, he said: 'I've got something to tell you. Jesus appeared to me and told me I was forgiven. I believe the blood of Jesus has washed away my sins.'

The chaplain rejoiced – an extraordinary thing to do a few minutes before the man dangled dead at the end of the rope. For twelve months the chaplain had spoken about repentance and forgiveness, but Crick's response had only been cold legalistic phrases which might have been customary for one who was a Doctor of Law. The only sign of progress had been when he said, 'We Nazis broke a divine law in persecuting the Jews. By it we were doomed to defeat!'

What about the other six who claimed forgiveness? Were they just doing it to escape divine wrath? The answer came when I remembered that two of them were those sentenced to imprisonment and not exe-

Figure 5.3. The Goering story: newspaper article as reported by the author about 1949.
Source: Daily Graphic

cution, so their motive could not be escaping judgement. Both had a sentence of twenty years, and one of them, Albert Speer, went to live in his house in Berlin when he was released.

Albert Speer was aged twenty when sentenced to twenty years' imprisonment. He had been Reich Minister of Armaments and war production and head of State production. The greatest manager Europe had ever known, Speer possessed remarkable powers of organisation and Hitler respected him more than anybody else. He mobilised a slave labour force of eight million people. A friend of mine, Fred Grossmith, went to visit him in Berlin and found that he was still an earnest Christian. He said, *'I cannot explain the change that came into my life when I accepted Christ.'*

I was telling a colleague of mine at UCB about him and that even before he knew his sentence he told his chaplain: 'The neglect of genuine Christianity [by the German nation] caused the downfall of the Nazi regime.'

Does that sound like a warning to Britain, I wonder?

The other Nazis who trusted in Christ were:

* Joachim Ribbentrop, Hitler's Foreign Minister and at one time Ambassador to London, condemned to death by hanging;
* Wilhelm Keitel, Chief of the German High Command, condemned to death by hanging;
* Wilhelm Frick, Protector of Bohemia-Moravia, condemned to death by hanging;
* Fritz Sauckel, Director of Manpower under the Nazis, condemned to death by hanging;
* Baldur Schirach, Youth leader responsible for indoctrinations and helping to deport Jews, condemned to twenty years' imprisonment;
* Hans Fritzsche, Goebbel's assistant at the Propaganda Ministry, discharged.

An eighth converted Nazi was the lieutenant colonel of the SS who attended prison services as the organist.

Those who Refused

Then of course there were those condemned to die who openly refused to accept the mercy of Christ, and scoffed at the offer. They were:

* Fieldmarshall Goering, Hitler's second-in-command, and Luftwaffe Chief who sent thousands of planes to bomb Britain's cities, condemned to death by hanging;
* Julius Streicher, the Jew-baiter and publisher of the provocative anti-Jewish newspaper, condemned to death by hanging (refused to

attend any meetings with the padre);
- Alfred Rosenberg, the propagandist of Nazism and evolution, condemned to death by hanging (refused to attend any meetings with the padre);
- Martin Bormann, Hitler's former Deputy, condemned to death by hanging;
- Alfred Jodl, Chief of Staff, condemned to death by hanging (refused to attend any meetings with the padre).

Several other Nazis imprisoned for various terms attended services led by the chaplain but made no commitment for Christ as far as we know.

The Chaplain

But who was the chaplain who was used to convert seven hard-bitten Nazis? He was Rev Captain Henry F. Gerecke. It was his report that I received within two years of the whole drama. I used it to reply in a newspaper to a report published by Airey Neave, MP that we do not know what passed at these interviews between the chaplain and the men condemned to die. The newspaper printed a half-page article with practically all I had written with only a few sentences omitted, under the title 'The Goering Story – What He Told the Chaplain', by Victor Pearce (Fig 5.3).

THE NUREMBERG CHAPLAIN

THE UNTOLD STORY OF THE
LAST DAYS OF HITLER'S
STRONG MEN AND THEIR
ENCOUNTER WITH GOD'S GRACE

'How can a humble
preacher, a one-time
farm boy, make any
impression on disciples
of Adolf Hitler?'

Henry Gerecke

Figure 5.4. Picture of Rev Captain Henry F. Gerecke, American padre to Nazi war criminals in 1946.

Source: F.T. Grossmith, The Cross and the Swastika, *Word Books, 1984*

With six or seven of the other Nazis he had more success, as I have said, but first he had to deal with his own misgivings. He was an American and both of his sons had been killed in the war; should not these Nazis receive the divine punishment which was due to them? The Chaplain General urged him to accept the task of chaplain to the most notorious group of men that perhaps the world has known. In many ways he was very suitable because he could speak and preach fluently in German, and he had a reputation for helping hardened men. Gerecke asked for two weeks to think and pray about it. He wanted to be sure that it was God's task for him. He reminded himself that Jesus said that he came to save sinners; he welcomed the repentant dying thief on the cross and said he would be with him in paradise.

St Paul described himself as the chief among sinners because he'd killed or imprisoned thousands of Christians but said that God had amazing mercy on him because he had had a misguided zeal for formal religion.

Eventually Henry Gerecke accepted the task looking for God's grace.

There was to be a daily service in the chapel lasting about an hour, but attendance was to be voluntary. Would any attend? Gerecke visited each cell and spoke encouragingly to each lone occupant saying that God had a message for each one and asking them to encourage one another to attend. Alfred Rosenberg, the tall, slender philosopher aged fifty-two, told the chaplain that he had no need of his help, and he never attended the services. He had dismissed Christianity and defined Nazi ideology in a book, *The Myth of the Twentieth Century*, which had sold a million copies and had greatly influenced Hitler. It propagated racial purity for German races, and because of this, evolutionary theories – especially 'survival of the fittest' – operated throughout the war, and elimination of inferior races such as the Jews was just one outcome. He believed there was a Jewish plot to rule the world.

Two others who never attended were Julius Streicher and Alfred Jodl the Chief-of-Staff. But, surprisingly, Goering attended all the services throughout the year during the time the trial was going on. He was heard to whisper that attendance could help their case but in any case it was a change to get out from the loneliness of their cells. Gerecke was relieved to find that all three attended regularly. (There were others who chose the Roman Catholic padre, who are not included here.)

- Ernst Kaltenbrunner, Himmler's Deputy and former chief of the security police, condemned to death by hanging;
- Arthur Seyss-Inquart, Commissioner for occupied Holland, condemned to death by hanging;

- Franz von Papen, diplomat and Ambassador to Austria and Turkey, discharged.

As I said in my newspaper article fifty years ago, if such gatherings were not the strangest in history, to cap it all, the one chosen to join the prisoners to play the organ for the hymns was a lieutenant colonel of the dreaded notorious SS guards. Nevertheless he accepted Christ as his Saviour at the end of the year's services. The chaplain wrote: 'Towards the end of the series of services, this organist trusted in Christ, and took part in the communion service. The simple Gospel of the Cross had changed his heart.'

Twenty-two Signatures of Appreciation!

You may still wonder if the lure to the daily service was just to get away from the cell, but a beautiful action was taken which showed that this was not so. For these details we are indebted to Fred Grossmith whose book gives fuller additional information which he gleaned from his visit to Germany in 1984. See his book, *The Cross and the Swastika* (Word Books, Milton Keynes, 1988).

In his book, he records that after eight months of the prison services the prisoners heard the rumour that their padre might be called back to America. Henry Gerecke had not been home to see his wife for two and a half years and naturally both badly needed the reunion and rest, and Henry himself had let out a moan about their separation. Consequently, his wife received a most incredible letter back home pleading with her to let her husband remain as padre to the end of their tenure. The letter had on it all the signatures of the prisoners which today must be the biggest collection of world famous – or infamous – signatures in history.

The letter was composed by Hans Fritzsche and translates as follows:

> Your husband has been taking religious care of the undersigned for more than half a year. We have now heard that you wish to see him back home after his absence of several years. Because we also have wives and children we understand this wish of yours well. Nevertheless we are asking you to put off your wish to gather your family around you. Please consider that we cannot miss your husband now. During the past months he has shown us uncompromising friendliness of such a kind that we cannot be without him in these surroundings in which – but for him – we find only prejudice, cold disdain or hatred. It is impossible for any other to break through the walls that have been built around us, in a spiritual sense even stronger than a material one. We have simply come to love him. Please leave him with us. Certainly you will feel this sacrifice and we shall be deeply indebted to you. We send our best wishes to you and your family. God be with you.

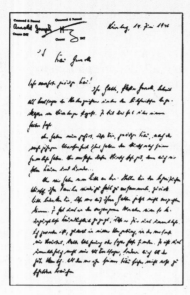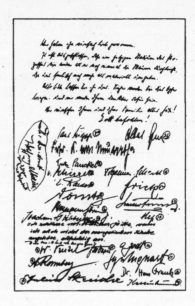

Figure 5.5. Letter containing 22 signatures of Nazis on trial for war crimes pleading with Mrs Gerecke to allow her husband to remain as padre during their trial.
Source: F.T. Grossmith, The Cross and the Swastika, *Word Books, 1984*

Amazingly all twenty-two prisoners signed this letter.

What had moved them to write in this way? Gerecke simply says: 'My congregation used to sing three hymns; we read portions of the scripture, and then gave a short address, closing with prayer. There was never any trouble or difficulty.'

What an amazing assembly! It was just as if the leading figures of a country's government were before him to hear the gospel clearly explained step by step, day by day. Most of the power figures of an important and talented country were before him to listen to the former farm boy who was now a chaplain. Most of them had degrees, had held high office and had exercised great power over millions of people. It was as if nearly all the country's cabinet were before him to hear the Good News of Jesus Christ which they had opposed and tried to destroy. Their faith in the gospel had been destroyed by Rosenberg's application of evolution, and by the German school of criticism of the Holy Scriptures, and now they came daily to hear the liberating truth.

Before Chaplain Henry Gerecke sat most of the former Government:

• The Chief of the Air Force, the Luftwaffe, Hermann Wilhelm Goering;

- The Foreign Minister, Joachim Ribbentrop;
- Chief of the Army High Command, Wilhelm Keitel;
- The Minister of the Interior, Wilheim Frick;
- The Director of Manpower and Employment, Fritz Sauckel;
- The head of the National Reichsbank and Finance, Walter Funk;
- Chief of the Navy, Erech Raeder;
- National Youth Leader and Governor of Austria, Baldur Schirach;
- Armaments Minister, Albert Speer;
- The Ambassador in London and Protector of Bohemia, Constantin Neurath;
- Chief-in-Charge U Boats, Chief-in-Charge German Navy, and Fuehrer succeeding Hitler, Grand Admiral Karl Doenitz;
- Minister of Economics, and Reichsbank President, Hjalmar Schackt;
- Propaganda Minister, Hans Fritzsche.

It is startling to realise that one day soon all the governments and cabinets of the world will be summoned to appear before Jesus Christ to hear their sentences when the Lord descends from heaven to settle the insoluble problem of Israel and Palestine. When he shall come in all his glory and with his mighty holy angels (to the Mount of Olives on the east of Jerusalem, Zechariah 14:4), then he will sit upon his magnificent throne. Before him will be summoned all nations and he will pick out individuals to separate them as a shepherd divides sheep from the goats (Matthew 25:31ff).

The rate at which Gerecke's audience showed response varied greatly. At first Von Ribbentrop made no response, resisting for a long time. He had been a product of the Nazi youth movement and had been brainwashed by their dogma.

We have always found that it is very difficult to win ex-members of Nazi youth to look at life from any other angle, let alone to consider Christianity. In their book of instruction they were told that they could not be a Nazi and a Christian, and the sayings of Nietzsche advocated by Hitler were quoted in the style of what Jesus said: 'Love your enemies and do good to those who ill-treat you, but I say to you hate your enemies and destroy them.' Hitler regarded Christ's principles of forgiveness as namby-pamby and weak; anyone practising them was inferior and not worthy of any consideration.

Very gradually, however, Ribbentrop realised that he had been misled by wrong propaganda, but when his wife knew of his changing attitude she threatened him. Gerecke felt that she was the most ungodly woman he had ever met. He discovered that originally they attended church and then withdrew. As the prison chapel services continued, Ribbentrop began to read the Bible until he became so fascinated with it that he read it every day for hours. He had progressed from cool indifference to a sincere Christian faith. This upset Frau Ribbentrop who wrote some very nasty letters to the chaplain saying she would offset all the influence he had exerted upon her husband in every way she could.

When the death sentences were pronounced the men were allowed to see their wives, and Ribbentrop pleaded with his wife, 'Have the children baptised, sweetheart.'

In the end she gave in, and later the chaplain heard Ribbentrop plead with her to bring up the children in the care and knowledge of Jesus Christ. For nearly a year he had heard the Good News simply explained, how the assurance of forgiveness could actually be experienced when a person was thoroughly sorry for what he had done and believed that Jesus had suffered the punishment for those sins on the cross. It was the Holy Spirit who applied that wonderful assurance. Ribbentrop could hold out no longer. He sought God's miracle of forgiveness and opened up his heart to Christ.

Sauckel the Slave-Driver First

Sauckel was the first to seek Christ. He was very burdened from the beginning of his imprisonment. In the main court among the evidence had been shown horrific scenes of cruelty for which he shared the guilt. He and Hans Fritzsche the propaganda minister, broke down in court and wept at the horrors projected onto the screen. He spent hours in his cell hearing from the chaplain how his guilt could be cleansed away. The Word of God was opened up to him step by step, and eventually he knelt down and cried: 'God be merciful to me a sinner!'

He gladly accepted a Bible and a Luther's catechism which he read constantly. He was a broken and changed man, but how could he alleviate the sufferings he had caused? He had a large family of ten children; at least he and his wife could bring them to faith in Christ and urge them to bring as much of Christ's kindness into the world as possible.

Sauckel was the first to ask if he could take Communion. Gerecke was deeply moved to see him take the bread and the wine which represented the precious body and blood which Jesus sacrificed for sinners like this convert – and for all converts, whatever their position in life.

The chaplain believed in hearing verbally a convert's testimony so that he would be quite clear about things. He would ask:

- Do you believe that you are a sinner?
  Yes, I believe I am a sinner
- How do you know this?
  From the ten commandments; these I have not kept
- Are you sorry for your sins?

Yes, I am sorry I have sinned against God.
- What have you deserved for your sins?
  His wrath, grief, eternal death and damnation.
- In whom do you trust for salvation?
  In my dear Lord Jesus Christ.
- What then has Christ done for you that you should trust in Him?
  He died for me and shed his precious blood for me on the Cross for the forgiveness of my sins.

Attitudes Begin to Change

Nearly four months went by and the chaplain began to notice a more earnest attitude among the others. The chapel services provided an opportunity for questions about all the important basics for personal salvation. A face-saving tactic by Doenitz was to argue about various aspects, but this seemed to be a cover to his own search. Others were asking for explanations about the passages of Scripture which had been read or spoken about. Fritzsche, von Shirach and Speer asked for a Bible each and a Luther's catechism to take to their cells to study. Friztche said he was deeply ashamed at having turned against the Church and was hoping to come all the way back to Christ. He asked Gerecke to list certain passages of Scripture which he should read in order to become clear and quite certain that salvation was complete in Jesus who had died for his sins.

Christmas came and fifteen attended the extra service. The story of the virgin conception was read in St Luke's account, and how it was brought about by conception through the Holy Spirit of God, just as it was foretold by God to the prophets centuries earlier. The scripture described how a very important angel told the virgin Mary how it would happen, and when it did the sky filled with angels singing with joy at this supremely important step God had taken. The unusual congregation listened intently.

Fritz Sauckel, the former slave-driver, stood stiffly to his feet and with emotion said, 'We never took time to appreciate Christmas in its biblical sense. Now here we are with no gifts or presents, but we have the only gift that matters!'

At the end of the service the organist played softly:

Silent night, holy night!
Son of God, O how bright.
Love is smiling from your face.
Strikes for us the hour of grace,
Saviour, since you are born,
Saviour, since you are born.
The musician played sensitively and tenderly; nobody would have

thought that he was once the colonel of the dreaded SS, callous, cruel and feared. He was a changed man now because even though he was not one of the prisoners, he had been deeply moved and changed in an earlier service which had told him that even 'while we were still sinners Christ died for us . . . While we were still enemies we were reconciled to God by the death of his Son' (Romans 5:8).

Figure 5.6. Cartoon of Hitler changing a cross into a swastika.
Source: Cross into Swastika? *Hodder & Stoughton*

'Stille Nacht,' the men hummed and whispered in German, and in spite of a closing prayer only one or two moved. Most sat still for five minutes or more with his own thoughts.

Progress

As I wrote in my newspaper article fifty years ago:

> Ribbentrop, aged 53, who was at one time Hitler's Foreign Minister and Ambassador in London, at first made no response, but later on the chaplain noticed that he commenced to read his Bible.
>
> Raeder, the chief of the German Navy, began to read his Bible zealously and would often come to the chaplain for help with difficult passages, and quite early in the course he asked if he might take Holy Communion.
>
> Keitel, the tough chief of the German Army Staff, asked the chaplain to convey his thanks to those who had so thoughtfully provided for their spiritual welfare, even though they were criminals. He could not keep back tears from his eyes as he said 'They have helped me more than they could have imagined. May Christ sustain me.'
>
> Many times a day the chaplain visited the cells of those who appeared to be making response. Field Marshall Keitel read and memorised many verses which spoke of God's mercy to repentant sinners. He selected a beautiful choice of Bible readings, hymns and prayers and read them himself aloud, so said Gerecke. 'He was unashamed to kneel at his bed and together with me make confession of his sins. Soon, he too wanted to be prepared for Holy Communion.'

The Lord's Supper

At the next Holy Communion service a small group took the bread and the wine, the sacred symbols of the sacrifice made by Christ once for all. Gerecke was moved to see those powerful men kneeling to receive the tokens demonstrating in their own hands that it was for them.

The chaplain had privately prepared each one, asking them, catechism style, if they had given themselves to Jesus, repented of all their many sins, and believed that the blood of Christ had washed them all away. The preciousness of the 'cleansing blood of Christ' came to mean a lot to them. This biblical expression was on their lips at various times. It seemed that their sins seemed so horrible to them that only the completely cleansing power of the precious shed blood of Christ convinced them that it fully saved them as the Scriptures said.

Counteracting Nazi Brainwashing

Nazi teaching has been called brainwashing because even those living today who were subjected to it find it difficult to break its influence. Among cuttings I have preserved I have found an article dated 1936 when all German youth were given the following anti-Christian and blasphemous list to learn:

1. Christianity is a religion for slaves, and stupid because it teaches the first shall be last and the last first.
2. Christianity puts Negroes and Germans on the same level.
3. The New Testament is Jewish filth from the four evangelists.
4. Before Christianity, German culture had reached a high standard which has been destroyed by Christianity.
5. Christianity has always been foreign to and at enmity with German unity.
6. The Bible is a continuation of the Talmud and has entirely a Jewish basis.
7. Everything that is against Christianity and racial mixture is good.
8. There is no Christian Culture.
9. Christianity is always unwanted and must always force its way in.
10. Christianity has spoilt the German because it first brought in the idea of sin (adultery, stealing) which was not known before.
11. Christianity is a substitute for Judaism and was invented by Jews.
12. The ten commandments are the expression of the lowest human instincts.
13. The thought of a world Messiah can only be imagined by a wicked people, because a good race does not need redeeming.
14. Nero was justified in his persecution.
15. Christianity has always hindered the development of medicine, science, etc.

Source: The Prophetic News, *1936*

Hitler himself was often making similar statements. He said, 'You are either a Christian or a Nazi. You cannot be both!'

Dr Robert Clark, the Cambridge scientist, wrote in his book *Darwin Before and After*, Paternoster 1966:

> Adolf Hitler's mind was captivated by evolutionary teaching – probably since he was a boy. Evolutionary ideas – quite undisguised – lie at the base of all that is worst in his book *Mein Kampf* – and in all his public speeches. In a speech at Nuremberg in 1933 he argued that a higher race would always conquer a lower. Hitler's hatred of the Jews was rationalised in the same way. The Germans were the higher race, destined for a glorious evolutionary future. For this reason it was essential that Jews should be segregated, otherwise mixed marriages would take place. Were this to happen, all nature's efforts 'to establish an evolutionary higher stage of being may thus be rendered futile'.
>
> (Quotation from *Mein Kampf.*)

Hitler's counterpart in Italy was Mussolini. He justified war by evolution and mocked at the concept of those who worked for peace, and in his public speeches he constantly used Darwinian catchwords. For him, those working for peace were hindering the evolutionary process. He said the reluctance of England to engage in war only proved the decadence of the British Empire.

A number of church ministers opposed such teaching, and said that Christ taught forgiveness, peace and happiness; but they soon disappeared into labour camps to perish. Hitler in reply would quote: 'Christ said, Love your enemies, and forgive those who insult you, but I say to you hate your enemies, and destroy them.'

From U-boat to Pulpit

The famous Pastor Niemoeller had the ability to withstand Hitler and even when he was put in prison, Hitler dared not kill him. Originally he was a U-boat commander but God called him to be a pastor. The popular *Answers* magazine of August 1939 called him 'The man Hitler fears' and in a full-page article said that was why he was in prison:

> For Martin Niemoeller has done no wrong, unless preaching the freedom-loving gospel of Christ is counted a sin! For two years he has been a prisoner of Nazi might. But all the forces of Hitler can't make this man pledge himself not to preach of Christ whose law is higher than Hitler's. And the Fuehrer keeps him under lock and key, fearful lest his doctrines of love and freedom should undermine the Nazi regime.

The Scenes at the End

As I said in my newspaper report, those condemned to death were allowed to see their wives for the last time, which was when Padre

ANSWERS, August 19th, 1939

The Man Hitler FEARS!

He's just a priest who wants to get back to his pulpit, but THAT MAN dare not set him free!

— By —
WALTER WHITMAN

It's more than two years si from his home, and they're s the whole Nazi machine ba bayonets, cannot force its gentleman, with no weapons,

I N the centre of the barb-wired camp the prisoners are moving round in a circle, watched by scowling, armed guards. Their faces all show signs of suffering and of that hatred which brutal and unjust treatment inevitably brings.

Except for one man.

He looks strangely serene and untroubled, and there's nothing of hate in his eyes. No, he seems gentle, kind, with that subtle dignity in his bearing which marks him out as superior to the bullying guards and the broken-spirited prisoners who surround him. Guards and convicts alike look up to him, hardly knowing why they do. *He's the man Hitler fears most!*

That's why he's there. For Martin Niemoeller has done no wrong, unless preaching the freedom-loving gospel of Christ is counted a sin! For two years he has been a prisoner of Nazi might. But all the forces of Hitler can't make this man pledge himself not to preach of a Christ Whose law is higher than Hitler's. And the Fuehrer keeps him under lock and key, fearful lest his doctrines of love and freedom should undermine the Nazi regime.

The Blow Falls

We must go back to the early days of 1937 for the start of the story. Crowds of eager Berliners throng the church where ex-submarine Commander Niemoeller boldly proclaims that Christ died for all; that all men of all races are of equal value; that Jew and German can be one in Him; that no State can set itself above His principles without ruining its people.

Warnings are given; the pastor must moderate his message or take the consequences. But still the services are held, and the crowds, eager to see

light in the midst of all the appalling darkness brought by Nazi rule, grow bigger, thousands devouring every word of the urgent message which falls from the eloquent lips of the Man the Leader fears.

Then, after a particularly striking sermon delivered to packed pews, Niemoeller returns to his home. Hardly has he entered it before four cars full of police dash through the Berlin streets.

"Wonder who's for it now?" say the citizens, who've grown accustomed to raids of all kinds.

The cars stop outside the home of the preacher, and fifteen sturdy policemen enter. They go from room to room, seizing every book, confiscating sermons and notes—anything which might help to sustain a charge of disloyalty against the minister.

Pastor Niemoeller before his arrest

lives into their hands, issued may seem fantastic," they organs of the Fatherland tu of Jesus Christ, but it is hap And what sort of man is t

Figure 5.7. 'The man Hitler fears', imprisoned in pre-war Germany for preaching Christ.

Source: Answers, *August 19th 1939*

Gerecke heard Von Ribbentrop ask his wife to bring up their children in the fear of the Lord and she consented.

As the solemn time arrived, Padre Gerecke went to each cell for a short time of prayer. As Ribbentrop left his cell with him he made it clear that he had put all his faith in the blood of the Lamb who took away the guilt of the world. At the foot of the steps he turned to Gerecke and said, 'I'll see you again.' His hands were bound; he mounted the thirteen steps of the gallows, and was no more.

When Sauckel's time came he was very upset. He thought he would collapse before the execution, and prayed out loud continually, 'O God be merciful to me a sinner!'

His wife promised him that their children would stay close to the cross of Jesus, and so he went to his death after a loving prayer and farewell with his wife and children.

Gerecke's final minutes with Field Marshal Keitel were drenched with tears. Keitel assured the padre that he was trusting the pardoning grace of God, and he added, 'I thank you, and all those who sent you with all my heart.'

As I have already said, when Frick's moment had come he gave the good news that Jesus Christ had appeared to him and told him that his sins were forgiven, and that he was trusting in the cleansing blood of Jesus. *A further example of divine guidance and mercy.*

One who remained deceived to the end by false science and false philosophy was Julius Streicher. He was the notorious Jew-baiter. On the morning of the execution he stood at the foot of the steps which led up to the hang rope. He made no reply when told to state his name, but marched up the steps, raised his bent arm salute, shouted 'Heil Hitler!' and went to his death. *God's miracle of forgiveness and salvation had been rejected.*

Disgraced but not Rejected

A very recent testimony of God's mercy was reported in the *Daily Telegraph* on June 10th, 1999. Jonathan Aitken, disgraced former cabinet minister, was sentenced to eighteen months' imprisonment for lying to the High Court. But while he was held in a cell on the day he was charged at Chelsea police station, he had spent five hours reading Mark's Gospel.

> This should have been a time of deep despair – the worst day of my life. Not so. For I had such an overwhelming sense of God's presence in the cell with me that I was at peace. However, I do not think I had fully appreciated the simple truth that being a Christian has little to do with external appearances and everything to do with internal commitment of the heart.

Aitken announced that he would be training for the Christian ministry after he was due to leave prison in the year 2000.

A CRUEL JAPANESE WAR CRIME TYRANT

In a condemned cell of Jehore's prison, Hayashi Sadahiko was talking:

> I was not forced to join the Kempeitai (military police). I was asked and urged to join. When I was first made to treat the men cruelly, I hated it. At my first turn of duty I loathed it. The second time, it did not feel so bad. On the third time I hardly felt it. After that I said to myself, 'They aren't people! They're just things! Things! I did not care what I did to them. Now I must die, and I'm only thirty-two years old. It isn't men who are punishing me. This is heaven's punishment. God cannot forgive me! I've been too wicked – too cruel – the spirits of the dead curse me! Yet I cannot die. The spirits of the tortured are waiting to pounce on my soul and tear me to pieces. I'm terrified of dying – but when will it be?

Miss Henty, the missionary, felt a pang of pity, yet he deserved what he was going to get. Why should he escape? Why should he get forgiveness from God? Why should she tell him how to get it? Yet that was her duty as a missionary. She was not the divine Judge. 'Return to your right function! Leave the rest to God – anyway he might not repent.' She rebuked herself: Did not the suffering Christ forgive the repentant dying thief while he was hung by his side nailed to the cross?

The Malayan jailer marched backwards and forwards in front of the prison's iron bars. Soon the half-hour allowance would be up, so Miss Henty commenced pleading to Hayashi to tell God that he was sorry – terribly sorry for all his sadistic cruelty, but there was no response.

How on earth had she been pulled in to deal with the case! This wasn't her area either – and not her job. There was supposed to be an Army chaplain somewhere. She'd come from seventeen miles away only to bring spiritual comfort to those emaciated shattered British soldiers, and to bring the Good News of new life in Christ to 24,000 Japanese prisoners who were gradually being repatriated back to their own country.

It was one of those British soldiers, a Christian, who pleaded with her twice to speak to the tormented tyrant and take a Japanese Bible to him. She objected that she was not allowed to. She had no authority. Even the governor of the prison was not allowed to give it. 'I'll ask God to make it possible,' said the soldier.

Then the miracle happened. She bumped into an old friend. In surprise she asked, 'What brings you here?'

'I've been made a member of the Crimes Commission!'

'Oh! Can you get me permission to visit the Japanese war tyrant?'

'Of course I can! But don't forget that his cruelty is notorious. The Crimes Commission are very unlikely to let him escape hanging!'

'That's not what I want to see him about!'

'Oh, I see, well you'll find him a tough problem! Do you really think you can get him converted?'

Well, she certainly tried. Three times a week she visited him and told him that Jesus had forgiven and changed the worst sinners. Look at St Paul for example. He'd murdered many Christians because he'd been deceived by false religion. As he said, 'I was originally a blasphemer, a persecutor and an insolent man, but I obtained mercy because I did it ignorantly in unbelief, and so the grace of our Lord was great beyond all measure. Loving and trusting me is typical of Jesus Christ. It is certainly true to say and to be accepted by anybody that Jesus Christ came into this world to save sinners among whom I was the very worst.'

But Hayashi continued to pace his floor in utter despair. 'I cannot sleep,' he groaned. 'At night this cell is full of those people I've tortured and killed. They seem to come up around me as if to strangle me. Sometimes I fancy I can feel their fingers tightening around my throat.'

Time was getting short. There were only three or four weeks to go. Soon he would be told the date and time of his execution, so Miss Henty pleaded and prayed with him. Then she remembered how she herself had been converted only two years earlier. Christ had appeared to her in a vision. Please Lord would you do the same for Hayashi? Please, please, would you do it?

The long night passed. With apprehension she reached the cell. What would she find? Would anything have happened? She entered the cell and there in front of her stood Hayasha. His face was glowing. His words were exultant, *'Jesus Christ came to me last night!' he said. 'I saw him, and he has forgiven me everything!'*

He told the jailers the astonishing news – three of them one after another – 'And I want to be baptised! Bring me some water! And my new name, my Christian name, is going to be PAUL!' So what St Paul wrote about himself being the worst of sinners upon whom the Lord had mercy, had sunk into his memory. It described him all over again! And here were the jailers bringing water rather like the jailer at Philippi.

Hayashi's last week had begun. He was to be executed the following Monday at ten in the morning, but surprisingly the week was a happy one. He had seen Jesus; he was at peace; he was ready to go. 'What a pity that I cannot live to tell others, but I shall soon have the joy of seeing Jesus again!'

The last full day before his hanging had come. It was Sunday. Miss Henty kept bursting into tears, so Hayashi said, 'You must not cry, this is a happy day for tomorrow I shall see Christ.' Next morning his face was radiant. Miss Henty was allowed only twenty minutes with him before he was to be hanged, and during that time Hayashi gave her a letter which he had written in pencil. 'I shall not be alive to tell others of Jesus,' he said, 'and so I have written this: *it is to Christians of the world.'*

Translation of the Former Tyrant's Last Letter

It is a fact that within this world of men, there is a world of God's Spirit. Those who do not believe this fact cannot understand it. These clever men of this world, men of wisdom in this world, are all foolish. All men have weak bodies; they believe death to be terrible. I would like to continue life's journey, giving body and spirit to God, never for a moment forgetting my repentance. In this world there are billions of men. All die less than a hundred years old. Only those who know God's Spirit, those who know heaven, only the Christians . . . see the Spirit of God as a reality.

They fear nothing not even death. It is the will of God that I should die at 32, but Christ is with me to the last. I am filled with joy. I know the happiness of death. I believe that my execution today is a punishment from heaven given by God.

Since I, Hayashi, have become Paul, I think like a Christian, my happiness is to become a spirit and pray. Although a man may live to become 70 without knowing thankfulness to God, he does not know even the preciousness of seven days of knowing God. Christians sing in church as larks sing in the spring, as angels sing. As you study my death you will clearly see that God's Spirit has been working. God has forgiven me – I who have sinned so deeply.

Moreover I do not fear execution. Through it I pray that peace may come to the world.

6   ANGELS IN WAR (THE FIRST WORLD WAR)

NEW LIGHT ON THE REASONS FOR SUPERNATURAL INTERVENTION

The classical examples of how angels have influenced battles, come from reports made during the last two World Wars. Many have read of these eyewitness reports. They come from military sources as well as from groups of soldiers and various individuals.

In case you have only a few details I will give you more later including new ones I heard myself. We will also consider why angels should have intervened, and if there were special reasons why God should favour one side in the war more than the other.

This is especially relevant to the two World Wars, because two important historical events arose out of them, and without them they might not have happened. What were they? A result of the victory in the First World War was the Balfour Declaration. This established a home for Jews in Palestine. Arising out of the Second World War was the creation of the State of Israel. These two events are still having their impact upon the world, and an even greater impact is still to come.

I will give you details to substantiate those statements, but initially it is obvious that if Hitler had won the war, Israel would have been wiped out. But is there any indication that it was God's intention that Israel should return to Palestine? We shall look at that too, but I only mention it at this stage because people find it easier to believe unusual phenomena if they can see a reason why they should have happened. When we look at events we begin to see that without divine intervention victory could never have been given to the Allies.

Hidden Mysteries behind the Two World Wars

This period of supernatural manifestations really began two weeks before World War I.

On Sunday July 21st, 1914, a remarkable vision appeared at Llanelli in South Wales. This was first described to me by George Jeffreys when I was about eighteen years of age.

I remember the details clearly, and they were confirmed to me years later when a history of Stephen and George Jeffreys was published in the book, *Seven Pentecostal Pioneers,* MMS.

George Jeffreys was holding a mission in Catford, south-east London, when he described how a vision appeared while his brother Stephen was preaching in Llanelli. Stephen could see that the crowd's attention was riveted in his direction but not at him. He was puzzled so he came down from the platform to see what the people were pointing to.

To his amazement he saw on the wall behind where he'd been standing, and above where his head would have been, the figure of a lamb. Then, after a few minutes, it changed into the living face of Jesus Christ as the Man of Sorrows, for tears flowed down his cheeks. It was a living face because people could see quite clearly his eyelids flicker. His hair was streaked with white so that he looked like a middle-aged man stricken with grief. Then it changed back again into the head of a lamb.

The lamb's head was alive and moving, then after a few minutes the lamb would change into the living, moving face of Jesus Christ again, the Man of Sorrows. George Jeffreys said that Jesus was weeping. Beautiful tears were rolling down his face and his eyelids flickered as the tears welled out. This indeed was the 'Man of Sorrows and acquainted with grief,' for certainly he bore our griefs and carried our sorrows, and the 'Lord had laid on him the sins of us all' (Isaiah 53:3).

Pastor Jeffreys had been preaching on the text: 'That I may know Jesus, and the fellowship of his sufferings.'

He began to appeal to listeners to respond to that love by forsaking their sins and receiving forgiveness, and during that appeal the face of the Man of Sorrows became enshrouded with glory.

An onlooker described Christ's face 'as most beautiful beyond description, kindly beyond words. And the eyes! They looked at you personally – those loving sad and glorious eyes which moved in the living face.'

George Jeffreys told us how long this vision lasted. It was not just for a brief time. It lasted through the night into the morning. Crowds of people came in to see it. Long after the meeting, it was still there. News spread throughout the town and hundreds more flocked in to see for themselves, and to hear yet another message from the evangelist.

Of course, some tried to explain it away. One man actually went to the wall and tried to wipe it off but without effect. So another man who was a painter and decorator took a cloth and held it over the vision but to his surprise the vision shone right through. Another tried to explain it by saying it was a hallucination caused by a flickering of the electric light. Stephen Jeffreys did not argue, he merely switched off the light, and there still shining out was the Saviour's face even more living and real.

Another thought that it must be that a bright light was shining through some sort of stained-glass window. Stephen tested this suggestion also. He had all the blinds drawn and so excluded all light, but that made no difference. The heart-rending vision still shone on through that night and into the day.

News continued to blaze around the town, and all kinds of people flocked in to see the vision. People of all ages and types – boxers, tradesmen, professional men, alcoholics and others with problems.

Little did they know that within two weeks the whole world would change for ever. The world's worst war would break out and hundreds of those young men who filed in to see the vision and had their doubts changed to faith would shed their blood on the fields of Flanders.

Even when the war broke out, it seemed to arise out of minor disputes. People in the streets were saying, 'It will be over in a few weeks!' It lasted four long years, during which millions died. Today one can go to Llanelli and see the names of the fallen, and among them would be a large percentage who'd filed past the vision, stopped to hear Stephen repeat his messages, yielded their lives to Christ and rejoiced in forgiveness from the Man of Sorrows.

Figure 6.1. War Memorial at Llanelli. Many of those who died in WWI would have seen the vision of the lamb and the Man of Sorrows two weeks before the war commenced.

I Saw the Zeppelin in Flames

As I write this account, the eightieth anniversary of the end of the First World War is about to be celebrated, but very few people will be told of the hidden mysteries which were behind why the two World Wars started and why they finished when they did.

Having been born before the First World War, I remember vividly, at the age of six, rushing to the top of the nearby hill with others to hear the guns of London fire salvo after salvo of rejoicing that 'the war to end wars' had ended and that the Armistice was being signed that very minute at 11 am on the 11th month in the year 1918. During the war, my mother entered me for a beautiful baby contest, while father was serving at the front in Mons and elsewhere with his Northants Regiment.

Figure 6.2. Author's picture as prize-winner in a pre-WWI beautiful baby contest. Caption reads: *Victor's daddy is at the front serving with the Northants Regiment .* Source: Mother and Home, *February 13th, 1915.*

Have you seen pictures of an early German Zeppelin? Heath-Robinson couldn't have designed one better! Air tactics were more primitive then. Still vivid in my memory is the sight of that quaint old-fashioned Zeppelin coming down in the night fog of London near Norwood. In the second year of the war it was intended to be a morale shaker. The bombs weren't very big. Indeed the crew merely lifted them out over the edge of the basket, to drop them upon the astonished citizens.

Unfortunately for Count F. Zeppelin's invention, a British airman in his army biplane shot it down. I saw it come down in flames in the dense yellow fog a little way from our backstairs landing window. I was roused by the shouts of folk in the house to see the sight. For me in my innocence it was better than a fireworks display.

On the whole I enjoyed the air-raids of the first great war, but certainly not in the Second World War, for then we were pounded mercilessly from the air by over a thousand Nazi bombers night after night as soon as darkness came and then when morning light dawned and the all-clear sirens blew their shrill sweet music we went out to pick the bits of bodies from among the rubble of what was once their homes. For part of this time I served as chaplain and then as vicar in a London parish.

In the First World War, raids were comparatively insignificant. I grew big enough to merit a pushchair and this was a source of wartime enjoyment because in the event of an air-raid warning when mother was shopping, the policeman would shout, 'Get into the doorway for shelter! Quick!' But for mother, the only safe place for an air-raid was home and as fast as you could get there, and so she would rush the pushchair over the cobbles at tremendous speed and I would go bouncing around like ice cubes in a cocktail shaker. It was great fun, better than a funfair crazy car, and by the time we reached home the air-raid would be over!

But as I grew I became aware of the great tragedies. Telegrams arrived at neighbour's doors and young women wept and names were added to long lists later to be chiselled into the cold stone of memorials in every village, town and city, and then one saw the newspaper clips of endless mud-filled trenches and saturation bombardments overseas.

ANGELIC INTERVENTION REPORTS

My father was in the first expeditionary force which fought in the dramatic battle of Mons, about which strange reports began to filter through of angelic intervention. Dad was one of the 'Old Contemptibles', so called by the Kaiser when he referred to Britain's small force of seasoned soldiers as 'a contemptible little army'. Dad wore a special medal on his chest.

When war broke out unexpectedly, Britain was unprepared, so this hurriedly equipped force was sent across the Channel. It was far weaker in guns and manpower than the opponents who had shocked the world by massacring helpless Belgian home-dwellers, but our army fought a dogged rearguard action as they fell back before the terrific impact of massed enemy attacks.

A big thrill was when Dad came home on his first leave, after the battle of Mons. I remember when he lifted me up on his broad khaki-uniformed chest. I did not know how many Old Contemptibles would never return.

Dad was surprised that the 'contemptible little army' managed to hold up the German advance during two days' fighting around Mons.

Those two days were vital, because the war could have been lost there and then. Those gallant Old Contemptibles did not know at first that there was more to tell about what happened behind the scenes.

The First Angelic Intervention

Individual stories and official reports began to filter through about strange happenings at Mons in Belgium. A lieutenant colonel reported:

> On August the 26th, 1914, the battle of Le Cateau [near Mons] was fought. We came into action at dawn and fought until dusk. We were heavily shelled by artillery during the day, and all our division had a horrific time of it. Our brigade, however, retired in good order. We were on the march all the night of the 26th; and on the 27th with only about two hours rest, the brigade to which I belong was rearguard to the division, so during the 27th we took up a great many different positions to cover the retirement of the rest of the division, so we had very hard work and by the night of the 27th we were all absolutely worn out with fatigue – both body and mental fatigue – but nevertheless we moved in excellent order and were not being routed.

There must have been a reason why they were not overwhelmed. What was it?

> I was riding along in the column with two other officers, and I became conscious of the fact that in the fields on both sides of the road along which we were marching, I could see a very large body of horsemen. These horsemen seemed to have the appearance of cavalry, and they seemed to be riding across the fields and going in the same direction as us and keeping level with us. The night was not very dark, and I fancied that I could see squadron after squadron of these cavalrymen quite distinctly. I didn't say a word about them at first, but I watched them for about twenty minutes. The other two officers stopped talking. 'Did you see anything?' one asked. I told him what I'd seen. 'I've been watching them for the last twenty minutes,' he said. When we reached the next halt, another officer took out a party of men to investigate the mystery. They found no one there, and yet the same phenomenon was seen by many men in our column.

The Sound of Marching

In the First World War, a soldier's wife received a letter from her husband, which said: 'During the battle I saw the angels all around. It's nothing short of a miracle.'

He then went on to describe how he'd been ordered to advance into a certain wood with his troops. On reaching the road, to his surprise, his horse stopped dead and nothing whatever could make his mount move. He turned to his ADC, but he found that the same thing had happened to him and to the whole troop. Nothing would make the horses move. The whole troop was at a standstill so they could do nothing else but return to their former position.

Later they discovered that a strong enemy ambush had been waiting for them along the road they were following.

The incident encouraged them greatly, but there were a lot of questions in their minds. Was it some instinct in the horses? They'd never experienced anything so unanimous amongst so many horses! Perhaps it was yet another supernatural intervention. Perhaps it was something like Balaam's ass in the Bible. The ass refused to go on because it saw an angel of the Lord standing in the way. Its rider was angry and tried to whip the horse forward time and time again and then the rider saw the angel blocking his path. The angel then rebuked Balaam for trying to twist religion to his own ends. If the war incident was similar then it was both horses and angels involved.

King David in the Bible was often seeking guidance. God told him, 'I will instruct you and teach you in the way you should go. I will guide you with my eye.' David was often in peril. On one occasion his country was invaded by the Philistines which threatened his very existence. David enquired of the Lord, 'Shall I advance against the Philistines?'

'Yes,' said the Lord, 'Go up and I will deliver them into your hands.'

There was a big breakthrough, and David destroyed all their idols and images.

But the enemy invaded again, and again David asked for guidance, 'Shall I advance against them?' This time God said:

> 'No! Circle round behind them, and then wait silently. Wait until you hear an angelic sound! The sound of marching in the tops of the mulberry trees. That sound will be the hosts of the Lord marching out before you. That will be the signal. The moment you hear that you must act promptly and burst out onto the enemy!'

David did and avoided a trap. He routed the invaders and pushed them out of the country.

Newspaper Reports

Reports began to come into the newspapers. The *Observer* of August 22nd, 1915, said that a nurse in a military hospital was told by a soldier that at a critical period in the retreat from Mons, a luminous angel with outstretched wings came between the Germans and themselves. At that moment the onslaught of the enemy slackened. Unable to credit the story she discussed it with a group of officers. A colonel looked

up and said: 'Young lady, the thing happened! You need not be incred-
ulous. *I saw it myself!*'

Confirmation also came from the enemy. In a Berlin newspaper it
was also reported on July 28th, 1915, that a regiment which was
ordered to do a certain duty in battle was censured for failing to carry
out certain orders. They reported that they did attempt to charge forward but were absolutely powerless. Why? Because *their horses
turned sharply round and fled like the wind* and nothing could stop
them.

A German lieutenant, a prisoner in British hands, said:

> I only know that we were charging full on the British at a certain place,
> and in a moment we were stopped. It was like going at full speed and
> being pulled up suddenly as if on a precipice, but there was no precipice
> there, nothing at all, only *our horses swerved round and fled. We could do
> nothing.*

Pax, a correspondent of *Light* dated July 10th, 1915 was enquiring
into the many stories of the visions at the battle front, which were
widely circulating. He quoted the following from an artilleryman: and
they absolutely vouch for the truth of it.

> Two English nurses at a hospital at St Germain-en-Laye, Paris, stated that
> the accounts were not only implicitly believed, but were absolutely known
> to be true . . . 'No French newspaper,' she said, 'would have made itself
> ridiculous by disputing the authenticity of what was vouched for by so
> many thousands of eyewitnesses.'

The paper *Universe* reported an officer's letter from the battlefront
about a party of thirty men and an officer who were cut off in a trench.
In order not to be trapped they decided to make a sortie against the
enemy, and although they were so few against so large a force, they
dashed out into the open shouting, 'St George for England!' As they
ran on they became aware of a large company of men going along with
them, and even leading them on against the enemy trenches.
Afterwards the officer talked with a prisoner whom they had captured.
The prisoner asked a very strange question:

'*Who was that officer on a great white horse who led them?*
Although he was so prominent, none of our men had been able to hit
him!'

G. G. Monck of Martock reported a young lieutenant in Oxford
who'd been all through the retreat from Mons and had been wounded
at Neuve Chapelle. He said it was simply miraculous, but was perfectly true. Almost the same thing happened at Neuve Chapelle.

A young woman who was at Stepney Soldiers and Sailors meeting, said she had just received a letter from her husband who was at the battle of Neuve Chapelle. He wrote: *'In the course of the battle I saw the angels all around us.'*

It's Happened Before!

Yes, it's happened before! Long ago in fact. It's recorded in the oldest book in the world. Compare these reports of Mons with a similar record in the Bible: 2 Kings 6:16,17, when Elisha was given the ability to see God's hosts of angelic fighters all around.

When the king of Syria was at war with Israel, he said to his officers, 'We will mobilise our forces at . . . (naming a place in secret)'. Immediately Elisha the prophet warned the king of Israel, 'Don't go near . . . (naming the same place), for the Syrians are mobilising their troops there!'

The king of Israel sent a scout to see if Elisha was right, and sure enough he had saved him from disaster. This happened several times.

The king of Syria was puzzled and called together his officers and demanded, 'Which of you is the traitor? Who has been informing the king of Israel about my plans?'

'It's not us, sir.'

One of the officers replied, 'Elisha the prophet tells the king of Israel even the words you speak in the privacy of your bedroom!'

'Go and find out where he is at once!' raged the king. 'We'll send our troops to seize him!'

The report came back, 'Elisha is at Dothan!'

So one night when it was very dark, the king of Syria sent a great army with many chariots and horses to surround the city. When the prophet's servant got up early the next morning and went outside, there were troops, horses and chariots everywhere.

'Alas, my master!' he cried out to Elisha. 'What shall we do now?'

'Don't panic!' Elisha told him. 'Our army is greater than theirs!'

The servant couldn't believe his ears. Was the prophet mad? In answer, the prophet prayed: 'Lord open the young man's eyes and let him see.'

The Lord opened the young man's eyes, *and he saw horses of fire and chariots of fire everywhere upon the mountain!*

As the Syrian army advanced upon them, Elisha prayed: 'Lord please make them blind!' and God did. Then Elisha went out and told them, 'You've come the wrong way! This isn't the right city. Follow me and I will take you to the man you're looking for!' He led them to Samaria!

As soon as they arrived, Elisha prayed, 'Lord, now open their eyes and let them recognise where they are.' The Lord did, and to their consternation they were in Samaria right by the strong capital city of Israel!

When the king of Israel saw that the Syrians were at his mercy, he shouted over to Elisha, 'Oh, sir, shall I slay them? Shall I slay them?'

'Certainly not!' Elisha told him. 'Do we kill prisoners of war? Give them food and drink and send them back home!'

Well the king did more than that. He made them a great feast and then sent them back home to their king. The Syrian raiders were quite flummoxed. They did not know how to react to such kindness, so they stayed away from the land of Israel.

Unbelief Leads to More Evidence

Of course there are many who find it difficult to believe such stories in the Bible. Such events are outside their everyday experiences. It was the same in the First World War. An outburst of discussion appeared in the newspapers. Some were suggesting naturalistic explanations. So because of this a private soldier, Robert Cleaver, swore the following affidavit. It was printed in the daily newspapers, and years later a copy of it was sent to me by Mr C. J. Atton of Prestatyn:

AFFIDAVIT. I, Robert Cleaver No. 10515, a private in the 1st Cheshire Regiment of His Majesty's Army, make oath and say as follows: That I personally was at Mons and saw the vision of angels with my own eyes. Sworn at Kinmel Park in the County of Flint this 20th day of August 1915. Robert Cleaver. Before me Geo S. Hazelhurst, one of his majesty's Justices of the Peace, acting in and for the County of Flint.

In an interview with Mr Hazelhurst, Private Cleaver explained that things were at their bleakest with our troops. If it hadn't been for this supernatural intervention they would have been annihilated. Suddenly the vision came between them and the German cavalry.

Debated in the Churches

The subject began to be debated in the churches. The following is taken from a detailed address given at Bridge Street Methodist Church, Mansfield, and was reported in the *Mansfield Reporter.* The information was given from a high source as it was given by the Assistant Chaplain General to the Forces, The Reverend Owen S. Watkins, CMB, CBE.

At the retreat from Mons, the only division of British cavalry was practically wiped out in a few minutes. It was a sad story which never has been told in full detail. The 'Charge of the Light Brigade' was child's play compared to that action. Out of a regiment of 500-strong only 12 men were left alive.

These figures were confirmed recently on BBC 1 TV on the eightieth anniversary of Armistice Day, 1998, when one of those twelve ex-soldier survivors gave his traumatic reminiscences. He was over one hundred years old, had lost the sight of one eye and was being pushed around in an invalid chair. On the screen we saw him take the presenter to the actual field. No one would have thought that such a tragedy had happened. Fresh green grass covered rising ground with a wooden fence on the far side behind which was a forest. With a sweep of the hand the survivor indicated where the 500 had perished, and the lower corner where the rain of exploding shells had missed him.

All the time a dogged rearguard action was fought by the British trying to hold back a mass of grey-coated 'Huns' advancing shoulder to shoulder. Without the angelic intervention the thinly-spread British would have been overwhelmed.

Another church where the subject was aired was St Mary-at-Hill, in the City of London. Dr Richardson, who I knew much later when I attended the church as a young man, advertised that he was going to speak on the 'Angels of Mons'. This beautiful Christopher Wren church was crowded and the result was reported in the well-known *London Evening News.*

'I would like to ask,' said Dr Richardson, 'whether there is anyone in the congregation who has letters in his possession or has seen such letters from soldiers who can tell of seeing angels on the battlefield.'

A lady at the back of the church stood up. 'I have seen letters from three different soldiers. In each one there is a clear and convincing testimony that the soldiers had themselves seen the angels. All the letters were written in convincing matter-of-fact statements. The soldiers declared that the invaders had been kept back by troops of angels. They also averred that the French soldiers affirmed that they had also seen the angelic forces.' Many others in the congregation added similar evidence.

Mrs Quest of St Leonards-on-Sea told how a nurse just back from France spoke to her on the train because she was wearing her son's regimental badge. The nurse was bringing with her three letters from different soldiers, each one firmly declaring that they had personally seen the angels, and that the French soldiers had seen them also. They described a powerful figure on a horse. He had golden hair and his face shone, as did his white garments, and he had a great troop of horsemen in white.

Many in church must have thought of Revelation chapter nineteen:

I saw heaven opened and behold a white horse, and him who sat upon it was named Faithful and True, and in righteousness he judges and makes war. His eyes were a flame of fire, and on his head were many crowns . . . His name is called The Word of God, and his armies followed him on white horses, clothed in fine linen, white and clean. And out of his mouth goes a sharp sword and with it he will smite the nations.

The Stampede

The soldiers' letters agreed that the intervention came at the height of crisis. It made the German horses stampede. German prisoners who were taken tried to account for it. Some said that the English must have had spies who tampered with their horses. Others said they just had to flee because large reinforcements for the English suddenly came up. But the English soldiers described it as a phantom army which appeared as they had no reinforcements; in fact they were so thin on the ground that they could only space one British Tommy for every fifteen yards to make a firing line.

Newspapers Continue the Debate

More newspapers came in on the debate. They were the *Manchester Guardian*, the *Daily Mail*, the *Observer* and many others.

Some reported that a dying soldier had said to a nurse, 'It's a funny thing, sister, isn't it, how the Germans say we had a lot of troops behind us.'

'Do they?' she said.

'Yes, the German prisoners ask "How could we break through your lines when you had thousands of troops behind you?" '

'Sister, I told them, "You must be joking! Thousands of troops! We were just a thin line of only two regiments, and nothing behind us." '

A sergeant major responded to this nurse saying that he'd heard an officer talking to a German prisoner who also spoke of the crowd of troops behind the British line. He said all the Germans had seen them.

The *Church Times* also published letters on this subject. One was from a Miss Campbell attending the wounded. She was bandaging up the head of a Lancaster Fusilier who was a Methodist when he told her, 'The phantom army was led on by a tall man with yellow hair. He was in golden armour and mounted on a white horse, and holding high his sword.'

A man sitting on the floor beside him butted in. 'It's true, Sister! We all saw it! It was just as the Germans were coming up over the hill like a solid wall in their thousands – then they all turned and fled, and although we were so few we rushed after them.'

Miss Campbell said that she also heard similar stories from Russian troops, two British officers, and three men of the Irish Guards.

The *Church Times* then published a letter by an objector named Mr Machin. In reply, a lieutenant colonel wrote: 'The British army was saved in a manner which puzzles the intellects of all soldiers.'

THE REASON FOR SUPERNATURAL INTERVENTION

Can we find a reason why God should have intervened in the First World War? There are a number of reasons, but the one I have already mentioned is that victory for the Allies made it possible for the British Government to promise a home to be established in Palestine for the Jews. We will look at the following questions:

1. What made the British government make this promise?
2. Had God said anywhere that he was going to bring Israel back to the 'Promised Land' after so long away?

Charter for a Jewish Commonwealth

Newspaper reports answer the first question. The *Kemsley National Newspaper* revealed years afterwards the following:

> Israel elects Weizmann. Dr Chaim Weizmann, the greatest figure in world Zionism, was elected President of the Provisional Council of the State of Israel in Tel Aviv last night. Dr Weizmann is 73. He helped to secure the Balfour Declaration of 1917 promising support for creating in Palestine a national home for the Jews. Dr Weizmann was once offered a seat in the House of Lords in recognition of his service as a chemist to Britain in World War I.

So what was that service? He invented TNT, the high explosive which made the British weapons more powerful and hastened victory. Here is another news clip from the time of the Second World War:

> It is well known that Dr Weizmann, the Zionist head, saved the situation for the Allies in the last [First] World War by inventing the cheap process of manufacturing acetone for TNT explosive. For this service to the Allied cause the Balfour Declaration promising the setting up in Palestine of a National Home for the Jews was made. Will he do it again? An Australian paper gives the news that Dr Weizmann has prepared a formula for a new super-bomb said to surpass anything yet invented, and to have created a sensation among military experts. Later news is that the Doctor has offered the United States Government a new method of producing synthetic rubber. Dr Stephen Wise says he would not be surprised if this new invention *wins for the Zionists a Charter for a Jewish Commonwealth in Palestine. (Source:* The Christian Herald.)

Soon after that promise of a home for Jews, victory was given to General Allenby over Turkey who governed Palestine. British forces then marched into Jerusalem without a shot being fired simply because the Air Force flew over Jerusalem. This made the Turks panic and flee out while there was time. The Turkish newspapers had the date at the heading: on one side it was 1335 in the Moslem date system. That was the figure given to Daniel in chapter 12 verse 12. On the other side of the heading the Western date was given. It was 1917. (See my book *Evidence for Truth, Volume 3: Prophecy*.) It is stated in Daniel 12:12 that the Israeli who reaches the year 1335 will be blessed. Dr Richardson commented:

> Our year 1917 is the year 1335 in the Moslem calendar when the Balfour Declaration established a home in Palestine. In 1886 Dr Gratton Guinness correctly interpreted these prophecies thirty-one years before fulfilment and wrote them in his book *Light for the Last Days,* Marshall Ltd. 'There can be no question that those who live to see the year 1917 will have reached one of the most important of these terminal years.'

You might wonder why God wanted to bring back Israel to Palestine after such a long time. Briefly the answer is, because he promised Abraham and Moses that he would do this. He also told many of the prophets that he would. In my book on prophecy I review all that God told the many prophets, so I won't enlarge upon it here except to give you an example from that well-known passage in Ezekiel chapter 37.

It starts with the dramatic vision of the valley full of dry bones. You may remember that Negro-spiritual song about the bones all clicking together again after lying so long in that old battlefield. Ezekiel asks God, 'What do you mean by this?'

The Lord replies, 'Behold, I will take the descendants of Israel from among the nations where they've gone, and will gather them from all sides, and bring them back to their own land.'

Then he explains that they will return as the united twelve tribes. They would not be divided into the ten northern and two southern tribes. Then he says, 'Take a stick and write on it "Judah". Now take a longer stick and write on it "Ephraim" meaning the ten northern tribes. Next, join them together with a quick hand movement so that they become one stick. This illustrates that when I bring them back to their own land they will return as one nation in Palestine. The united twelve tribes of Israel.'

That is why today it is ISRAEL which is on the map not Judah, the two tribes. Judah returned after only seventy years of exile as God told Jeremiah they would but were scattered again to join the rest of Israel after they rejected Christ. The longer time when all the tribes would be scattered among the nations of the world is called by the Rabbis 'The Diaspora' meaning the dispersion which Ezekiel 38:8 says will last a very long time until the end of the age.

How the Churches Got Excited in 1917

When the news came through about the Balfour Declaration all the churches were thrilled and said, 'This means the end of the age is near!'

Huge meetings were started teaching about the second coming of Christ. But God's timing is not man's. This was only the 'eleventh hour'. It was not the 'twelfth hour' when 'Behold the bridegroom [Christ] comes' (Matthew 25:6).

To mark the eleventh hour the Armistice was signed on the 11th hour of the 11th day of the 11th month, and each year since the Remembrance trumpets have sounded reveille – wake up! – before the last trumpet sounds the 12th hour.

Although this enthusiasm lasted a long time it gradually faded in the following decades just as that verse says it would, so Christ's return will take many by surprise.

THE SECOND ANGELIC INTERVENTION

Four weary years of war had dragged on. Millions of young soldiers had lost their lives leaving young widows to grow old and die (although some are still with us and have led happy lives of service).

In the spring of 1918 the Germans were determined to end the war by a massive assault. They broke through the Allied line. Heavy casualties were sustained. Reserves were practically exhausted. Mr W.B. Grant supplied the following report to me.

The White Cavalry of Bethune

Describing how the German advance was checked, an article in the journal of the Brigade of Guards (*Households Brigade Magazine*) states:

> At the focal point of the enemy's advance, at Bethune, the Germans concentrated on a slight rise beyond the town, yet the ground there was absolutely bare and none of our men were there; nevertheless, enemy machine guns and shells raked it from end to end with lead. As suddenly as it had started the enemy's fire ceased, and in the complete silence there rose a lark's thrilling song of thankfulness. The dense line of German troops which had started to move forward to their victory in mass formation, halted dead. As the British watched they saw it break! The Germans threw down everything they had and fled in frantic panic!

What caused such an amazing turn of events?

A senior German officer who was taken prisoner immediately afterwards gives this extraordinary explanation (taken from the account of the Staff Captain, 1st Corps Intelligence, 1st British Army Headquarters, 1916–18, who was present and himself took the statement):

> The order had been given to advance in mass formation, and our troops were marching behind us singing their way to victory when Fritz, my lieutenant here, said, 'Herr Kapitan, just look at that open ground behind Bethune. There is a brigade of cavalry coming up through the smoke drifting across it! They must be mad, these Englishmen, to advance against such a force as ours in the open! I suppose they must be cavalry of one of their Colonial Forces, for look! They're all in white uniform and are mounted on white horses!'
>
> 'Strange,' I said. 'I've never heard of English having any white cavalry whether Colonial or not. Anyway, they've all been fighting on foot for several years past and in khaki, not white.'
>
> 'Well, they're plain enough,' he replied. 'But look! Our guns have got them in their range now; they'll be blown to pieces in no time.'
>
> We actually saw the shells bursting among the horses and their riders which still came forward at a quiet walk trot, in parade-ground formation, each man and horse in his exact place. Shortly afterwards our machine guns opened a heavy fire, *raking the advancing cavalry with a hail of lead*; but on they still came and not a single man or horse fell. Steadily they advanced, clear in the shining sunlight, and a few paces in front of them rode their leader, a fine figure of a man, whose hair, like spun gold, shone in an aura around his head. By his side was a great sword, but his hands lay quietly holding the reins, as his huge white charger bore him proudly forward.
>
> In spite of heavy shelling and concentrated machine-gun fire the white cavalry advanced, remorselessly as fate, like the incoming tide on a sandy beach. Then a great fear fell over me. I turned to flee; yes I, an officer of the Prussian Guard, fled panic stricken, and around me were hundreds of terrified men, whimpering like children, throwing away their weapons and accoutrements in order not to have their movements impeded . . . all running. Their one desire was to get away from that advancing white cavalry; but above all from their awe-inspiring leader whose hair shone like a golden aureole.
>
> That is all I have to tell you. We are beaten. The German Army is broken. There may be fighting, but we have lost the war; we are beaten by the white cavalry . . . I cannot understand . . . I cannot understand.

During the days that followed, many German prisoners were examined and their accounts tallied in substance with the one given here.

Letter from Mrs Peggy Main of Ascot, Berkshire

The 'White Cavalry of Bethune' was recounted by Captain Hayward. He was Intelligence Officer to Staff Headquarters on the Western Front. He was the officer who interviewed the German soldiers who were retreating for fear of what they had seen – white cavalry with a leader who had a halo round his head and was mounted upon a huge white charger. Captain Hayward later examined a number of German prisoners, all who had a strained look on their faces, and all told basically the same story. Strangely, Captain Hayward himself had seen nothing on that empty open ground!

This story was confirmed when my husband and I were attending a fellowship conference. An elderly lady there said her brother had been present when the Germans in question had been brought in. They were absolutely terrified by what they had seen.

Mrs Peggy Main added, '*I have heard that this vision followed a national day of prayer in Britain.*' It was the only one that Britain had in the First World War. The churches were holding prayer meetings throughout the war, but it was only when they urged the government to have a National Day of Prayer that defeat was turned into victory. Germany had no national days of prayer in either war. A further report tells me that the USA also joined in that national day of prayer, and that it had been called jointly by Parliament and US Congress.

The Vision as Seen from the British Area

Captain Cecil W. Hayward tells us how the Bethune angelic intervention appeared to the British ranks. He says that Germany's furious attack was intended to win victory before the American forces arrived later in July, 1918. The noise of the gun barrage was so terrific that even three miles away Captain Hayward felt the ground heave under his feet.

A section of the trenches had been taken over by the Portuguese because there were very few relief troops available. The British had been holding the line for the Portuguese. It was their first taste of battle. The intense rain of shrapnel raining down upon them blotted them out completely. This made a gap in the front line through which the Germans came pouring. The few Portuguese still alive threw down their weapons and came staggering through to the British who were retiring in good order, keeping up a stiff rearguard action as they went.

It was then that a report reached Captain Hayward: 'Fritz seems to have gone barmy, Sir!' The enemy had suddenly stopped firing at the British and were raining down their fire on 'empty naked open ground rising just outside Bethune'.

Captain Hayward was puzzled and anxious to see what was happening, so he reached a lookout point and saw that the enemy was raking that empty area backwards and forwards with heavy bursts of massed machine-guns.

Hayward was astonished and moved to see better. There were no troops within sight against whom they could be firing with increasing fury. Then the shattering noise of bombardment suddenly ceased. There was a pause. Then to the amazement of all, the Germans threw down their arms, haversacks, rifles, coats and anything which would hinder their flight and ran back in panic.

A deathly silence settled upon the Bethune mound, and then it was that the lark arose. It soared up and up singing its thrilling message of triumph.

It was unbelievable that those well-drilled, disciplined Germans who were advancing in mass formation as a victorious army, suddenly broke up into groups of frightened men on the run. A sergeant brought in German officers as prisoners two at a time. They spluttered out stories of white cavalry led by their awesome commander on a great white horse whose hair was like spun gold shining like a halo round his head. They described his great sword, and how the white cavalry advanced remorselessly on, untouched by the hail of missiles and bullets firing through them.

Yet Captain Hayward said: *'We could swear that we saw no cavalry in action, neither did any of us see so much as a single white horse, either with or without a rider!'* So what did the Germans see? A vision?

Shortly after this the American forces came into action, and from July 11th, the Allies advanced, and by November 11th the war had ended at the 11th hour, on the 11th month – 11 months after Israel had been promised a homeland in Palestine.

> I saw heaven opened, and behold there was a white horse! He who sat upon it is named faithful and true, the Word of God. He judges justly and makes war. Heavenly armies in fine white clean linen, follow him on white horses. (Revelation, concerning the end times, chapter 19)

Only the First Stage, Making a Second War Necessary

But that home in Palestine was only the first stage. God told Jeremiah that he would bring back Israel in two stages. First, it would be a pleasant prospect attracting many Jewish pioneers who would change a desert land into prosperous fertility as foretold by many scriptures. Then the second stage would be a desperate one. The Jews would be hounded back. That stage started with the Hitler gas chambers in which six million Jews perished, causing a mass exodus to Palestine and the creation of the State of Israel. Here is what God said about this in Jeremiah 16:14–16:

> 'Look! The days are coming,' says the Lord, 'when the main saying will no longer be, "The Lord lives who brought up the people from the land of Egypt." It will change to, "The Lord lives who brought up the people off

Israel out of the North country, and out of all the other countries where he had driven them." For I will bring them back to their own land which I gave to their fathers.'

Then the two stages are described:

'Look! I will send for many fishers and they will entice them back with bait, and afterwards I will send for many hunters and they will hound them back from every mountain and every hill, and out of the clefts of the rocks.'

Here is something for you to think about: *If Hitler had won his war he would have continued into Palestine to wipe out the Jews! There would have been no Israel!* That's why there had to be supernatural intervention in the Second World War, and the Jewish gas chamber holocaust motivated the United Nations Organisation to create the State of Israel after the Second World War.

It is my view that if governments had read the prophecies, believed God's declared purpose, and acted on it, there would have been no horrific World Wars.

7 THE SECOND WORLD WAR MIRACLES

THE SUPERNATURAL EVENTS RESULTING FROM NATIONAL PRAYER

Yes, there were some angels seen in the Second World War, but so far as one can tell, not so dramatically as in the First World War. It was evident that the main acts of God came after each national day of prayer. There were seven of these, and I kept a diary record of the events which followed each one.

We will look at the angelic incidents first. During the Second World War, I collected clippings from the newspapers which reported manifestations.

Angelic Appearances

The *News Chronicle,* a national newspaper, reported the vision of Christ crucified followed by angels in the sky over Sussex. The paper described it as the strangest event yet of the war and compared it with the Angels of Mons (see Fig 7.1).

My second cutting is from 1943. It is headed: 'Vicar interprets the vision in the sky'. A similar vision to the one seen at Lewes 200 miles away three years earlier had been seen at Ipswich by the Reverend Harold Green.

A report in the *Christian Herald* at the time said:

Wide publicity was given to the truth of our Lord's return in the London and provincial press recently when the Rev Harold Green, vicar of St Nicholas' Church, Ipswich, preached to an over-full church just after a vision had been seen in the sky by several people in the parish. A white cross, on which was a figure of Christ, was said to have been seen by several people quite independently of each other, and the vicar took the opportunity to proclaim the truth of the coming of Christ and the setting up of his Kingdom, basing his remarks on Matthew 24 and Luke 21.

My third cutting is from the *South London Newspaper*: this was reported on September 8th, 1944, and headed: 'ANGEL' SEEN IN PECKHAM DURING AIR RAID.

Mr D.L. Phillips said, 'The figure was perfect; there was no mistaking it.' Mr Halsey says that he was surprised when he looked up into the sky to see a large angel holding out his arms as if to shield the

Strangest Story Of The War

THIS STORY, AS TOLD TO THE NEWS CHRONICLE LAST NIGHT, IS THE STRANGEST YET OF THE WAR AND IS A PARALLEL OF THE FAMOUS "ANGEL OF MONS " LEGEND OF THE LAST WAR:

MR. FOWLER of Firle, Lewes, was attending his sheep on the Sussex Downs when he noticed a white line spreading slowly across the sky.

Gradually to his eyes it took the shape of Christ crucified on the Cross. Then six angels took form.

The apparition lasted for two minutes, then faded.

Mr. Fowler rushed down the hillside to tell the village, but found he was not the only witness.

Villagers working on the land said they had also seen it.

A Newhaven evacuee, Mrs. Steer, of The Street, Firle, and her sister, Mrs. Evans; said: " We could see the nail in the crossed feet of Christ, and one of the angels with arms upstretched appeared to be praying."

Similar statements were made by seven other villagers.

The comment of the Rector of Lewes, the Rev. A. G. Gregor, when interviewed by the News Chronicle, was: " I only wish that I could believe it, but it seems to me that if such a thing really occurred more people would have seen it."

Figure 7.1. Newspaper cutting of Sussex vision of Christ on the cross attended by angels.
Source: News Chronicle, *August 1940*

inhabitants from flying bombs which were coming over. There were at least eight others who also saw it.

Victories after each National Day of Prayer

The big features of the 1939–45 war were the seven national days of prayer and the dramatic events which followed each one. They saved Britain from disaster.

My record of these days of prayer as they occurred from 1940 to 1945 provided the details of each deliverance or victory which followed. Why did I do this? Because I knew that it would be useful for reminding Britain and the world in future years, and here I am doing it at the age of eighty-five! The fiftieth anniversary of D-Day was observed without any mention of those prayer days, when at the call of King and Parliament, the majority of the population crowded into the churches and overflowed outside, because they knew our position was desperate. The only acknowledgement so far as I know, was a report I gave on BCC Radio Stoke which they have repeated since, and on the United Christian Broadcasters' European network, and on TransWorld Radio.

Seven National Days of Prayer in Six Years

Of seven separate days of prayer called by King and Parliament in the six years of war, as many as three were held within the first twelve months because the situation was known to be so desperate. In gratitude for deliverance after the war, the government passed a law making Christian teaching in schools compulsory. Now it is difficult to

A VISION IN THE SKY

, Wide publicity was given to the truth of our Lord's return in the London and provincial press recently when the Rev. Harold Green, vicar of St. Nicolas' Church, Ipswich, preached to an overfull church just after a vision had been seen in the sky by several people in the parish. A white cross, on which was a figure of Christ, was said to have been seen in the sky by several people quite independently of each other, and the vicar took the opportunity to proclaim the truth of the coming of Christ and the setting up of His Kingdom, basing his remarks on Matthew 24 and Luke 21.

Figure 7.2. Newspaper cutting of Ipswich vision of Christ on the cross.

get permission even to mention the name of Christ, and many children lack ethical and moral teaching. The results in our community life are obvious.

Yes, Britain was in a desperate situation. We were quite unprepared for war and humanly speaking we were left in an impossible situation. That situation worsened when France fell to the Nazis, and the British Army of only 350,000 men were hemmed in with backs to the sea at Dunkirk. All the protection that was left in Britain was a 'Dad's Army practising drill with broomsticks'.

Before calling the nation to the first national Day of Prayer, Winston Churchill said he had, 'Hard and heavy tidings to announce'. The commander of the British Forces, Lt General Sir Frederick Morgan, said there was no way out barring a miracle. That miracle happened after the first Day of Prayer.

A

FORM OF PRAYER

TO

ALMIGHTY GOD

AT

THIS TIME OF WAR

TO BE USED ON
SUNDAY, MAY 26th, 1940

Issued under the Authority of
THE ARCHBISHOPS OF CANTERBURY
AND YORK

LONDON, 1940
Printed by EYRE AND SPOTTISWOODE LIMITED
Printers to the King's most Excellent Majesty
and published by
THE SOCIETY FOR PROMOTING CHRISTIAN KNOWLEDGE
Northumberland Avenue, W.C.2

Figure 7.3. Cover details of a 20-page leaflet for prayer in time of war, issued by the Archbishops of Canterbury and York for the Church of England's own call to prayer. The 20-page order of service included prayers 'for those who fight against us' beseeching God to 'turn the hearts of our enemies, and to help us to forgive them'.
Source: SPCK

Figure 7.4. King George VI calls the nation to prayer.
Source: The Christian Herald, *May 1990*

1. *The first National Day of Prayer was called for by King George VI on March 27th, 1940.* The miracle took place during the week following. Most people have heard how the English Channel was absolutely calm all the days during which thousands of private boats and yachts, including my father-in-law's boat, went to and fro rescuing from the sands of Dunkirk 338,000 men of the British Expeditionary Army, leaving only 12,000 sadly to become prisoners or killed.

Drama of the Little Boats

The following details are supplied by Lt Commander E. Keble Chatterton:

Things happened quickly; immense possibilities widened. Instead of, perhaps, a lucky 25,000 or so, more than ten times that number might be saved. But how? It all resulted from a marvel of detailed organisation. Already the Admiralty had with great foresight given notice that all privately owned motorcraft of 30 to 100 feet in length were to be at their disposal. So, likewise, by means of a licensing system for all coasting vessels, the Ministry of Shipping were kept aware of movements and could lay their hands on suitable vessels almost instantly. The congregating of a vast improvised fleet numbering nearly 1,000 units therefore was just a matter of telephoning and telegraphing. Nothing like it had ever been devised. Trawlers, drifters, Thames sailing and motor barges, little cargo carriers, colliers, motor-boats, motor-yachts, 17 of the Royal National lifeboats, open skiffs, oared boats from liners, sailing boats from Southend beach usually employed for pleasure parties, tugs from the Thames, even the six motor bawleys that gather up cockles from the estuary; pleasure paddle steamers accustomed to ply their trade along the Clyde or at Llandudno, or Margate; one of the LFB fireboats, steam yachts that were veterans when fighting U-boats in the last war; Dutch schooners and Belgian craft, swelled this extraordinary list till they numbered 665, in addition to the 222 naval units. Cross-channel steamers with ample passenger accommodation and high speed, normally carrying from seven to fourteen deck-hands, now received additional volunteers to man the boats which would have to be used as ferries from the beach. One amateur yachtsman assisted by his son, sailed his yacht all the way from Southampton to Dunkirk on his own initiative, and fetched home a batch of tired soldiers.

Figure 7.5 . Father-in-law's motor yacht *My Beth* used in the Dunkirk evacuation.

So then the army was back in Britain having lost their armaments, as helpless as sitting ducks for Hitler.

It was a miracle that Hitler didn't follow up his victory immediately. That first Day of Prayer was followed up by two more within five months, so within five months we had three national days of prayer, not called by the Church, but called by the King and Parliament. But did the nation respond as a nation? They did! Hardly anybody stayed away. The churches and halls were crammed full and overflows outside were sometimes bigger than the crush inside.

The Cabinet's Words of Encouragement

At this time the war cabinet sought to inform clergy in Britain of the serious situation while at the same time providing a positive message of hope and encouragement. The first of a series of letters from Duff Cooper at the Ministry of Information was circulated on 21st June, 1940 advising what Hitler was seeking to do that autumn and to prepare the congregations to fight 'side by side for the fields and villages and cities that we love'.

Tunbridge Wells Empty!

Resulting from the inspiration of the call to prayer, we have the story of 'The Town That Stood Still'. A local greengrocer put forward the idea that every shop should close one morning in July 1940 for an hour of intercession. It received the enthusiastic support of the local Traders' Association so the people of Tunbridge Wells, as never before in their history, put themselves in God's hands.

Figure 7.6. The town that stood still: local traders stop to pray.
Source: The Christian Herald, *July 25th 1940*

Any communication in connection with this letter should be addressed to :—

Letter sent to
Clergy & Ministers

THE SPECIAL SECRETARIAT,
MINISTRY OF INFORMATION,
MALET STREET,
LONDON, W.C.I.

21st June, 1940.

Dear Sir or Madam,

This is the first of what I hope will be a series of letters that I shall address to you from time to time. People in positions of responsibility such as you occupy are in constant touch with different types of your fellow citizens and it is but natural that they should look to you for information, comfort and guidance in a time such as this. I have no desire whatsoever to influence your own judgment or to intrude upon your personal convictions. Yet I feel that it may sometimes be of value to you to receive a letter from myself indicating the proportions of the situation as I see it myself and suggesting certain lines of encouragement or reassurance which may help you to advise those with whom you are brought into contact.

The war is entering upon a new phase. The enemy has begun to deliver heavy bombing attacks, which are likely to continue. The anxiety and distress which this will cause to the civilian population can to some extent be mitigated by people of authority such as yourself. In particular you can reassure people regarding the state of defences and the efficiency of our Air Force and point out that even if the German bombers are sometimes able to pass through our defences we are also able to penetrate theirs. It is also useful to point out to people that an air attack sounds far worse than it is. The Germans deliberately exploit the factor of noise in order to exaggerate terror, and they attach to their machines and bombs devices which increase that noise tenfold. Actually the physical and material effects of air bombardment are nothing like as serious as the effect upon the nerves. Remind those with whom you come into contact that Hitler's main object is but to undermine their courage. Remind them that courage is as infectious as cowardice.

There is the probability also that Hitler will seek to invade Great Britain. People should be encouraged to look forward to that invasion without any apprehension— to prepare for it but not to fear it.

continued overleaf

We are fortunate in the fact that the greater part of the B.E.F. is safely home in the island. All those men are confident in their ability to defeat the Germans —and they constitute the largest armed force we have ever had in Great Britain.

Our Air Force is as strong to-day as when the intensive war began six weeks ago. Fighting in France and Belgium they have never failed to bring down two, three or even four enemy 'planes to every one of their own. Fighting in their own country they will be at a far greater advantage and we may look forward to Germany's numerical superiority in 'planes being rapidly reduced to equality and then to inferiority.

Moreover it is a great advantage to have our men fighting on their own soil for their own homes. There will for the present be no more Expeditionary Forces with all the anxiety that separation entails. Our loved ones will be near us and we shall have daily news of them. So fighting side by side for the fields and villages and cities that we love we shall have greater confidence, knowing that our cause is just, that the life of our country is at stake and that we shall never surrender.

Hitler's belief is that he can frighten the British people into surrender before the autumn. If he fails to do that he will have failed to win the war and the great tide of power will begin to turn upon our side.

These are the sort of things which, in my opinion, you should be able to say to people and thereby to bring them comfort and strength. I shall be writing to you again shortly giving you further suggestions.

Yours truly,

Duff Cooper

Figure 7.7. Circular letter from the Ministry of Information to all clergy explaining the gravity of the situation in mid-1940 and at the same time providing words of encouragement.

Tennis Courts Empty!

2. *The second Day of Prayer was on Sunday, August 11th, 1940.* This was a national youth call to prayer. The King had called all the young people to pray. I was walking past a large area of tennis courts on the way to church. The tennis courts were deserted except for a perplexed young man holding a tennis racket. He was completely alone.

'Where have they all gone?' he exclaimed.

'They're all in church praying for national deliverance,' I said. 'Why don't you go!'

'I can't believe this! My pals have never gone to church even once in their lives!'

The Answer

Britain could not know that within the week that followed, the over-weight Nazi, Air Field Marshall Goering, commenced the first stage in the Battle of Britain. It failed. The relatively small British force of Spitfires and Hurricanes shot down 180 Nazi bombers over south-east England. The rate of interception excelled by far anything that could be expected or explained by radar, said our air commander.

3. *The next national Day of Prayer was only a month later on September 8th, 1940*. Calling for another Day of Prayer so soon showed how desperate Parliament knew the situation to be.

The answer again was immediate and it was during this period that people in the streets began to see angels in the sky. A more determined Nazi air attack was made by sending five fighter planes to accompany every single bomber during the week following. Yet against all odds, as many as 185 Nazi planes were shot down. It was sad for us padres to see the empty canteen tables of those who did not return, but they had shot down a far greater number than our own losses. In fact Air Chief Marshall Dowding said: 'I will say with absolute conviction that I can trace the intervention of God . . . Humanly speaking victory was impossible!'

And that was during the week following our third National Day of Prayer, and the newspapers were not afraid to print that statement by Dowding.

Goering, the Nazi commander, expected success and in anticipation Hitler had prepared invasion barges at Bremen. But I see in my notes taken at the time, that a terrific storm in the channel and North Sea blew away those invasion barges. The result was that the invasion of Britain was postponed. This was vital, for it gave Britain more time to manufacture armaments to re-equip our depleted forces.

Remarkable Guidance for the Fourth Day of Prayer

4. *My diary records that the next National Day of Prayer was only six months later.* It was called by King and parliament for March 23rd, 1941. The guidance of God must have been evident, for we did not know at the time that this was Hitler's next date for invading Britain.

I have before me Hitler's plan of invasion which was discovered after the war and published in the national newspapers.

My notes record the following events which followed the fourth National Day of Prayer:

1. A great earthquake created waves with terrific gales which blew Nazi ships 80 miles of course.

2. That same week, Yugoslavia which had surrendered to Hitler changed its mind and organised resistance.
3. Ethiopia was liberated from Mussolini, Hitler's co-partner.
4. The British Navy fought the Italian fleet in the Mediterranean. Italy lost many cruisers and destroyers and their newest battleship was badly damaged. There was no damage to the British Navy, and no men were lost.
5. The Ethiopian ports were liberated. Haile Selassie, Ethiopia's Christian Emperor, said when no help was coming, 'Then I put my cause into God's hands'.
6. Hitler changed his plans entirely as a result of the submarine earth-quake. *He gave up invading Britain*, and against all the advice of his generals, *he turned his attention eastwards to invade Russia*.

This was a turning point in the war. We learned later that Hitler had put off the invasion of Britain four times. A full account was given by Mr Attlee in 1946 as reported in the *Daily Telegraph:*

> This Operation Seelowe (sea lion) was based on a landing of two armies with 25 divisions in all between Folkestone and Worthing. Ten divisions were to go ashore on the first four days to form the initial bridgehead. The preparatory phase, an air offensive, was to have begun on August 13th, but the Germans decided that the actual invasion could not take place until September 15th. D-Day was eventually put off until September 21st. Altogether, Hitler postponed the plan four times between September 1940 and the Spring of 1942, after which 'it did not seem to be seriously considered again'.

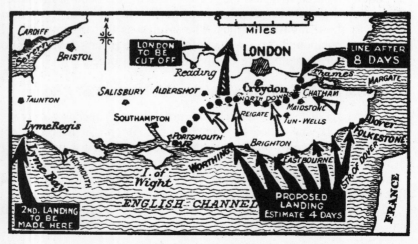

Figure 7.8. Map of the German invasion plan based on information released in 1946.

Source: Daily Telegraph

Significant Events after the Fifth National Day of Prayer

5. *The fifth National Day of Prayer was on September 3rd, 1942.* It was the third anniversary of the outbreak of war. The very next day at Palermo in the Mediterranean, the whole Italian fleet was sunk. Very significantly, the next month in the North African desert, the Eighth Army under General Montgomery saved Egypt (and therefore Israel) from being invaded by Hitler's powerful tank commander Rommel.

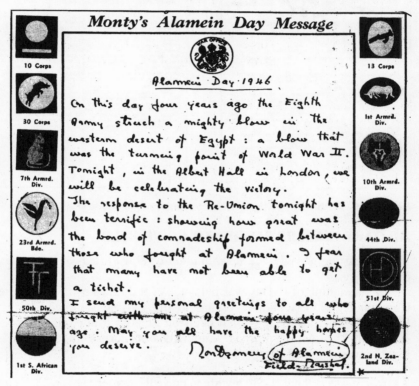

Figure 7.9. Monty's Alamein message, on the fourth anniversary of a turning point in the Second World War.
Source: Daily Graphic, *October 23, 1946*

Italy Surrenders, Mussolini Murdered

6. *The sixth National Day of Prayer was held on September 3rd, 1943.* It was a weekday, chosen at the time because it was the fourth anniversary of the outbreak of war. Italy surrendered to the allies that very night, and the dictator Mussolini was murdered.

It was Mussolini who had invaded Abyssinia (Ethiopia). Emperor Haile Selassie's prayer had been answered. The Ethiopians were liberated, and Haile Selassie became a popular speaker saying, 'I glory in the Bible'.

THE EMPEROR HAILE SELASSIE'S STRIKING TESTIMONY
Address delivered at the Royal Albert Hall, London, at the Annual Public Demonstration organised by the Bible Testimony Fellowship

I AM indeed grateful to the organisers of this meeting for having given me this opportunity to add my testimony to the greatness of the Bible.

As you probably know, we have one of the oldest versions of the Bible, but however old the version may be and in whatever language it might be written, the Word remains one and the same. It transcends all boundaries of Empires and all conception of race. It is eternal ; and one of the most complete proofs of this can be found in the body of the Bible itself.   You are all familiar with the incident recorded in the Acts of the Apostles of how Gamaliel, one learned in the law, warns Israel of their attitude to the Apostles and their teaching. " Refrain from these men," he says, "and let them alone : for if this counsel or this work be of men it will come to nought : But if it be of God ye cannot overthrow it." And so we see to-day the Bible with its wonderful message reaching the remotest parts of the earth.

No doubt you all remember reading in the Acts of the Apostles of how Philip baptised the Ethiopian official.   He is the first Ethiopian on record to have followed Christ ; and from that day onwards the Word of God continues to grow in the hearts of Ethiopians.   And I might say for myself that from early childhood I was taught to appreciate the Bible, and my love for it increases with the passage of time. All through my troubles I have found it a cause of infinite comfort. " Come unto Me, all ye that labour and are heavy laden, and I will give you rest "—who can resist an invitation so full of compassion ?

Because of this personal experience in the goodness of the Bible, I was resolved that all my countrymen should also share its great blessing, and that by reading the Bible they should find Truth for themselves.   Therefore, in spite of great opposition, I caused a new translation to be made from our ancient language into the language which the old and the young understood and spoke.   It must not, however, be understood that this opposition was due to narrow conservatism : it was rather because in her long history our Church had painful experience of attempts from abroad to change the faith which she had retained for many centuries, and it was consequently thought that this new translation was dictated by the same foreign influence.

To-day man sees all his hopes and aspirations crumbling before him. He is perplexed and knows not whither he is drifting. But he must realise that the Bible is his refuge, and the rallying point for all humanity. In it man will find the solution of his present difficulties and guidance for his future action, and unless he accepts with clear conscience the Bible and its great Message he cannot hope for salvation. For my part, I GLORY IN THE BIBLE.

Figure 7.10. Testimony of Emperor Haile Selassie of Abyssinia (Ethiopia).

MILITARY LEADERS TESTIFY TO GOD'S HELP

7. In the spring of 1944, the seventh and last Day of Prayer was called by the King.

The launching of D-Day was delayed several times by the Supreme Commander G. Eisenhower owing to the terrible weather. At last Eisenhower had to make a final decision or miss it altogether, so on June 5th the Allied Forces launched out across the Channel. Eisenhower reported later:

> If there was nothing else in my life to prove the existence of an Almighty and Merciful God, the events of the next twenty-four hours did it. The greatest break in a terrible outlay of weather occurred next day and allowed that great invasion to proceed. You may say to me 'The nation prayed on this last National Day of Prayer but what did the Army do about it?' All officers were called to church services, and all ranks came to pledge themselves to God. 'But how deep did this go,' you may ask, 'knowing the varied types of characters?'

I can only quote to you part of the address given by the deputy chaplain-general. He did not merely urge religion. He urged faith in the Lord Jesus Christ. The actual services of dedication were held on the eve of D-Day: The deputy chaplain-general was Canon Llewellyn

With a Prayer on Our Lips...

A READER HAS SENT US *THE FOLLOWING* REMINDER OF THE DAY OF NATIONAL PRAYER IN THE CRISES OF 1918:—

In 1916 Admiral Beatty wrote: "England still remains to be taken out of the stupor of self-satisfaction and complacency into which her great and flourishing condition has steeped her; and until she can be stirred out of this condition and until religious revival takes place at home just so long will the war continue.

"When she can look out on the future with humbler eyes and a prayer on her lips, then we can begin to count the days towards the end."

Beatty's words were literally fulfilled. The spring of 1918 called forth Haig's "Back to the Wall" order. The National Day of Prayer was held on August 4 (the only one during the war). By November 11 Germany was defeated and the Armistice was signed.

So let us to-day pray, as His Majesty asks, in the name of Jesus Christ Our Lord.

Figure 7.11. Suporting the King's call to prayer during WW2.

Source: Daily Exprress, *1944*

Hughes. He said:

It is not enough for an army or a nation to have a vague faith in God. It is not enough for us to rest content that our commanders are godly, and that God's flag is publicly flown. Faith in God is useless until it governs action. What does God want done? We believe in God – as what? As a nonentity, content to be recognised, and then ignored? As a vague power, meaningless, purposeless, inarticulate, and therefore unfit to command a platoon, let alone a world? No. We believe in God who wants, and means to have done, all that Christ embodied, taught, lived out. Let an army and a people learn what God stands for, and then they will know when they are for or against His purpose, and support or oppose with confidence as His commissioned servants. That is where the solid toil of consecration comes in. The character of Christ must be known; His goodness perceived and loved; Himself accepted as Master. No special effort thrown off in an emergency will accomplish that; and there is no short cut.

So the chaplains are going forward with the forces preaching the simple Gospel of Christ, the Author and Finisher of all the fine qualities of men ...

There is no ideal of character better than the one God sent to us in Jesus Christ our Lord. Read the New Testament again.

This is typical of the spiritual leadership given by officers and commanders of the armed forces.

My memory of that seventh National Day of Prayer is that the nation did not turn out for prayer in the same overwhelming numbers as on previous occasions. What was the reason? Was it that the fear of defeat had vanished? If so it would be typical of human nature, unfortunately.

Earlier in the war, everybody understood the hopelessness of our situation and fled to God for deliverance. Even newspapers had given tips on how to pray. See the example from the *Daily Express* early in the war (Fig 7.13).

The Miracle of Malta

General Sir William Dobbie, the hero of Malta, gives some personal insights into the real faith of many top military authorities. Malta was

'We commend the Gospel of Christ our Saviour, for it alone can effectively mould character, control conduct and solve the problems of men and nations, and thus make life what it should be.

'Faith in Christ the Lord, and loyal obedience to His will as revealed in the Bible, ensures peace of mind and brings satisfaction in service to God and man.'

ANDREW CUNNINGHAM,
Admiral of the Fleet.

JACK C. TOVEY, *Admiral.*

H. R. ALEXANDER, *General.*

B. PAGET, *General.*

E. L. GEORGE, *Air Marshal.*

The above statement was signed by these Commanders-in-Chief of the Royal Navy, Army and Royal Air Force early in World War II as a foreword to one of the Gospels distributed to members of the Forces.

Figure 7.12. Statement of faith in Christ and the Bible by leaders of the armed forces in WW2.
Source: Church of England Newspaper, *1945*

HOW DO YOU PRAY?

DAILY EXPRESS 1940

MANY of us have started to pray again for the first time, perhaps, since we were children. And we don't find it easy. We flop down on our knees and say, "O, God, please don't let there be a war, and if there must be a war, don't let them kill me and my family."

A petition like that is not really a prayer, but a wish, and, when you come to think of it, rather a selfish one. Why should you in particular be exempt from danger?

Those who get up from their knees after a prayer like that probably feel, "Well, now I've asked God to do what I want. If He doesn't do it I shall feel that He doesn't exist and that it is no good praying."

This frame of mind leaves such people very much where they were before they started praying, in a state of despairing half-belief. It is reducing God to the level of a lucky mascot.

All the same, half the battle is won by the willingness of people to trust something more than just clever wits and material strength. The most encouraging signs recently have been those of the public distaste for war. The question is : When you pray to God, what ought you to pray about?

The first thing for you to do is to acknowledge the existence of evil. This should not be difficult. The dogs of war have rather barked their way into prominence over the last few days.

The next thing is to remember that it is not for you to condemn any human being as wholly evil. You are not to pray for the destruction of those of whom you disapprove. God will destroy them. In the end, if they ought to be destroyed. God always triumphs over evil, because He is all-powerful and evil is only negative.

BUT God has more time to work His will than our short lives. Even Communists or dictators or Conservatives or whoever they may be whom you personally dislike must one day die.

But you can work against the will of God and assist evil and war by wishing destruction of people rather than of things. So when you pray, pray for justice, right and grace.

JUSTICE for all in the decisions which are being made today, not the sort of justice that was made at Versailles, but divine justice.

Right triumphant over wrong.

Grace working in the hearts of all men, to bring about the triumph of good over evil.

And here you can dedicate yourself to God, to let Him use you as He wills. In this way, even if the prayers of the faithful cannot avert a war, you will be submitting yourself to the will of God and He will tell you what to do.

And if you want words in which to express all this and more, you will find them in the Lord's Prayer.

Hugh Shields

Figure 7.13. Tips on how to pray during WW2.
Source: Daily Express, *1940*

under siege, and seemed unlikely to survive. General Dobbie wrote:

> At about this time, I was greatly encouraged by a telegram I received from the Chief of the Imperial General Staff, General Sir Edmond Ironside (later, Field Marshall). The telegram, which was addressed to me personally, contained the reference Deuteronomy chapter 3, verse 22. I looked up the reference in my Bible, and I read: 'You shall not fear them, for the Lord your God, he shall fight for you.' God certainly did so that the outcome was popularly called 'The Miracle of Malta'.

I bought General Dobbie's book, *A Very Present Help* (Marshall, 1944), as soon as it was published because I had met him two years earlier when he told the remarkable deliverance of Malta. The visit was reported at the time in the *Dorset Daily Echo* as follows:

> General Sir William Dobbie's visit to Dorchester on Wednesday can be placed without qualification in the category of memorable events. It brought about a unique mobilisation of religious leaders of the town, sounded the highest notes of spirituality and left scores of Dorchester people feeling better for having met one of the outstanding personalities of the war. He brought into the crowded hall some of the rock-like attributes of Malta itself, and it would be true to say that the majority of the audience were more deeply moved by his simple unaffected confession of faith, than by the story, even, of the Island's defence, glorious as it was . . . In addition to the dignitaries already named as present, our thanks are due to Mrs Victor Pearce for her solo, 'I know that my redeemer liveth'.

Four Days to Save HMS *Illustrious*

One of General Dobbie's reports was on how the new aircraft carrier HMS *Illustrious* was saved: In January 1941, a convoy was brought to Malta. It was escorted by a considerable portion of the Mediterranean Fleet, and in the escort was a new aircraft carrier, HMS *Illustrious,* a magnificent and very valuable ship. The German Luftwaffe had recently come to Sicily in considerable strength, in order to reduce our offensive activities at Malta. They attacked the *Illustrious*. In spite of heavy losses by the Germans they pressed the attack and obtained a number of hits causing severe damage. That evening after dark *Illustrious* limped into Malta and made fast alongside the dockyard. When they saw that *Illustrious* was in the dockyard, the German airforce came over Malta and persisted relentlessly to bomb the ship. She received several more hits, and near misses caused underwater damage. The situation was very serious, and the chances of saving the ship were very small. However, the dockyard authorities said that if there was no further damage for four days it might be possible to get the ship to sea.

General Dobbie bade many people in Malta to join him in prayer. The attacks started again the next day, but strangely all the bombs missed! Why was that? It was the same for the next three days. They all missed! Apparently, the Germans had changed tactics and bombed from a much greater height, and missed every time, and *Illustrious* sailed out safely.

Other similar instances were described by General Dobbie, but a very significant statement was made concerning difficulties in the terrible First World War, and about the delay for D-Day in the Second War. It emphasises my remark that the nation did not turn out in the same way on the seventh Day of Prayer as they did when Britain was in peril.

The Sinking of the *Bismarck*

The following extract appeared in the *Daily Sketch* on April 9th, 1946 concerning the testimony of the importance of prayer by the Vice-Admiral of the Fleet, at the time of the sinking of the *Bismarck* on May 27th, 1941.

When the *Bismarck* was hamstrung by our torpedoes in mid-Atlantic, Admiral of the Fleet Lord Tovey [then Vice-Admiral Sir John Tovey] knew he could bring her back into action next day at his convenience. 'But although she was damaged, her guns and instruments were in perfect condition,' he said. 'Although I was going to bring her into action with the *King George V* and *Rodney*, if you had asked any informed person what the result would be, he would have said, "You'll sink the *Bismarck* but one or both of your ships will be mauled."

'THAT EVENING I WENT DOWN TO MY CABIN AND SAID A PRAYER ON MY KNEES. WHEN I HAD SAID IT I KNEW EVERYTHING WAS GOING TO BE ALL RIGHT. I took those ships in to attack the biggest battleship in the world, far bigger than my two . . . I closed in to 3,000 yards – and the Bismarck never scored a hit on either of my ships. I have no doubt of the explanation of it.'

Lord Tovey told the story at the parish hall of the Church of the High Seas, St Dunstan's, Stepney Green, where he handed over to the rector the flag he flew in the action.

The capital letters above are as printed in the *Daily Sketch*. According to *Everyman's Encyclopædia,* 1978, 'The action was a triumph of co-ordinated movement'.

The Miracle of the Fog

General Morgan referred to other miracles great or local which others reported. Here is one concerning a platoon in the American General Patton's Third Army. It is from a soldier's letter to his mother, who lived in Pleasantville, New Jersey. His name was Joel; he was six foot four inches and weighed 215 lb. Facing the enemy in Luxembourg, he braved everything they could fire at him and his platoon.

He and the fifty men of his platoon were in real danger. They were working in observation lines, and in a few patrols.

> One of my best friends, Tom, with his whole platoon were pinned down by mortar and artillery fire. They were given the order to move but they couldn't because the enemy had full view of them from a hill and were zeroing their fire on them accurately. Tom is the most conscientious Christian boy I have ever met in the services. He knew something had to be done to save the fifty men. He crawled from his foxhole and looked things over. Seeing the hopelessness of the situation, he laid down behind a tree and prayed earnestly for God to help him. This is true mother . . . after he prayed a mist or fog rolled down between the two hills, and the whole platoon got out of their foxholes and escaped. They reorganized in a little town behind the lines where there was a church building. They all went in and knelt down to pray and thank the Lord, and then they asked Tom to take the service. This is true mother, and it just shows how much prayer can mean. If that was not an answer to prayer, I don't know what is. You can bet Tom is respected by his buddies.

The mother reported that both Joel and Tom had an experience with the Lord – that's when they received his salvation and came to know him personally.

THE IMPACT OF PUBLIC PRAYER AND FAITH OF LEADERS

In the 1914–18 war the ding-dong struggle went on backwards and forwards. People have said, 'It seems as though God was withholding success from us, yet keeping us from disaster.' Until, that is, an official government move to authorise the National Day of Prayer. The churches were praying all the time of course, but God was waiting for a national commitment. It was not until July 1st, 1918, that a decision was taken by the Government to issue such a call. Immediately that decision was taken, a remarkable change came over the situation . . . there was a series of brilliant victories which led up to the Armistice.

It might be asked, 'Did Germany not have any official prayers?'

The answer is that they did not. Moreover, Hitler contradicted Christ's words. He said, 'Jesus taught love your enemies as yourself and be kind to those who insult you. But I say, hate your enemies and destroy them. Let the German Master-Race dominate!'

He was following the teaching of Nietzsche, the demented son of a Lutheran pastor, and none of Hitler's youth movement was allowed to be a Christian.

It was very different with Dobbie and with others like him. As the

Dorset Daily Echo reported, 'He made a confession of faith' as they called it:

> At the age of fourteen years I came to know Jesus Christ, before that I only knew him in my head, but at half-term holiday at Blackheath . . . I then and there accepted Jesus Christ as my Saviour, on the grounds that he had settled my debt of sin once and for all, and that therefore I went free. Having taken that step, my first reaction was one of intense relief. The heavy burden was lifted for good and all. I could face the past, present and future with confidence.

What is very significant was the eagerness of the commanders-in-chief of all the three military services that all ranks should possess and read The New Testament. At the back of that little khaki Testament each commander-in-chief of the Navy, Army and Air Force had added his signature to the words: 'We commend the Gospel of Christ our Saviour to every member of His Majesty's Forces.'

One of many stories told tells of a dying soldier. He lay face down and under his hand lay an open khaki New Testament. His finger was stuck to the page and the print came off as they lifted him up. He was buried with these words to which he had been pointing, transferred to his finger:

> Jesus said, 'I am the resurrection and the life. He who believes in me, although he were dead, yet shall he live.'

Lt General Sir Frederick Morgan was head of the British and American Planning Staff that made plans for the invasion, that led to the surrender of Nazi Germany. He wrote two years after the surrender and end of hostilities. 'Miracles happen still,' he wrote. 'How many of them have we not seen enacted before our eyes in these past few years?' Then he lists a few and adds others:

> 1. There was Dunkirk and its flat calm sea. Who planned that? We saw no way out barring a miracle. Then came the miracle.
> 2. Two years later, the British and American military convoy was sailing in order to land in North Africa. All the enemy submarines were on the lookout. A breathtaking moment was when a U-boat caught sight of the tall ship of one convoy, the rest being obscured by a squall that seemed to be travelling with our ships and providing cover. The Nazi observer thought that what he saw was merely worthy of routine report.
> 3. Then just as General Patton was due to land on the Casablanca beaches, open to the full Atlantic swell, just as it seemed inevitable that the whole affair must be called off, the wind changed from on-shore to off-shore and let the small craft in successfully. There was surely more than human planning here too!

4 The history of other theatres of war tell many similar happenings, but I doubt if any will compare with the miracle of D-Day in 1944.

He goes on to explain that had that been delayed, the enemy could have held up operations in time to perfect secret weapons which we now know were in the making. General Morgan ends by asking to whom do we owe these miracles?

Prayer and the Angels

What goes on behind the scenes concerning prayers in wartime and the angels? There are a number of passages in the Bible which indicate that behind the earthly conflicts there exists a conflict between spiritual powers of good and evil, and earnest prayer can influence the outcome which becomes reflected on earth.

The prophecies of Daniel reveal some of what goes on. The relationship between prayer and the angelic powers is partly revealed in that mystical chapter ten of the book of Daniel. It is in verses 5, 12–14:

'Then one day early in April,' Daniel says, 'as I was standing by, before me stood a person robed in linen garments, with a belt of purest gold around his waist. His skin had a lustrous glow, and from his face came blinding flashes like lightning.' . . . Then he said, "Don't be frightened, Daniel, for your request has been heard in heaven and was answered the very first day you began to fast before the Lord and pray for understanding; that very day I was sent here to meet you. But for twenty-one days the mighty Evil Spirit who overrules the kingdom of Persia blocked my way. then Michael, one of the top officers of the heavenly army, came to help me, so that I was able to break through these spirit rulers of Persia. Now I am here to tell you what will heppen to your people, the Jews, at the end times – for the fulfilment of this prophecy is many years away."

8 **T**HE UNSEEN BATTLE FOR NATIONS

PRAYER AND THE ANGELS

Daniel chapter 10 is an eye-opener to the spiritual battle behind the scenes. This passage is linked with historical events so we know it is true.

Daniel was told that the answer to his prayers was held up by a spiritual enemy which had dominance over Persia. It had been a three-week battle — a spiritual battle in the unseen spiritual realm which influenced the earthly nation of Persia.

Fortunately, Daniel had been guided to set aside three weeks of intense prayer. He did not know that this battle was going on in the unseen. He did not know that his prayers were helping the angels of God win through. Actually, he wondered why no answer to his prayers seemed to be coming through to him, until it was all explained to him later. He had been heard in heaven right from the beginning. Here are the words the angel spoke to him in Daniel 10:12:

'Fear not, Daniel, for from the first day that you set your heart to understand and to chasten yourself before your God, your words were heard, and I have come for your words.'

Then follows the eye-opener. It is obvious that he is speaking about an unseen spiritual power behind a nation's events. In this case it was one of Satan's evil principalities. The angel said in verse 13:

'But the Prince of the Kingdom of Persia opposed me for 21 days, but lo, Michael, one of the chief princes, came to help me, and I retained the upper hand with the kings of Persia [Iran].'

It becomes obvious as you read on, that the Prince of Persia is a spirited unseen power, an evil prince spirit which fights to destroy the soul of the nation.

Greece Was to Be Next

The angel then spoke of Greece in verse 20. That also has an evil spiritual spokesman trying to claim the soul of this nation. Then in chapters 11 and 12 the events of succeeding history down to modern times are given in remarkable detail which was then, in Daniel's time, in the future. Much of it has been fulfilled, but there is still some to be fulfilled concerning Babylon.

The point of all this is that behind world events there are spiritual powers fighting for the souls of various nations. What evil spirit is fighting to destroy our nation? This aspect is the background to Ephesians 6:12. I'll give you Berkeley's translation:

> Our wrestling is not against flesh and blood opponents, but against the rulers and authorities of darkness; against the spiritual forces of evil in the spiritual sphere.

Daniel was told that he was greatly beloved by God because he set aside three weeks to pray earnestly against these hidden forces of evil.

When you look around and see Satan's deception claiming the soul of various nations, like Daniel, who set aside three weeks for earnest prayer, you can help the victory of truth. For this he was told, he was a man greatly beloved by God.

Have you heard the expression 'Wars and rumours of wars'? That's what Jesus said would happen before his return. The Greek for rumours could also be 'reports' of wars. The Bible says that the real war is fought in the unseen. Ephesians 6:12 tells you that some of these forces are very wicked:

> For we are contending . . . against principalities, against powers . . . against hosts of wicked spirits in the heavenly places. We are contending against the planned strategies (wiles) of the devil.

Yes, that word in the old English, 'wiles', is the translation of a Greek military word. It means a general plan of strategy. It tells you that Satan, the devil, does not work in a haphazard way. He has it all very cunningly planned out. He knows the weaknesses of the forces for good and truth. He knows your weaknesses and where you're most vulnerable. He has thousands of years experience. That's why you need the victory of Christ who has defeated the devil. All that happens on earth is but a reflection of the spiritual unseen conflict.

As Soldiers of Jesus Christ, How Do We Engage the Enemy?

Well first, in the air by prayer says verse 18, but there are other spiritual weapons that you need as well – in fact you need the whole armoured equipment – the whole armour of God (v 13). Its high tech equipment is devastating to the wicked one if you use it fully, but the trouble often is that Christians don't use it fully – for example, we should practise sword drill with the Sword of the Spirit. 'The Sword of the Spirit is the Word of God', the Bible. Satan has struck it out of the hand of many Christians. Many a discussion is on 'What I think', instead of 'What the Word of God says'.

Satan has also struck it out of the hand of some leaders. How? Well many theological courses teach the idea that the Bible is the word of man – not the Word of God. Trainees leave with a damaged faith, and most of the evidence for truth has been denied them. Destructive theories of the Bible's origin were thought out in ignorance 200 years ago before most of our discoveries of science and archaeology, and before the literacy methods and cultural routines of Bible times were known, and secular lecturers have withheld these facts. Satan's first attack was on the Bible.

Many Christians have not learnt to use the Sword of the Spirit as a weapon against Satan's lies. Instead of quoting the Bible's answers, they discuss its problems or humanise it.

Beware of using such expressions as 'The prophet thought this', or 'Isaac said that', when in fact it was God who said it. What the scripture actually says is, 'God said this to the prophet', 'God revealed that to the prophet' and 'God said to the prophet, "Write this down with a pen and paper that he who reads it may run to obey." '

Many things that God said to the Bible prophets, the prophets themselves sometimes did not understand. That shows that the ideas were not from the prophets themselves, but from God. 'I heard, but did not understand,' wrote Daniel, in chapter 12 verse 8, 'but God said to me, "Go your way Daniel, for the meaning of these words is closed and sealed until the time of the end . . . none of the wicked shall understand, but those who are wise will understand." '

Satan's Devices

The battle in the unseen is real, says the Bible; we are not ignorant of Satan's devices, says the New Testament.

How well do you use your spiritual radar detection, and God's high tech? Did you detect what the devil was up to when two Christian TV programmes in America were brought into disrepute? The occasion was seized on in Britain as an opportunity to restrict Christian broadcasting. It was just when possibilities were opening up for Christian stations and real biblical teaching was likely to be allowed in the nationally-controlled media.

Of course the devil had it all beautifully timed and worked out. 'We wrestle against wicked spirits in high places,' says Ephesians 6:12, so be fully armoured. Now in that list of Christian armour in Ephesians the Bible is the only weapon for attack. The rest are protective against the vicious missiles of the devil, says verse 16.

So the armour-plating is the breastplate of righteousness and the buckle of truth; righteousness and truth should be buckled on. The devil is always eager to pounce on the slightest lapse. Policemen are sometimes caught being lawless, but the world does not say therefore, we need no policemen. Unfortunately, sometimes there is news of a doctor who breaks the code of conduct, but the sick don't say abolish all doctors. There have been cases of political corruption, but people don't say do away with governments. But when a Christian slips up, that is taken as an excuse to be godless.

A solicitor once told me that he really wanted to go into the ministry, but he knew how people pounced on a minister for any slip up. He went on to say that his legal profession gave him an insight into percentages of misdemeanours. Subsequently he was astonished to find how low the percentage was among Christian ministers. The percentage of misdemeanours among other professionals against their own code of conduct, was much higher.

Remember your part in the battle of prayer. Remember that witches' covens all over the country pray to Satan especially against Christian ministers. They pray that their families may break up, or worse. So let that challenge you to use the spiritual intercom of prayer. Every time you tune into God on the wavelength of Jesus, that gives victory, 'for at the name of Jesus every knee shall bow'. It's the world's most powerful transmitter and heaven's too, because Jesus said, 'All power is given unto me, all things in heaven and on earth and under the earth.'

Yes, let your Jesus-prayer blast out the bunkers of badness. Because Ephesians chapter 6 says:

> We manoeuvre not against flesh and blood, but against wicked spirits, against rulers of the darkness of this world. So pray all the time with all kinds of prayer-supplication with observation and perseverance.

The Mystery of Micaiah

One of the astonishing stories in the realm of the supernatural is the mystery of Micaiah (1 Kings 22).

Micaiah was the prophet whom wicked King Ahab did not like because he was always loyal to God's Word. So Ahab summoned 400 **false** prophets. Why? because they would advise what he wanted. (There are often more false prophets around than true prophets.)

Ahab was a successful warrior. He is actually mentioned by the king of Assyria on the Black Obelisk, which was dug up by archaeologists. He was confident of victory over Syria especially as he was joined by the powerful king of Judah, King Jehoshaphat, who was faithful to the Lord. He was not happy at Ahab heeding the false prophets, so he suggested calling in Micaiah. Ahab's response was: 'I hate him because he never prophesies good for me!' No wonder! Ahab never wanted **God**'s good.

An officer fetched Micaiah. Now what was mysterious about Micaiah? It was the vision which God gave him. The question is, did Micaiah actually see these spirits on each side of God's throne, or was it just a vision in order to give the required guidance?

In the vision the Lord said, 'Who will entice Ahab to go to battle and be killed?'

One said this and another said that and then a spirit came forward and said, 'I will entice him.'

The Lord said 'How?' and the spirit said, 'I will go out and be a deceiving spirit in the mouth of Ahab's prophets.'

Micaiah then turned to King Ahab and said, 'Look! The Lord has put a deceiving spirit in all your 400 prophets, because God's judgement is coming upon you in this war.'

To avoid disaster, Ahab put on an ordinary soldier's armour, but in battle an archer shot an arrow at random and it killed him.

My question is this; and I would be glad of your answers. Was this just a vision to Micaiah or did God really commission a spirit to deceive the false prophets? Perhaps that spirit was Satan who also asked permission to afflict Job, but in his case Satan was allowed only to go so far.

In our days several witches who have been converted to Christ declare that as Satan-worshippers they did actually see Satan. Doreen Irvine was one, and there were two others recently reported in an evangelical paper. In any case, false prophets who don't want truth are always open to deception. The Bible says this will increase in these last days. One passage is 2 Thessalonians 2:9–11. I quote:

> A lawless one will come with the deceptions of Satan, with wicked deceptions for those who perish because they did not receive the love of the truth so as to be saved. For this reason, God will send on them a strong delusion for them to believe the lie.

Does this sound to you like a New Testament example of that Old Testament mystery of Micaiah? Are Satan's lies believed today?

AUTHOR'S WARTIME PREDICTIONS WHICH CAME TRUE

The remainder of this chapter is a transcription of my book *Advent or Atom?* republished by Prophetic Witness Movement International in 1980.

In July, 1944, I wrote in *All Saints Herald* predictions of events which have since been fulfilled. Prophecies of the Bible concerning these significant times were carefully interpreted by me as follows:

> This is what the Bible says will be the international arrangements in the final phase (of this age), and towards which present events are moving.

There will be two great amalgamations of nations, the States of Europe and a Northern Confederacy. Included in the first will be Britain, France, Belgium, Holland, the Rhineland, Austria, Switzerland, the Balkans, Italy, Spain, N. Africa, Turkey and the Levant; while the Northern Confederacy will be led by Russia with most of Germany probably up to **Hamburg** [i.e. East Germany].

This was fulfilled on April 26th, 1945, when Russians met the Allied Forces at **Hamburg** and the **Elbe**. The Council of Europe commenced about 1947, and the 'Iron Curtain' divided the nations exactly as described. It had taken a year for the British and American forces to reach the Elbe. All the plans and forecasts had been that we would reach the Elbe and beyond Berlin before the Russians got there, but I had studied certain prophecies in the Bible about the end times which indicated to me that we would only reach the Elbe, and Russia would occupy Berlin.

My article continues:

The above will be the settlement which will exist before the return of the Lord Jesus, and if it arises out of this war, peace will be settled on those lines or develop later. This makes the present battles significant, because if conquest becomes the basis of settlement, Russia should be in Berlin before us, while we should only just be getting into Western Germany.

This was fulfilled on April 18th, 1945, in spite of the Allies expecting to be in Berlin first.

Figure 8.1. The newspaper map of 1945 shows how Russia did get to Berlin first and the allies only reached Hamburg and the Elbe as prophesied by the author a year earlier.

RUSSIA TO HOLD HALF GERMANY

———•———

DETAILS ANNOUNCED OF CONTROL ZONE

U.S. TROOPS TO MOVE BACK 150 MILES

BRITISH WILL OCCUPY KIEL AND HAMBURG

BY OUR DIPLOMATIC CORRESPONDENT
The Moscow newspapers, clearly acting on official information, yesterday published details of the zone in Germany to be occupied by the Red Army.

On a rough estimate the area to be garrisoned by the Russians is equal to about half of the total territory of the Reich.

A map issued to the Russian Press shows that the zone extends in some places far to the west of the present line of demarcation between the Red Army and those of the Western Allies. It includes the whole of the German States of Thuringia, Saxony, Mecklenburg and Anhalt.

This means that American troops now in some parts of Thuringia and Saxony will have to withdraw over 150 miles to the west, abandoning the towns of Leipzig, Chemnitz, Halle, Dessau, Weimar, Jena and Eisenach.

Figure 8.2. Half of Germany officially controlled by Russia as predicted by the author in 1944.
Source: Daily Telegraph, *June 7th, 1945*

In May 1940, when Italy was hesitating to enter the war, I wrote: 'She will come in against us, be defeated, and then become a co-belligerent.' This was fulfilled in June 1944.

Writing in 1944, I said: 'England will relinquish India to home rule.' This was fulfilled in 1947.

The God-given prophecies which enabled the foregoing deductions to be made are to be found in Daniel chapter 2 and Ezekiel chapters 38 and 39. Read these passages and see if you can tell how it was working out. By interpreting these and similar passages as early as 1886, Dr Gratton Guinness accurately foretold many happenings of our days.

In July 1944, I wrote:

One of the outcomes of this war will be to give opportunities to Jewish emigration . . . the suffering of the Jews will have greatly expedited the movement . . . to settle in Palestine. Ezekiel 39:23–39.

This was fulfilled May 15th, 1948 and onwards with the establishment of the State of Israel.

Why is the Bible so interested in our times?
It is because God is working out a plan which will lead up to the return of the Lord Jesus Christ in power and great glory.

SHOCK OF THE ATOM BOMB

When news of the Hiroshima atom bomb was announced in the papers on August 7th, 1945 it was a great shock to people. There were conflicting opinions on whether a whole Japanese city should be wiped out in this manner. Many wrote to the newspapers protesting against it even though the Japanese had committed so many crimes. The usual reply was that it saved millions of soldiers' lives – both Japanese and those of the Allies – by shortening what would have been an extended Eastern War.

That day I was taking a men's meeting in London, and after it one of the men came up to me and said: 'Doesn't it make Joel's prophecy about the latter days significant, about wonders in the sky and on earth blood and fire and pillars of smoke!'

Those pictures of the mushroom-shaped pillars of smoke were soon to appear in our papers and the man was very smart to notice the connection. Here is an extract from the *Daily Sketch* of August 8th, 1945:

> Captain William Parsons of the US Navy, who worked on the development of the bomb, rode in the Super-Fortress [which dropped the bomb] to observe the effects. He said: 'The whole thing was tremendous and awe-inspiring. After the missile had been released I sighed, and stood back for the shock. When it came, the men aboard with me gasped, "My God," and what had been Hiroshima was a mountain of smoke like a giant mushroom.'

Jewish Scientific Weapons Turn the Tide

You may have noticed in my records that at critical points in both world wars, Jewish scientific weapons helped to change defeat into victory. Dr Chaim Weizmann's TNT explosive chemical helped the Allies to victory near the end of the First World War. In recognition, he was granted a home for Jews in Palestine.

The sudden end to the war with Japan was the result of the atom bomb. Another newspaper cutting I preserved was about a Jewish woman who was the inventor. She was Professor Lize Meitner. She escaped from Hitler's control and brought her secret to the Allies. So Hitler's persecution drove from him the secret he was seeking. Churchill referred to this when the war was a year old:

> Since the Germans drove out the Jews and lowered their technical standards our science is definitely ahead of theirs.

The Hidden Hand

How remarkable are the issues behind the world dramas of the last century! Are you beginning to see them? God told the prophets that after a long period, he would bring Israelites from all over the world back to Palestine. The Balfour Declaration established the home for the Jews in the Holy Land.

In the Second World War, the Jewish woman scientist brings the secret of the atom bomb to quickly end the war, and the United Nations meet and then contrary to expectations, established the State of Israel in Palestine.

There appears to be a reference to this by Jesus. He said that after his crucifixion the Jews would never govern their city of Jerusalem again until the appointed time of Gentile rule ends. Then there would be a 'united nations' trying to find a solution to the troubles there, and the 'power of uranium' (atoms) would be released.

I wrote an article about it immediately after the dropping of the atomic bomb in 1945. It was copied in many magazines.

ATOMIC WEAPONS AND THE STARTLING ACCURACY OF JESUS

Uranium, the element from which atomic weapons are made, is actually spoken of in the Bible, when describing the conditions that will herald the return of Christ with power. Dr J.E. Shelley, of Cyprus, says of my article, which appeared in four different periodicals:

> Victor Pearce has dealt with the significance of the word Uranium in his splendid article, 'Jesus and Nuclear Fission . . . Our Lord's Prophecy in Luke 21:25–26'. Pearce suggests that it could be translated: 'On earth a banding together of nations in impassable straits of roaring seas and billows, men breathless for fear and expectation of what is about to come to civilization, because the power of uranium (heaven) shall be shaken.'

My article had also said:

> We can at least describe it as a strange coincidence if nothing more, that the word 'heaven' in the Greek is ouranon. The name Uranium comes from this Greek word which we usually translate 'heaven', but let us translate it as 'uranium' and we find that our text says that men will fear and nations will coalesce, because the powers of uranium will be released . . . St Peter also uses the word, so let us see how 2 Peter [3]:12 reads if we translate it in the same way. It says: 'Looking for and hastening unto the day of God, wherein uranium being on fire shall be dissolved and the elements will melt with fervent heat.'

Look at that word 'element'. It is used today to describe a primary substance composed of one kind of atom, and we find that the old Greek word *stoicheia* has exactly the same meaning. The Greek lexicon tells you the following: 'In physics, it means the primary matter, elements.' An atom bomb is made up from the element uranium. The word 'atom' was an equivalent used by Leucippus as long ago as 400 BC.

Uranium, from which atom bombs are made, is an element. Man has made it unstable by separating the two uraniums, U235 from

U238, and by doing so has made it terribly dangerous. The separating of the two makes plutonium, and it is this that is used to start the chain reaction of nuclear fission in an atom bomb and will also do so in the even more powerful hydrogen bomb and neutron bomb. The world-wide threat, which such weaponry makes, is plainly spoken about by St Peter. Furthermore, the terrific heat which accompanies the melting or disintegration of the element uranium is accurately described by as strong a phrase as possible – 'with fervent heat'. The heat released by nuclear fission approaches the temperature of the sun. In the Mexican desert tests it fused the surrounding sand for miles around into a sea of green glass.

In my original article I wrote, 'Some may feel that this is pressing the meaning of the Greek word *ouranos* too literally, and that the application of the English text as it stands is sufficiently impressive. To my mind it appears to be an instance of the Lord's foreknowledge of history which itself would lend deeper meanings to his words as prophecies unfold, and for this reason I would say that it was more than coincidence that when uranium was discovered it was given the name of "uranium". It was discovered by a German scientist who named it "heaven" (uranium), because of its heavenly translucent colour. The *Oxford Dictionary* relates the etymology of uranium with "Uranus and the Greek *ouranos*".'

The prophecies of Daniel imply that history would give deeper meanings to prophecies; 'Go your way Daniel, for the meaning of the words is closed and concealed until the time of the end . . . None of the wicked will understand, but they who are wise will understand.'

It could be objected that we may not know when to translate *ouranous* with the word uranium, or when to use the original meaning 'heaven'. For an answer look at how other words with secondary meanings are translated according to the context. The Greek word *pneuma* meaning 'wind', later took on the secondary meaning 'spirit', and so in St John's Gospel 3:6, it is translated 'that which is born of the spirit is spirit,' but in verse 8 the same word is translated 'wind', its original meaning, i.e. 'The wind blows where it wishes.'

When the agnostic scientist H.G. Wells heard of the atomic bomb he said, 'This is the end. The human race will destroy itself.' The Bible is more optimistic than this, or it can be for you, because in that scripture where Jesus described atomic fission, he said to those living at that time, 'Be uplifted for your deliverance is near.' He was speaking to those who had taken him as their Saviour. He would return for them, with great power. He would stop the world destroying itself and judge the nations responsible. He would then establish a wonderful millennium of peace and good living. The actual destruction of planet Earth would be a long time after this.

ANGELS AND ISRAEL

Something Symbolic about the Discovery of the Scrolls

We have said it was only because Hitler was defeated that the 'home for the Jews' was preserved, and the State of Israel was created by the United Nations.

You have probably heard of the Dead Sea Scrolls. Scores of large earthenware jars were discovered in the caves near the Dead Sea, and sealed inside them were all the sacred scrolls of the Old Testament. There were also other writings by the religious sect which had hidden them for safety when the Roman invasion was threatened in AD 66.

Among those other scrolls one was found which was dramatically significant. It was called 'The Assumption of Moses', and it prophesied that the scrolls would be preserved in those jars 'until the liberation of Israel'. The writer of that prophecy must have been thinking of a similar action by the prophet Jeremiah. He buried documents in a jar which he said would be discovered when Israel returned to Palestine (Jeremiah 32:13–44). The remarkable thing is that it was at the time of the creation of the new State of Israel that the sacred scrolls were found. Listen to Professor Yadin's report.

Professor Yadin is the son of Professor Eleazar Sukenik who bought the first three scrolls for the University of Jerusalem. He wrote on page 14 of his book *Message of the Scrolls:*

> I cannot avoid the feeling that there is something symbolic in the discovery of the scrolls and their acquisition at the very moment of the creation of the State of Israel. It is as if these scrolls have been waiting in caves for two thousand years until the people of Israel had returned to their home . . . The first three scrolls were bought by my father for Israel on the *29th of November 1947, which was the very day upon which the United Nations voted for the re-creation of the Jewish State after two thousand years.*

Yadin then quotes a paragraph from the 'Assumption of Moses' scroll in which it instructed the original preservation of all those scrolls as follows:

> Preserve the scrolls which I shall deliver to you . . . Anoint them with oil and put them away in earthen jars until God's name shall be called upon, until the day of repentance, in the visitation wherewith the Lord will visit them in the consummation of the end of days.

This reflected the words of Jeremiah's prophecy:

> Put them in an earthenware jar . . . for I the Lord will gather Israel from

all countries where I have driven them. I will plant them back in their own land. Is anything too hard for the Lord to do?'

Nothing was too hard for the Lord. Is not this the reason why the angel armies intervened to give victory to the Allies? They were enabled to make a home for the Jews at the end of the First World War, and create a State of Israel after the Second.

The White Cavalry for Israel

I have preserved some newspaper cuttings which are reports made at the time of the invasion of the newly born State of Israel. They state that within two days of Israel's birth as a state, she was invaded from all sides. The aggressors aimed to demolish this work of the United Nations Organisation. In spite of that no member of UNO did anything to stop this flagrant reversal of decree. The world just sat back and watched, expecting the State of Israel to be wiped out.

The newspaper reported it with an air of a *fait accompli*. The invasion is shown to have come from all quarters:

- Egyptian forces invaded Palestine from the south-west, captured Gaza and were thrusting along the coast to link up with –
- Arab legion troops driving from the west towards Tel Aviv, the capital of the new State of Israel.
- Another Egyptian column thrust 30 miles across the southern desert and entered Beersheba.
- Lebanese and Syrian forces are shown to be attacking from the north.
- Iraqi and Trans-Jordan forces advanced from the north-east.
- An Arab legion column striking west from Jericho were only ten miles from Tel Aviv.

So, humanly speaking, the case for Israel looked hopeless. Some of the nations had actually forbidden any armaments or weapons to be sold to Israel. In contrast, the crack Arab Legion forces were trained and led by British Army officers. *Yet within days, all the invading forces were routed!*

The Egyptians were flung back to the Nile. Jordan's legions lost all their area on the west side of the Jordan River. Israel occupied Lebanon and the Golan Heights.

What Had Caused Such a Dramatic Reversal?

Strange rumours were coming in. Invaders from the south reported that they were confronted by legions of unknown troops clothed in white.

The Israeli troops reported similar stories.

The manifestations were all similar to the Angels of Mons accounts of the First World War, and like the many reports about the 'white cavalry of Bethune', as they came to be called.

It also seems significant that the same news extract records that the first president of the new State of Israel was Dr C. Weizmann who was instrumental in obtaining the Balfour Declaration in 1917. He had been involved in the Allies' war efforts after inventing acetone for TNT explosives.

The Six Day War Was Also Significant

The Six Day War of 1967 was very significant because, for the first time for 2,520 years, Israel captured and governed Jerusalem. For all those years, Jerusalem was governed by non-Jewish powers, but their control was prophesied only to continue 'until the times allotted to the Gentiles are completed,' Jesus said (Luke 21:24). So Christians everywhere got very excited at the significance of this event.

The attack on Israel was again very sudden, so how was it that Israel gained such a rapid victory? Of course their efficiency and bravery were evident, but I received this interesting note from Mr C.J. Atton of Prestatyn:

> God's cavalry were also in evidence in the Six Day War in 1967. Arab generals said, 'They did not know that Israel had large cavalry units.'

Why should Israel be so favoured by such intervention? Is it because they deserve it? The answer is 'No'. In the Bible God says, 'Don't think I am doing this because you are better living than any other nation. It was because of your sins that you were scattered among the nations. It is because I am honouring my promise to Abraham.'

Furthermore, God says he will eventually bring blessing to the Egyptians and Arabs as well as Israel. Here are his words in Isaiah 19:24:

> In that day Israel will be the third with Egypt and Assyria [Iraq], a blessing in the midst of the earth, whom the Lord of angelic forces has blessed saying, 'Blessed be Egypt my people, and Assyria the work of my hands, and Israel my heritage.'

The Sign in the Sky in 1973

I have quoted reports of supernatural intervention related to the 1948 and 1967 Palastinian wars. A similar overruling seems the only explanation for the 1973 Yom Kippur deliverance.

Yom Kippur is a major Jewish festival in the autumn. It is the Day of Atonement. The Israeli army was on leave, and the invasion from all sides was a complete surprise. Lance Lambert informs us that something stopped the invasion, yet the Israeli garrisons had only a few hundred men against Syria's massive tank attack. Syria had more tanks than Hitler's offensive against Russia. On the Golan Heights in north Israel on a twenty-mile front they had 1,200 tanks. Egypt attacked from the south-west with 3,000 tanks, 2,000 heavy guns, 1,000 aircraft and 600,000 men, according to a report to the United Nations.

The Egyptians crossed the Suez Canal and drove on. The whole of central Israel was at their mercy, and only half an hour's drive away. Yet something stopped them.

When the Syrians launched their attack in the north with 1,200 tanks the Israeli Golan Brigade commander reported that he had only two tanks and ten men on duty. Wave after wave of Syrian tanks bore down on them but when only one mile away, within sight of the Lake of Galilee, they stopped. What stopped them?

An Israeli captain without any religious beliefs said that he looked up into the sky and *saw a great grey hand pressing downwards as if it were holding something back.*

These tremendous forces were held back until the Israelis could be called out of their synagogues to man their tanks. Then ensued what were described as 'the greatest tank battles in world history', greater even than the battle of El Alamein in the Second World War. The Yom Kippur war was the first wholly technological war in Middle East history, in which 4,000 tanks of 900 batteries were thrown into action. Soviet Russia had organised a massive airlift of arms to Syria and Egypt.

The great hand in the sky was a sign that God was holding back the forces until Israel was alerted to leave her Day of Atonement prayers and get back into action. Then against all odds the invaders were driven right back. They had expected to wipe out Israel, but they did not know that that was impossible because God had told the prophet Amos concerning these latter days:

> 'I will restore the fortunes of my people Israel . . . I will plant them upon their land, and they shall never again be plucked up out of the land which I have given them,' says the LORD your God.
>
> (Amos 9:14,15, RSV)

ELIJAH AND ANGELS

Well do you believe in angels? Then here's some food for thought. In fact I'm thinking of when an angel brought food to Elijah. He did it twice, why?

Elijah was absolutely exhausted. He was drained physically and emotionally. He'd come through a great crisis – a crisis for his country. He'd rescued Israel from backsliding from God's revealed truth and accepting a false religion. He'd stopped them from being dominated by satanic Baal worship.

Inspired by God, he'd won a great victory over 950 false prophets; 450 of them were prophets of Baal and 400 of them were prophets of a goddess.

God had honoured Elijah's great faith by sending down fire from heaven and consuming the offering made by Elijah. This made Israel shout, 'The Lord Jehovah he is God. The Lord is God!'

Now this infuriated the Queen who'd introduced this false satanic religion. Her name was Jezebel. Elijah was a real he-man; he feared no man and very few women – but Jezebel was one of the few women he did fear. He was victorious over 950 men but when Jezebel threatened his life, Elijah ran for cover. Sometimes a surprising setback after victory has that effect on you. Elijah was exhausted in body and in mind.

He lay down under a tall evergreen tree and fell into a deep sleep. It was then that God showed a deep tenderness to his champion. 1 Kings 19:5 says, 'An angel came and touched him, woke him up and said, "Sit up and eat!" ' Yes, it was an angel of the Lord! 'Sit up and eat,' he said.

Elijah looked and on a hot stone near his head was a delicious cake still warm after baking and a jar of water. Elijah was ravenous and gorged the lot, and then fell into a deep sleep, unconscious of time.

The angel came again, touched him and pointed to more food that gave him amazing strength. This enabled him to make the long journey back to God.

9   WHAT HAPPENS AFTER DEATH

WINNING BACK THE ASHES

A lady in her letter asked about the ashes, referring to cremation, 'How can God raise from the dead the bodies burnt to ashes? I suppose I should find an answer in that the martyrs were burnt to ashes at the stake.'

She has hit on the right clue. Ashes cannot rob God of his saints – believers I mean. If so, thousands who have been burnt for their testimony would have perished. God will win back the ashes, so to speak! But if the body has dissolved and disappeared, how will God raise their bodies from the grave?

That is exactly the question Paul answers in 1 Corinthians 15:35 onwards. He replies that when a person is buried, you are not putting into the grave or burning into ashes the material of the body which God will give it in the resurrection. You only sow the character of the body. It is like sowing the seed, the seed of wheat or some other grain. Now a seed does not contain the substance of the future wheat with its stalk, leaves and head. It only contains the genetic fingerprint! It is the same with a human being. God has your genetic fingerprint. You know what science says about that, don't you; it says that you are unique. There is no one else like you. Jesus puts it in a more homely way. 'He calls his sheep by name', or again, 'Every hair of your head is numbered'.

He also says, 'He who believes on me will never perish but I will raise him up at the last day.'

That is the real you that he will raise up. Look at it another way. Did you know that even while you are alive, the substance of your body had changed by the time seven years has passed? Your muscles and organs have been replaced by new proteins and amino acids all the time but they make up the same shape and tissues as dictated by your genetic fingerprint – or the seed.

So Paul is quite scientific when he explains that at death you only sow the seed. As God has the record of the characteristics, he will supply substance to it at the resurrection. Of course, with the Lord Jesus, his body was only in the tomb three days, so the substance had not disappeared. As the Old Testament prophesied, 'Thou will not allow your Holy One to see corruption.'

Nevertheless, God changed that same body into a resurrection body. It still showed the scars of his suffering for you but it was no longer limited by material limitations. Neither will you, if you believe. You will be 'changed in a moment and the twinkling of an eye at the last trumpet'.

THE BEMA COURT

I wonder if you've ever had to go to court. Depending on the legal problem you might go to the criminal court, the civil court or the crown court.

I know little of these definitions as you may detect and not much about our legal system; but I do know about the Bible law system.

Did you know that there are different courts of justice for different categories of people? The Bible tells me I shall come to the Bema of Christ, and I hope you will too. I will not appear before the great white throne of justice, and I hope you won't either.

Where do we read of the Bema? The word is in the original Greek. It's usually translated as the judgement . . . of Christ. Only those who belong to Christ will appear before it.

In 2 Corinthians 5:10 we read, 'We must all appear before the judgement seat of Christ.' That is the Bema, it says in the Greek original – the Bema of Christ. If you go to the remains of the city of Corinth to which this letter was written, you can see the Bema, the local court where cases were heard for citizens.

Only those whose sentence has been cancelled will appear at the Bema of Christ. That is those who have accepted forgiveness from Christ. They will not be judged for sin, they will be judged for reward. Because their sins are forgiven they will not come to be sentenced at the judgement day of the great white throne.

Jesus said so in John 5:24: 'He who hears my word and believes . . . has everlasting life and will not come to the judgement, but has passed from death to life.' So if you believe Christ's words and accept his salvation you will not come to the judgement of God at the last day described in Revelation chapter 20.

That's why I said I hoped you will not. Why? Because I hope you will have accepted Christ as your Saviour.

The Bema is the citizen's court where a reward is given for service. But God's high court gives penalty for sin. You can't be judged for sin if Christ has forgiven your sins can you? So that's the difference between those two courts.

The Bible says that some of the believers will not have given very good service for Christ. They will get very little reward and they'll be very sorry, and yet they will be saved because they were born again into God's family, and as citizens of heaven they will not come to the judgement. But those who have not been born again not only get just sentence for sin, they cannot enter heaven. Jesus said, 'Flesh and blood cannot inherit the kingdom of heaven, only those who've been born again by God's Holy Spirit into God's family.' The Holy Spirit gives you rebirth when you accept the Lord Jesus Christ as your Saviour. So be born again by God's Holy Spirit.

IS THERE A SOUL?

Some question whether there is a soul as distinct from the body. This is important because if there is no soul, the Christian ceases to exist when he dies. Death would mean oblivion until resurrection.

This would contradict Christ's promise in John 5:24 that he who believes the gospel would never die. If death meant oblivion, the Old Testament saints also would cease to exist, but Jesus quite clearly said that Abraham was alive and rejoiced to see Christ's day. This was his reply to the Jews who asserted that Abraham and the prophets were dead.

'No,' said Jesus, 'your father Abraham rejoiced to see my day and he saw it and was glad' (John 8:56). He must have rejoiced with the angels at the birth of Jesus. Moses and Elijah rejoiced to see Christ's day. They discussed it with him on the Mount of Transfiguration.

On another occasion, Jesus corrected the Sadducees (in Matthew 22:32). He said that, 'God is the God of the living, and is the God of Abraham, Isaac and Jacob because all live unto him.' He used the present tense to show that their souls were alive as he spoke.

The same is made clear about the New Testament believers, for example in Revelation 6:9 John saw the souls of those who were killed because of their witness for the Word of God and for their testimony. They were obviously conscious too, because they cried out to God asking how long it was to be before judgement day when persecutors would be punished.

Notice here that their bodies had been killed, yet their souls were alive and conscious. That is quite clear.

This fulfilled the words of Christ in Matthew 10:28 where Jesus had clearly stated, 'Don't fear those who can only kill your body, and **cannot** kill your soul'. He was warning believers that down the ages Christians would be persecuted and killed. But they were not to be afraid, because murderers cannot kill the soul.

The one they **were** to fear was God. Why? Because he alone could destroy both the body and soul in hellfire. Yes, you're advised by Jesus to fear hellfire and come to Christ for salvation. That's why Jesus says to you, 'What shall profit a man if he gains the whole world and lose his own soul.'

Some have argued about the word for soul and translated it as 'life'. The Greek word for soul here is psyche. It is the same word that Jesus uses to distinguish it from the body. So it must mean the soul.

Therefore it means that if you are not saved your body can die, but your soul lives on to be judged and lost for eternity if you have not accepted salvation. No wonder Jesus wants you to fear. Fear God who can destroy your soul in hellfire, he said.

But for the believer, when his body dies, his soul goes to be with Christ, which brings wonderful happiness, as St Paul says, 'I have a desire to depart, and to be with Christ which is far, far better.'

Paul repeats that word 'far'. It's a pity the translator didn't do so. Paul was emphasising the wonder of being with Jesus his beloved Saviour.

Sleeping Seed

A lady wrote to ask, 'What does the Bible mean when it refers to death as falling asleep?' She asked if this means that a dead person ceases to be conscious.

It was the Lord Jesus who first referred to death as sleeping. Do you remember that when he went to the little girl aged twelve who had died, he said, 'She is asleep!'

Yes, and they laughed at him, knowing that she was dead.

He also said Lazarus was asleep, when he had been dead four days. From then onwards, the disciples always referred to death of a believer as being asleep in Jesus. But this must refer only to the body, not to the soul. For example, Paul says that to depart this life is to be with Christ which is far better. If his soul was also asleep and not conscious, he could not know that it was bliss to be with Jesus.

Concerning the death of the body, Paul says it is like sowing a seed. The plant dies, but the seed is left to bring a new plant of the same characteristics. In 1 Thessalonians 4, Paul says that those who are asleep are with Jesus in heaven and God will bring them with Jesus when he returns at the second coming. So here again the sleeping part must refer to their body, because their soul is in happy fellowship with the Lord Jesus. But, as regards earthly troubles, Revelation 14:13 says, 'Blessed are they who die in the Lord, for they rest from their labours'.

The Lord Jesus promises you that, 'He who believes on me will never die'. Because the body does die and fall asleep in Christ, that promise must refer to the saved soul.

Someone who was sadly bereaved of her husband in middle life said: 'His body was just a cloak which he had cast off. My real beloved husband is with Jesus, rejoicing in his presence. I know, because he took Jesus as his Saviour years ago and trusted the precious promise.'

'He who believes on me will never die.'

Ghost in a Machine?

Wasn't it Immanuel Kant who said that to think of a soul in the body was like saying there is a ghost in the machine! That was an ironic description. There are a lot around today who say there is no separate soul and body, they say when the body dies you cease to exist – until the resurrection. They say that the word **soul** only means **'life'** – the life of the body.

Are there scriptures to show this idea is wrong? Yes, definitely, and we are looking at some. It's sad that people can overlook them if they don't want to see them.

It is also interesting to look at scientific tests on the difference between the brain and personality.

Two scientists, Cosgrove and Schmidt carried out experiments that showed that behind the mechanism of the brain, there was also a personality using and reading it. They quote Penfield. He writes that the brain is a computer, which must be programmed and operated by a personality which is capable of independent understanding. Because of that he is forced to accept that man's being consists of two basic elements.

What he's saying is that, scientifically, man consists of body and soul, which is what Jesus said. That's what settles the matter.

Jesus gave up his spirit on the cross into his Father's hands, but his body was laid in the tomb until the Spirit returned for it.

Peter, when preaching about it on the day of Pentecost, quotes the Old Testament prophecy: God 'will not leave Christ's soul in Hades – that is the place of the departed – neither will he allow his Holy One to see corruption..'

Peter then interprets it in Acts 2:31: 'He spoke of the resurrection of Christ that his soul was not left in Hades neither did his flesh – that's his body – see corruption'

Yes, the Lord Jesus experienced the separation of soul and body.

He came to save your soul. He valued your soul and gave his life to purchase it from being lost forever. What a tragedy if you value your soul less than Jesus did.

Think of the man who retired on his wealth in Luke chapter 12. He'd made provision for his body only, but that night God said. 'You fool, this night I will require your soul.'

SAVED TODAY

We have seen the scriptures which clearly say that every person has a soul, a soul which does not die when the body dies, such as the statement by Jesus in Matthew 10:28 where he said that persecutors can kill the body but cannot kill the soul. This is why Paul could say that when his body died, his soul would go to be with Christ which is far far better.

This was why Jesus told the dying repentant thief that he would see Jesus that same day in paradise; 'Truly I say to you, this day you will be with me in paradise.'

Now some have said that Jesus was not saying that the soul of the repentant thief would 'be with him this day', but that Jesus was saying to him this day (comma), that he would see him in paradise. In other words that the comma should come after the words 'this day' instead of before it. The people who contend this have deliberately altered the place of the comma. Why? Because they contend that the repentant thief had no separate soul to exist after the body died, to see Jesus.

Those who wrote to me did not realise that there were punctuation marks in the original Greek and the punctuation is before the words 'this day' and not after it.

Some have even contended that original Greek had no punctuation marks, but I have sent to them copies of the original Greek showing them punctuation marks in the text. W.E. Vine in his *New Testament Greek Grammar* says, 'There are four punctuation marks: the comma (,), a dot above the line, the full stop as in English and the question mark which is like an English semicolon.'

A very ancient copy of a page of St John's Gospel – or part of it – showed punctuation marks. This is called The Rylands fragment and is dated at only about twenty years after the apostle's death. Also I have photocopies of secular Greek letters which were written in Christ's time. They show Greek punctuation marks so you see, one must be aware that there are those who can mislead you. The Lord said that there would not be a jot or a tittle of the law that will not be fulfilled. The jot and tittle were the smallest marks of the Hebrew; the same principle applies to the Greek New Testament.

So, the dying repentant thief, **did** have a soul which would survive the death of his body, and which would see the Spirit of Jesus that same day. 'Truly, truly, I say it to you (comma), this day you will be with me in paradise.'

What wonderful grace, that the first to be saved, the first to see his Saviour, was a murderer who repented and believed at his death. By this, God showed the extent of his full and glorious salvation.

With Christ?

The need to be clear about Bible teaching on life after death is apparent from many letters we receive.

One writer said he did not know that the Bible says that when a Christian dies he goes to be with Christ. I directed his attention to what Paul said in Philippians 1:23: 'I have a desire to depart this life and to be with Christ which is far better.'

Now notice that in this statement, the moment of death is given as the time when the believer (in this case St Paul) goes to be with Christ. Somebody once said to me, 'That might apply to St Paul, but I could never be as holy as him.' But the Bible says that it does not depend on how holy we are, but whether we have asked God to forgive us for Jesus' sake.

'While we are at home in the body, we are absent from the Lord. We are willing rather to be absent from the body, and be present with the Lord.'

So what does that pronoun 'we' represent? It represents the souls of the believers. We are willing to be absent from the body, but what is it that would be absent from the body? It is the soul. The souls of believers are described as 'we' – the real self.

The believer is willing because salvation was received by him as a free gift. Free, because the price was paid by Christ's suffering. The believer is willing for his soul to be with Jesus because he knows that in the presence of God there are joys for ever more. The Bible says John got a vision of them in heaven rejoicing, he says, 'I looked, and behold a great crowd which no one could number stood before the throne and before the Lamb of God. They were dressed in white . . . They praised with a loud voice "salvation to our God . . . Worthy is the Lamb who was slain to receive power, riches, wisdom, strength, honour and glory and blessing . . . For you have redeemed us to God by thy blood out of every family, language, tribe and nation." '

OVERCOMING EMBARRASSMENT WHEN VISITING THE DYING

Do you feel awkward when visiting someone with terminal illness? That's understandable, yet the Lord Jesus told us to visit those who are ill. Perhaps some advice may help.

You may be afraid of saying anything which suggests they're dying. As a matter of fact, it's been shown that most terminal patients know that they are dying. They don't like this conspiracy of silence. Why? Because they would like to be ready for death. They'd like to leave their things in order and their soul in order. Also conspiracy to silence robs families of their most precious moments.

But how do you broach the subject? Sometimes the patient will hint himself, but if not, an easy way is to ask him if there's anything worrying him. Get him to give you the lead. He may mention material things at first, but then you can ask him if he is at peace.

First, is he at peace with other people, or are there memories which trouble him? Does he need to ask somebody's forgiveness? Does he want you to write to someone on his behalf? Forgiveness brings peace with man and God. You can then ask if he's asked God's forgiveness.

This question can open up all his soul's need. Depending on how much he knows of the gospel, you can explain the way of salvation. Perhaps he did not realise that he could be certain of salvation because Jesus bore his punishment for him in his place. He needs to tell God how sorry he is and accept Jesus as his Saviour, and the free gift of full forgiveness. 'The wages of sin is death, but the free gift of God is eternal life through Jesus Christ your Lord' (Romans 6:23).

But what if the patient is in a coma. He seems unconscious. Some people make the mistake of thinking people in comas can't hear and they talk about all kinds of unwise things in front of them.

Don't do that! Talk to him in loving and kind words, just as if he can hear. Explain salvation to him. Say slowly a prayer of acceptance of Jesus. I've known some who've been brought back from death's door and who've then told me they heard all that I said.

Patients have said that they felt their spirit had left their body, but could hear all that was going on for a short time. If this is true, the one you are with could hear you telling him how to be saved.

TAKING AWAY THE FEAR OF DEATH

People avoid the subject of death, and nobody wants to tell a person that he's dying – so they say; and yet a questionnaire reveals that eighty-one per cent are anxious to know how it affects them – I mean in the **after** life.

Do you think that this reveals a hidden fear?

Hebrew 5:7 tells you that the Lord Jesus knew this fear. It reads: 'In the days of his flesh, Jesus offered up prayers and entreaties with strong entreaty and tears to him who was to save him from death, and was heard in that he feared.'

So you see, he experienced your natural fear of death. Of course it was for a different reason. For you the cause of fear may be uncertainty, or if you're saved it's just a fear of a new experience.

With Jesus it was knowing that in dying, his pure spotless soul was going to have the foul sins of the world laid on him, and then with them on him he was to have the excruciating pain of slow torture and exposure to ridicule.

How did God the Father answer his cry of fear? By Jesus knowing that he could trust his Spirit safely into his Father's hands. 'Into your hands I commend my spirit.' That's what you can do – trust your spirit into God's care after death. You can do that if you trust in the cross for forgiveness. That which caused Christ agony and fear is the very thing which can bring you comfort and peace. Your sins were transferred to him, they caused him pain and fear, but by believing that, that can bring you the joy of assurance that your sins are gone, taken away by your Saviour, who takes away your fear. Here are some more letters from readers who have seen people die with joy in their faces.

After Death – Christ's Experience

How moving it is to read of a child's death. Here is a letter from Swindon about a child who was only two years old, but she was dying. Suddenly she lifted up her arms as if to be carried to heaven and said excitedly 'Door! Door!' The mother believed the gates of heaven were opening to the child.

We have seen, from the Media Services Agency, that eighty-one per cent of the British public want to know what happens to them after death. Thirty-four per cent wanted to know about heaven, thirty-one per cent about after death and sixteen per cent how to get to heaven.

The Bible gives you information about this, but an important clue is what happened to the Lord Jesus Christ after death. It tells you that the Spirit of Jesus descended into Hades.

I had a letter from a listener asking about this: 'How can you say that Jesus descended into Hades, when the Bible says he descended into hell?' The original Greek in which the New Testament was written, says, 'Hades'. It is only the Authorised Version that says he descended into hell. We love the Authorised Version, but you must remember, it is only a translation – a very good one it is true but it must always be checked with the original language.

What does the original tell us? It tells us that it is only after the judgement day that the unsaved will be cast into hell, Gehenna or hell-fire. Until then the unsaved are held on detention. The saved section was called paradise. It was to that part of Hades to which the Spirit of Jesus descended. Luke chapter 23 tells you that Jesus saw the repentant thief there. Let me quote it: 'Truly I say to you, this day you will be with me in paradise.'

Yes, the Lord Jesus was telling him that the same day of the crucifixion, the Spirit of the Lord Jesus and the spirit of the saved thief would meet in paradise.

The spirit of that man saved at the last minute would not go to the place of the lost.

Some try to cheat God and say that they will repent on their deathbed. Little do they realise that it is the Holy Spirit who convinces a man of sin (John 16), and he will not always strive with a man. The Bible says. 'God is not mocked; whatever a man sows that will he also reap.'

If you feel urged to receive salvation, then don't put it off. 'Procrastination is the thief of souls.' In 2 Corinthians 6:2, God says to you, 'Behold, now is the time to accept, now is the day of salvation.'

WHY RAISE THE BODY?

Somebody came up with the question 'Why raise the body?' They said, 'If the saved soul is so happy at going to be with Jesus at death, why bother with a resurrection of the body? What's your answer to that?'

It's surprising to note that evil spirits and demons crave to possess a body. That's why it is so dangerous to meddle with the occult or with mediums. Those deceiving spirits will imitate past relatives or make other deceptions in order to gain possession of you if you let them. Remember how the devils in the possessed man of Gadera wanted to possess the bodies of pigs when they were cast out. They'd rather do that than go into the abyss.

The human soul may have a sense of incompleteness until his resurrection body is available.

But there is another reason why body and soul must be reunited. What did the Lord Jesus do when he arose from the grave? He was able to have fellowship with earthlings. He ate a meal with them and yet he was able to pass through rock, through doors and through walls. He was able to appear and disappear. Scientifically we know that if a body was changed to neutrons, this could happen. Neutron atoms can replace the proton and electron atoms and look like similar material.

The resurrection body may be similar in appearance. The extraordinary thing is that in 1 Corinthians 15:52 you are told that the sudden change of your body at the resurrection will be a change in the atom. 'Atom' is the word used there in the original Greek.

Now why would the saved believer need such a body when he comes with Christ to judge the world? This only makes sense to those who take the Bible millennium literally. 'Shall not the saved judge men?' asks Paul. Yes, during that 1,000 years reign on earth they will be able to mix with the inhabitants. Like the Lord Jesus they will be able to inhabit heaven and inhabit earth.

'See,' said Jesus, 'a ghost does not have flesh and bones as you see I have,' and he ate a meal in front of them.

Paul certainly took our part in the millennium literally. He said, 'Shall not you saved Christians judge the world.' Scripture says in many places that Jesus will come with all the resurrected people to judge and establish his kingdom on earth. What a fascinating time that will be if you're saved!

LIFE AFTER DEATH

The Cruelty of Reincarnation Belief

Do we live more than one life? Have we been in this world earlier as some other person? This sounds an innocent enough question until we realise the consequences of such an idea. Glen Hoddle the English football manager caused an outcry against remarks he was said to have made saying that invalids suffered for sins done in their former life. This added to the sufferings which invalids already had to bear. I am sure Glen Hoddle never meant it that way because he is known to be very generous to the invalid cause.

Yet in some philosophies the theory of reincarnation has actually excused some from helping the downtrodden and unfortunate. Their misfortunes are regarded as a punishment for sins in an earlier life even if they are unaware of them! They are experiencing only what they deserve! So why help them? Such an outlook has kept the low caste in their miserable state.

So what is this theory of reincarnation? It is that the spirit of a human existed in many lives before the present one, perhaps even as an animal.

Does the Bible have anything to say about this?

Yes it does. Look at Hebrews 9:27 in the New Testament. There we are told, 'It is appointed for a person to die only once and after this the judgement'. Other scriptures teach the same: 'We must all appear before the judgement seat of Christ so that everyone will receive the things done while we were in the body according to whether they were good or bad' (2 Corinthians 5:10).

Now this is really good news because it means that the tyrants won't get away without just retribution. Think of all those cruel despots who have tortured millions. Would you like them to escape?

God repeatedly tells you that he is a just and fair God who on the judgement day will give rewards to those who have done good and appropriate punishment for evil deeds. And as regards our attitude towards invalids, the homeless and starving, look at that story Jesus told about the rich man and the beggar.

There was a certain rich man who dressed in luxurious clothes of important purple and of the best material, and who feasted gluttonously every day, but there was a poor beggar named Lazarus who was dumped at his gate full of open sores, and he craved to be fed from the crumbs which fell from the rich man's table. What is more, the dogs came and licked his sores. Now it came to pass, continued Jesus, that the beggar died, and his spirit was carried by the angels into paradise. The rich man also died and had a grand burial.

In the Place of the Departed he lifted up his eyes, being in torment, and saw paradise a long way off and there was the former beggar Lazarus in luxury. The former rich man cried out, Have mercy on me! Send Lazarus to me that he may dip the tip of his finger in water and cool my tongue because I'm tormented in this flame.

But the answer came: Remember! Remember! You in your lifetime (notice that there was only one lifetime) received all your luxuries, but in contrast Lazarus suffered all those evil things. But now, what a contrast! He is comforted and you are tormented.

But there is a reason why Lazarus cannot come to you. Between you and us there is a great impassable gulf fixed. This prevents anyone who wanted to pass from here to you from doing so. Neither can anyone pass from you to us.

Then the former rich man said, I plead with you! Send Lazarus to my brothers to warn them! Send him to my father's house where my five brothers live, so that he can give them his testimony to stop them from coming to this place of torment.

The reply came, THEY HAVE THE BIBLE! LET THEM HEAR WHAT THAT HAS TO SAY TO THEM! But the former rich man said, Oh, no, no! They won't listen! But they would if one returned to them from the dead. Yes, they'd repent.

The reply came to him, If they will not listen to the Bible from Genesis to Revelation, they will not be persuaded even when Jesus rises from the dead!

WHAT HAPPENS AFTER DEATH

What questions do you think worry the general public? We saw that from a sample of 5,000 non-churchgoers, when asked: 'If you could ask God any questions except any on the Bible, what would they be?' eighty-one per cent wanted to know about things after death. They are concerned about it and don't forget that young people and middle-aged people die as well as old people.

Their own questions were these:

- What is heaven like?
- What happens when we die?
- How do you decide who goes to heaven?

Only nineteen per cent asked other questions. Is this surprising in this sceptical age? In spite of unbelief constantly pumped out on the media, people all over the world would like assurance about conditions after they die. I was told this story.

A senator in the Australian Parliament was strongly averse to being approached with the gospel of Christ. One day he realised he had a malignant growth in one of his ears. His wealth and medical treatment were of no avail and he became confined to bed. When visited he said, 'Oh Mr B, I hope God will not forsake me.'

Mr B placed his arm about his spent frame and said, 'He will not forsake you, senator, if you place your trust in him.'

He read a few verses from Psalm 103 to him, 'Like as a father pitieth his children, so the Lord pitieth those that fear him. For he knoweth our frame, he remembereth that we are dust.'

'Read that again,' said the senator, which Mr B did, and then he asked him to kneel and pray for him. At the conclusion of the prayer, he raised his arms and said, 'Now I place all my trust in him.'

He enjoyed peace for the remainder of his earthly life.

Heaven Is Beautiful

There was a paediatrician whose duty was to sit by a child aged five who was dying of leukaemia. Instead of it being a heart-rending strain, it turned out to be a glimpse of glory. The child sat up just before she died and said, 'Mummy, what lovely music, and all those angels singing! Oh, how happy it is and how beautiful. The music, lovely, lovely!'

We have had so many stories sent in by listeners to my programmes of children with similar experiences. It seems that Jesus, with his great love for children, relieves their suffering with special visions of joy.

A little boy was knocked down in a motor accident. He suffered from a fractured skull and severe concussion. The doctors gave a hopeless prognosis and said that if he recovered, which was most unlikely, he 'would only be a cabbage'.

His parents, however, who were strong of faith, called in many friends and prayed continuously day and night for his recovery and healing. After several days, the boy regained consciousness much to the surprise of the doctors, and was discharged from hospital. Later, he told his mother that he had a dream that he had died and went to heaven. He said it was a beautiful place and that Jesus came to meet him, welcomed him and had a place for him, but after a while he said that although he was ready for him, he had changed his mind and would let him go back home. He made a rapid and complete recovery.

Concern for Loved Ones

One day I was visited by a young lady who had a very anxious question. It was about her older sister who had died of polio two or three years earlier. Now she was very anxious. It only just started to worry her, she said, because she had been converted only recently. She had given her heart to the Lord; she had received the free gift of salvation and she was full of joy. Then she thought of her sister who had died; did she die unsaved? Then she remembered that I had been there at the side of the iron lung which was keeping her sister breathing. She remembered me talking with her and reading a passage of Scripture. So now, two years later, she came with her urgent question.

'Oh please, oh please could you tell me. Do you remember whether she responded and did she accept Christ's salvation?'

Fortunately, I could remember the girl and her name quite clearly. So it was with great relief that I was able to say, 'Yes, your sister came to the Lord easily and readily. She did not know that she would not recover but she heard the way of salvation with great appreciation and joy. She thanked the Lord most earnestly and accepted full salvation through the cross.'

This news was received with tremendous joy. She said, 'You see, before I was saved, I did not know how important it was.'

Reflected Glory

Perhaps I am speaking to one who is holding back from giving his life to the Lord Jesus. O friend, if you think of no one else, think of your family. They have probably been praying hard for you. So many think with great sadness of their loved ones who have died. Why? Because they cannot be sure that they were saved.

It is quite illogical that anyone should hold back his life from God who loves him. God loves you. The Lord Jesus has paid the price for forgiveness of your sins. He would guide you into the ways of blessing and eternal life if you would let him. I have known some people who have held back for years and then have come to Christ and so regretted that they did not do so before. Did you know that it is part of your fallen nature which keeps you from God? As soon as Adam sinned he hid from God and God said, 'Adam, where are you?' You are a child of Adam.

Don't grieve your loved ones any more. They have been praying for you and if you died unsaved they would be very greatly saddened. But what if your loved ones aren't saved either? We pray they will be.

A believer in West Lothian describes two occasions when the face of a dying Christian lit up as they were passing over to the Lord. The first was a relative who loved the Lord and was a help to many. As he died, his face reflected the glory of Jesus. The second was a sister who saw the Lord as she died and glory shone in her face. In Acts 6:15, the face of Stephen shone like the face of an angel before he was martyred. Paul saw it and no doubt it prepared him for his conversion. Afterwards, he saw the Lord Jesus himself on the road to Damascus.

Disabled in Body or Character

We have spoken of the beauty of heaven. We have spoken of the need of the cleansing blood to admit you there. But what of your character? Will that be lovely or will it spoil everything. And what of your body? If you are crippled, disabled or arthritic, will your joints still creak?

Billy Graham tells of his grandmother in his book, *Facing Death*. As she was dying she sat up in her bed, smiled and said, 'I see Jesus and he has his hand outstretched to me and there is Ben and he has two eyes and two legs.'

Why did she say this? Because Ben had lost an eye and a leg in the battle at Gettysburg.

Have you wondered whether there would be cripples in heaven? Cripples will be in heaven if they are saved but they will no longer be cripples. The blind will not be blind. I asked a blind woman what she looked forward to in heaven. She said, 'The wonderful advantage I have over others, is that the first person I will see is Jesus.'

She was of course a Christian. She was even glad she was blind because it was her blindness which brought her to Jesus. She was with the Torch ministry for the blind; it was they who showed her how to be saved.

Problems of the Body

Every idea has to be tested by Scripture, so does the Bible say that there will be no physical handicaps in heaven? Well, in the first place it is the soul which goes to heaven. That carries no injuries with it. What about the body at the resurrection when soul and body are reunited? The Bible says God will give us a new body, 'Thou sowest not the body that shall be' says 1 Corinthians 15. By the sowing it means the burial of the body at death. What kind of body is it which is raised from the grave? Colossians 3 says it will be a glorious body, like Christ's resurrection body. On hearing this, someone said to me that Christ still bore the scars, the wounds, the nail prints, and that Scripture says when he returns with power and glory all nations will see those wounds. (That would only be possible, of course, with close-up TV. It could be that God wants all the world to see 'him whom they pierced'. He may be an exception.)

Whether or not, the important thing to note is that Jesus was characterised by his marked body but not handicapped by it. Remember that in his resurrection appearances he walked eight miles to Emmaus on his wounded feet. On that long journey he revealed prophecies to the two disciples which all foretold his death and resurrection. In the Upper Room he showed them the gaping wound in his side but it was not handicapping him. In fact he began to eat a meal with them and then gave them a long thrilling insight into all the Old Testament prophecies which he had now fulfilled.

So you see, although his wounds were devastating and he had died in agony for our sins, he was alive and well three days later. When the handicapped get to heaven, they will enjoy new bodies and when you get to heaven you will be young again. That is the significance, I think, of the angel in the tomb being young. People sometimes refer to when they were young; when you get your new body and talk of the past, you will say, 'When I was old'! So that is the real secret of eternal youth. Why not put your faith in the risen Saviour who says, 'He who believes on me will never die!'

Your Improved Character

What a grand message for all born-again Christians. At the resurrection you will all have new bodies, perfect bodies and they will be resurrection bodies like Christ's. This will happen at the resurrection of the saved or 'those who belong to Christ' as Paul calls them. In 1 Corinthians 15 we read that the change will come in the twinkling of an eye, or in an atom of time. The Word of God is always up to date – as I have already explained to you, all the world today goes by what is called the Universal Time Clock and that works by the throb of the atom. The atom clock measures the tiniest fraction of time, even less than a billionth of a second. 'That,' says God, 'is how quick I shall be in changing your bodies into glorious resurrection bodies – that is if you are born again.' Wonderful isn't it!

But what about grumbling, difficult Christians? Everyone is improved in character by conversion but we all need to be sanctified as well, otherwise we would spoil heaven, wouldn't we? Well, our characters will be completed at the resurrection, too. This is what St John says. In 1 John 3, it says, 'Beloved we are God's children now; it does not yet appear what we shall be, but we know that when he appears, we shall be like Jesus.'

Isn't that grand! Paul says something similar in Philippians 1:6. He was thankful for the enjoyment of the fellowship of those Christians and then says, 'The Lord has begun a good work in your characters and will bring it to completion at the day of Christ.'

The day of Christ means his second coming. So isn't that encouraging if you are saved: at your resurrection you will have a perfect body and a beautiful character!

With Christ

We have been looking at reports from listeners to my radio programme on the peaceful and beautiful deaths of friends they knew. You may have noticed a common feature in those experiences. When they were dying they actually knew that they were going to be with Jesus. Many of them actually saw the Lord Jesus Christ. This is then one answer to that question 'What happens after death?' The answer is, the saved believer goes to be with Jesus. Paul said this in Philippians 1:21,23 (NIV).

Even to the dying thief when he repented and believed, Jesus said, 'You will be with me in paradise.'

The fact that the Lord said this to a wicked man who was now truly sorry, but who had no opportunity now to live a good life, demonstrated that it is by free grace you can be saved. Yes, it is Christ's sacrifice which saves the believer. His suffering on the cross has won forgiveness from God for all your sins. Sing with John Newton:

Amazing Grace how sweet the sound,
That saved a wretch like me,
I once was lost but now I'm found,
Was blind but now I see.

Marriage in Heaven?

Some religious leaders in Christ's time came to tell Jesus a funny story. They were actually trying to make him look a fool! In the end, they made fools of themselves. They came with a trumped-up story of a woman who had been married seven times.

'Yes,' they said, 'this woman went on marrying one by one, and one by one they died!'

Makes you wonder why, doesn't it! Anyway, they came to the point. It was an imagined difficulty. They asked, 'When she gets to heaven, whose wife shall she be?'

Now I have been asked this question by one who was widowed three times. She was really worried about it. Well, Jesus came straight out with the answer. He knew all about heaven of course. He told them that there was neither male nor female in heaven and no marriage and, he added, 'Don't take it for granted that you will get to heaven.'

Luke 20:34–36 says, 'And Jesus answering said unto them, the children of this world marry and are given in marriage, but they which shall be accounted worthy to obtain that world, and the resurrection from the dead, neither marry nor are given in marriage.'

Are you saying, 'Oh, I have had such a wonderful married life. All the loving affection, the closeness of two loving personalities, the beauty of doing things together, the deep emotions shared in confidence – I'm sorry if there is no marriage in heaven!'

Wait a minute. The Bible shows that in heaven you get all the advantages of marriage and none of the disadvantages! Now that is different isn't it? Also, you will meet that perfect husband in heaven if he is saved and you will meet that perfect wife if she is saved. Oh, you might say, my partner wasn't all that good. Ah, but he will be in heaven because you are told in 1 John 3 that he will be changed into the lovely character of the Lord Jesus Christ. All those nasty irritating habits will have gone. He will be an absolute saint – and so will you, thank heaven!

There is another thing. There *will* be a marriage in heaven. Oh yes, a wonderful one for all those who love Jesus and are part of the Church of the saved. You are called the bride of Christ and the next thing you will know after the resurrection is that you will be married to him. Those who have remained single for the sake of Christ will find this makes up for everything. It means that God chooses all the most wonderful delights of marriage to be a spiritual equivalent in our relationship with the Lord Jesus Christ. All the most tender expressions of delight, spiritually, in the Song of Solomon will be yours. 'My beloved spoke and said to me, rise up my love, my fair one and come away.'

Separation

What encouraging reports we have had about Christians seeing the glory before they went to be with Christ. We have seen that although people avoid talking about death, when asked secretly, most want to know what happens to them after death. We have read reports and excerpts from readers' letters. They have told us of many cases in which the believer has seen the Lord. This was just before going to be with Christ. Now there is the vital question, does everybody go to a happy heaven when they die? Sadly, the answer is no.

A neighbour whom I had known from a small child was an atheist. He hated all Christians. When he was dying he was fighting the devil. It was very upsetting for his family. His wife did not dare go back into the house to sleep for a long time afterwards.

What a contrast that is to the death of a believer – another listener writes, 'When my grandfather was dying he said, "There is the Lord, can't you see him? Oh, he is beautiful, he is beckoning for me." With that remark, Granddad passed into his presence.'

Psalm 116:15 says, 'Precious in the sight of the Lord is the death of his saved.'

I ask again, would the gentle Jesus refuse admission to his heaven? He will refuse all people who refuse him. Let the Lord Jesus answer himself in Matthew 25: 41. He says, 'Then shall he say to those on his left hand, depart from me, you who are cursed, into eternal fire prepared for the devil and his angels. Then they will go away into eternal punishment but the righteous to eternal life.'

This separation is clearly taught throughout the Bible. Eternal punishment for the unsaved and heaven for the righteous. But who are the righteous according to Jesus? He tells Nicodemus that it is those who have been born again by the Holy Spirit, that unless you are born again by the Holy Spirit you cannot see the kingdom of God. Our wicked nature has to be changed by the rebirth. Another passage about separation is in Matthew 3:12, 'He will gather his wheat into his barn, but he will burn up the chaff with unquenchable fire.'

The Lord Jesus was so convinced that only his sacrifice could save you, that he willingly suffered for our sins. Listen again to his conviction about you. In Matthew 13, he says the wheat means the saved. They will be reaped at the end of this age, but what happens to the weeds? They represent those who kept ignoring the warnings. They avoided salvation. Here are the words of the Saviour concerning you if you are still unsaved:

> As the weeds are pulled up and burned in the fire, so it will be at the end of the age . . . The angels will throw them into the fiery furnace where there will be weeping and gnashing of teeth. Then shall the righteous shine like the sun in the kingdom of their Father God.

It is in love for you that the Lord Jesus is frank. He was so convinced that you would go to hell if you were unsaved that he faced torture on the cross to save you. The fact that you can hold out against such loving entreaty shows how sinful your heart is. Pride and obstinacy stops even religious people from accepting Christ's free gift of salvation. The Lord Jesus wants you to be among those who shine like the sun in the kingdom of their Father. Think of all those quoted in letters we have read who pleaded on their deathbeds with neighbours and relatives and loved ones to receive Christ, so that they will meet them again in glory. I end by quoting one who on his deathbed said, 'Tell my unconverted sister to receive Christ so that I can meet her in glory.' Then he looked up with a lovely smile and said, 'Yes, Lord, I'm coming, I'm coming.'

Scripture Teaching of Life After Death

After all those wonderful experiences of those who saw the Lord as they died, you might like a summary of what the Bible, God's Word, teaches about life after death. First, we will look at the events for a believer. It is as follows: At death the spirit of the believer leaves the body and goes to be with Christ.

The body is cremated or buried and the bodily remains wait for the time called the resurrection of the body. The spirit of the believer rejoices with great joy in the loving presence of the Saviour. When at the end of this age, Jesus Christ returns from heaven, the believer's spirit accompanies his Saviour Jesus Christ to return to the sky. That's at the second coming of the Lord. Then, the resurrection of the believer's body takes place.

This resurrection body is reunited with the believer's spirit. All those resurrected are Christ's Church. Christ gives a loving welcome to his bride, the Church.

Next follows the prize-giving time while still in the sky. The believer's works for the Lord are examined, for the deeds done in the body. For these he or she is rewarded and given their praise, 'Well done good and faithful servant!'

They are allotted their suitable function in the coming kingdom.

Next comes the tremendous earth-shaking event. Jesus descends with his believers to judge the nations. He descends to the Mount of Olives just outside Jerusalem. He banishes all wickedness and establishes his happy kingdom on earth for a thousand years.

The Lord's prayer will have been fulfilled, 'Your kingdom come, your will be done, on earth just as it is in heaven.'

At the end of the 1,000 years, the rest of the dead will be raised for their judgement. Then the whole universe will be cleaned up and a wonderful era of blessing and happiness will be fulfilled. Sin and Satan will be banished and the universe will be the glorious realm of happiness which God intended, but which was spoilt by the rebellion of Satan and then by the disobedience of the human race.

As it says at the end of the Bible: 'Nothing unclean will enter, nor anyone who practises filth but only those whose names are written in the Lamb's book of life.' So do ask the Lord to cleanse you and put your name in his book of life.

Is your name there?

Visions not Enough

Have you felt you wanted to be alone after something shattering has just hit you? Paul was shattered when he met Jesus Christ. So he went away into the desert. In the Arabian desert Paul saw visions which gave him the full truth of the gospel, yet he gives a warning which makes us ask, Can Satan give visions as well as God? Paul is speaking about his experience. Galatians 1:8 says: 'There are some who trouble you and want to pervert the gospel of Christ, but even if we, or an angel from heaven should preach to you a gospel contrary to that which we preached to you, let him be accursed.'

Strong words aren't they? We ask, then, has Satan or a fallen angel given a twisted gospel or a false religion? History says yes. The Lord himself said there would be false prophets and false Christs, especially in the latter days. Paul said that Satan likes to appear as an angel of light. He even said that he would get false ministers of religion into the Church. That makes you think doesn't it! Read 2 Corinthians 11:3–15

What then is the real test? – not visions, but the Bible. What does the Bible say? – that's the test.

There have been instances down the centuries when a vision given by Satan has started a false religion or a false cult. How are you to judge whether it is false? Paul says, if it incites you to preach a gospel which is contrary to the gospel of Christ, it is a false gospel. It is false even though it would appear to be an angel from heaven who misleads you.

A vision to worship anyone else but Jesus Christ and God is a false gospel. A vision to worship a saint is a false gospel. John was about to in Revelation 22:8 but he was stopped. He fell down to worship at the feet of the angel, but was told, 'You must not do that! I am a fellow servant with you and with those who keep the words of this book Revelation. Worship God only.'

In 1 Kings chapter 13 we read an extraordinary story of a prophet who was told to go straight home after he'd delivered God's word to a wicked king. On the way home a false prophet met him and said, 'I am a prophet as you are, and an angel spoke to me by the word of the Lord, saying bring him back with you into your house.' But he lied to him.

The prophet was deceived, so the word of the Lord came to him, 'Thus saith the Lord, you have disobeyed the word of the Lord and not kept the commandment which the Lord your God commanded you.'

On the way home a lion pounced on him and killed him.

Satan is depicted sometimes as a roaring lion seeking whom he may devour, but more often he prefers to appear as an angel of light. He finds it more effective to deny gospel truths through an unconverted minister of the Church. The worldling scoffs and ridicules when Satan causes a minister to parade his unbelief to the world. So don't let Satan deceive you.

Satan Unmasked

I had a letter from a man who said there was no such person as the devil. It was God who was blamed for all the suffering in the world.

That remark reveals why the devil wants to persuade people that he does not exist. It's to blame God – and he gets many to do it.

The devil, or Satan, is fully unmasked in God's Word, the Bible. The Lord Jesus clearly said in John chapter 8 that the devil was the father and originator of all evil and murder. Here are the words: 'The devil was a murderer from the beginning and there is no truth in him. When he makes lies, he speaks according to his own nature, because he is a liar and the father of lies.'

Paul says that the devil fell from being good to being evil through pride.

In Ezekiel chapter 28 we are told that God created the devil as originally good but pride caused his fall. Matthew 4:9 tells that Satan craves to be worshipped.

Isaiah chapter 14 tells how he tried to become greater than God. He was expelled and started to wreck God's earth and creation.

Genesis chapter 3 tells how he caused the ancestor of our human race to rebel against God.

Job chapters 1 and 2 tells how he hates good people and tries to spread scandal about them, and afflicts them with disease.

Mark chapter 8 tells how Satan afflicts people with illness.

2 Corinthians chapter 12 tells how he afflicted Paul. In chapter 11, we're told that the devil disguises himself as an angel of light by putting unconverted ministers into the Church to deny the truth, and by starting false religions.

Revelation shows how he deceives the whole world by his lies.

An example of this was a series on British television. The speaker said that Jesus was not mentioned anywhere in history. This was very misleading because Jesus is mentioned seven times by seven Roman historians of the time, nine Jewish antagonists speak of him as well as eight other writers of the time. Also there is the full story of Jesus by the four Gospel writers who declare themselves eye-witnesses. More mention of Jesus is made than of any other historical character.

All efforts to reply to this outstanding lie were blocked by the television authorities. But, praise God, the Bible tells how the devil will be banished to hell, and so will all his fallen angels. Then all the world, including nature, will be at peace. Meanwhile the born-again Christian is given authority over the devil.

St James says, 'Resist the devil and he will flee from you.'

Revelation chapter 12 says that 'the ancient serpent who is called the devil and Satan, the deceiver of the whole world will be conquered by the blood of the Lamb and by the word of God and the testimony of believers who loved not their lives unto death'. Instead, the Lord Jesus has given believers authority over the devil. The Lord Jesus has defeated him, and Jesus assures you in Matthew chapter 28:18 that, 'All power is given unto him in heaven and earth, and everywhere.'

So take courage, if you are a believer, you are on the winning side.

Satan's End

The final chapters of the Bible are solemn, exciting and joyfully triumphant. Good triumphs, but first the source of all evil has to be banished for ever. That is Satan and his two false religions. Revelation 20:10: 'Then the devil who had deceived them will be thrown into the lake of fire burning with sulphur where the Creature and the False Prophet are.' Notice that the devil was the great deceiver to the end. But the trouble is, mankind wants to be deceived and therefore is very gullible.

Jesus had said earlier in Matthew 25:41 that the devil and his fallen angels would be thrown into this everlasting fire and that it had been prepared for them. Unfortunately, he will take with him all who did not become the sheep of the Good Shepherd, Jesus Christ. But please notice that the chapter in Revelation which describes the lake of fire says that everyone will be judged according to their works whether they be good or bad. So it will be a just judgement and nobody will be able to say that they have been treated unfairly. But only those who've had their sins forgiven will enter heaven. No one will be allowed into heaven it says whose mind or tongue is filthy or who is immoral or trades in prostitution, or is a murderer or makes lies or worships idols, unless Jesus has changed their lives and forgiven them. These are the words used in chapters 20 and 21:

> I saw a great white throne and the one who sat upon it, from whose face the earth and universe speeded away . . . and I saw the dead, great and small, standing before God, and the recording books were opened, including the book of life, and the dead were judged according to the things written in the books, each according to the deeds they had done, whether good or bad.

Before Satan's final end, he will have been chained in the bottomless pit for 1,000 years. That was so that he would not deceive the nations any more until the end of the 1,000 years. Those who think that this millennium comes *before* the coming of Christ, must ask themselves whether the last 1,000 years has been completely free from Satan's deceptions. The answer is surely no. Did not Jesus say that there would be false prophets and false Christs who would deceive many before he returned.

Notice, too, that the two major false religions in the book of Revelation 19:20 were active **before** the millennium starts. At the end of the millennium the devil joins them in the lake of fire.

What are those two false religious systems? They are described as the beast and the false prophet. Jesus described them in Matthew 24:26 as the false Christ in the inner rooms and the prophet of the desert to whom pilgrimages are made into the desert.

These deceptions will be destroyed in two stages according to Daniel 7:26 and 1 Thessalonians 2:8–12. First, gradually by the Word of the Lord, the Bible. Radio and television are bringing this worldwide. Then, suddenly at the second coming of Christ so that the nations will not be deceived any more during the 1,000 years which follow.

The Old Testament prophets say that when those deceptions of the devil are abolished, the veil of blindness over all nations will be removed. Here are Isaiah's words in 25:7 about that day:

'The Lord will remove the blindness which covers all peoples, the veil which is spread over all nations. He will swallow up death forever.' 2 Corinthians chapter 4 says: 'If our gospel is veiled it is veiled to those who are lost. Satan has blinded the minds of those who don't believe.'

According to Isaiah chapter 14 the nations will say to Satan, 'So you were the cause of all the trouble.'

What an eye-opener that will be. But first let God open your eyes to the truth now.

Peter's Glimpse of Glory

What stands out in your memory above anything else?

Peter had a glimpse of glory that he never forgot. The memory of it was bright in his mind in old age: for when he wrote his second letter, in chapter 1, he speaks of that spectacular transfiguration of Christ – it's when the person of Jesus glowed with light on the mountain:

> We did not follow cleverly devised myths when we made known to you the power and coming of our Lord Jesus Christ but we were eyewitnesses of his majesty. [Take note those who think that the New Testament Gospels were not written by eye witnesses.] We were eyewitnesses of Christ's majesty, for when he received honour and glory from God the Father and the voice was carried to him by the Majestic Glory, 'This is my beloved Son in whom I am well pleased,' we heard this voice from heaven, for we were with him on the holy mountain.

The description of this glimpse of glory is given in *all* of the first three Gospels. Mark who wrote down Peter's description says in Mark chapter 9: the garments of Jesus became glistening, intensely white, whiter than any launderette could bleach them. The Gospel writers grope for words. Luke says, 'As Jesus was praying on the mountain, the appearance of his face was altered, and his clothes became dazzling white.' Matthew says, 'His face shone like the sun and his garments became white as light.' Jesus was transformed in front of them.

It was then that Peter, James and John were astonished to see two men talking with the Lord Jesus.

Were they angels? No. They were two famous characters in Old Testament history: Moses and Elijah – but how did they know? They'd never met them before and they'd had very little description of what they looked like.

This opens up the questions again – shall we recognise our loved ones in heaven? If so, then how?

Remember the little girl aged eight who, as she was dying, recognised her baby brother? Now that baby brother died before she was born, and what is more that baby brother was only a few hours old when he died – so there is a marvellous mystery. Had that newborn babe matured in heaven? Had he come with Jesus to welcome her?

10   STRANGE MIRACLES

A PRAYER THAT FELLED A TREE

I was greatly surprised when God made a tree fall down in answer to a wish. Did an angel push it, I ask myself, or did God use some other means? But let me tell you more.

I had been broadcasting the story of Jonah – the angry prophet who got swallowed by a whale or great fish. You remember that God sent him to warn the biggest city of his time that God's judgement was coming upon it, because they were an extremely cruel and bitter people. As they were enemies, Jonah wanted the city to perish and so he disobeyed God. He booked onto a passenger ship which went in the opposite direction and, to cut a long story short, God brought him back by having him swallowed whole by a whale.

Back home, God gave him the same order: 'Get up! go to Nineveh! Proclaim to that great city the message I tell you!' Jonah still wanted the city to be destroyed by an earthquake or some calamity, so he sat on a hill overlooking this huge city, and hoped it would soon be demolished.

While he sat, he was almost overcome by the scorching heat, so God made a fleshy plant to grow up to give him shade. To Jonah's chagrin this plant shrivelled up, so he was angry again – at being scorched by the heat.

Well, I had been giving the evidence that this had actually happened. It is recorded in my book *Evidence for Truth, Volume 2: Archaeology.* Remembering Jonah's experience, I talked with God. The idea suddenly struck me: why don't I ask God to do something similar for me? That would be further proof of a miracle.

There was a row of large fir trees outside my bedroom window. One of them was blocking the lovely morning sun from shining into my room.

I read Christ's promise in Matthew 21:21 about a fig tree which had withered up. Jesus said, 'If you ask in prayer and full faith, not doubting, God can do the same for you', so I prayed that evening. 'Dear Lord, show that you can do it for me; that tree is blocking out my morning sunshine.' I then went to bed and forgot all about it.

Imagine my utter astonishment in the morning when I looked out of the window and there was the tree fallen flat on the ground. Not one of the other trees was affected and there had been no gales during the night. It was a stout tree in private ground well away from public access.

Some friends came and we took photos of it: lying flat on the ground, photos of the gap it had left letting the sun shine through, photos of how it was torn up by the roots.

I was thrilled. I said, 'Thank you, Lord. I have written this book proving your miracles and you have graciously done a miracle for me.'

He seemed to say to me, 'What did I say that the conditions were?'

I said: 'Praying with faith. Yes! Praying, not doubting in your heart.'

'Yes! What else? Forgiving anybody who's done you a dirty trick.'

I blushed and said 'Lord I have forgiven.'

Figure 10.1. Author standing beside tree which fell down overnight in answer to prayer, Eastbourne 1994.

HOT AIR WHALE AND THE GHOST FROM THE SEA

Did you know that in Palestine there is a plant which grows up in one day and disappears the next morning? It is called the palmcristy. Some who do not know this have doubted Jonah's story in the Bible. Anyway it is only a problem for those with a small God; and more knowledge has corroborated the unlikely stories of Jonah.

A favourite obstacle to belief is that Jonah could have lived in a fish for three days before being coughed up onto the Palestine shore. Some used to say that a whale could not swallow a man, because it had a grill at the front of its mouth. But that is only one kind of whale. The kind which frequents the Mediterranean is the catchelot which has no grill. Large sharks have been found in its stomach. Moreover there are as many as five cases where fishermen have been swallowed by a catchelot whale and have come out alive.

One was an Arab who cut his way out of the whale's stomach with a sharp knife which he had in his belt. But a famous case was that of James Bartley. He was pulled overboard into the sea when the crew harpooned a whale off the Falkland Islands. The crew wondered where he'd disappeared to. They succeeded in hauling the whale on board and began the usual process of cutting it up, saving the oil and the blubber. After eight hours work they got down to the stomach.

They put a chain round it and hauled it out of the carcass onto the deck. To their surprise the stomach started wriggling. They rushed to cut it open and out fell James Bartley. He was fully alive, even after many hours in the whale's stomach, but was raving mad. The sailors had a quick remedy – they threw several buckets of sea water over him which brought him to his senses!

Figure 10.2. The fish-man god Nina, found on a wall at the site of Nineveh. The experiences of Jonah, who came out of the belly of a 'big fish,' would have frightening impact on the Ninevites who worshipped their fish god.

He had a strange story to tell, which was similar to Jonah's account. He realised he'd been swallowed when he felt himself being drawn forward in the dark soft slimy gullet. Then he flopped into a bigger cavern. The slimy hot walls shrunk away at his touch. It was terribly hot. The sauna-like atmosphere seemed to draw out his vitality from every pore of his body. But he could breathe, this surprised him – he could breathe!

Therefore Jonah could breathe for all the three days he was in the stomach. His words are graphic. 'I cried to God out of the belly of hell, and you heard my voice! I promised to do what you said, you can save me!' God acted promptly. He spoke to the fish, and it made for the shore and vomited up Jonah onto dry land.

So Jonah went to Nineveh in the end. But why did the king and the people take any notice of him? Look at the case of James Bartley again for an answer. We saw how that sailor was in the whale's stomach for eight hours. During that time the whale's strong gastric juices had a big effect on his skin; it parched it and shrivelled it a deathly white, so when he was cut out of the whale's stomach he looked like a ghost. So Jonah looked like a ghost as well. No wonder the population rushed out and took full notice as he shouted. 'In forty days' time, the God of heaven and earth will demolish your city!' The citizens knew they were wicked and cruel with their horrible tortures, and that their king was a violent despot.

Another discovery reveals why the despot was anxious when Jonah appeared – he declared that he'd come out of a fish. The king would be startled. Nineveh was named after the fish Nina – their fish god! Had Jonah come out of the mouth of their fish god?

As he had told the sailors earlier, so Jonah told the king, his God was far greater than any of their gods which were no gods at all. The God who'd sent him was the God of creation, the God of the sea, the God of the heavens and the God of fish, the God of the earth from which he could overthrow Nineveh with an earthquake, just as he'd overthrown Sodom and Gomorrah for their wickedness. The tyrant was terrified. 'Let man and beast be covered with sackcloth and cry mightily to God. Yes, let everyone turn from his evil ways, and turn away from the violence he commits. Perhaps God will turn from his fierce anger so that we may not perish!'

Now here's a question, does God do such earth-moving marvels these days? This is an extract from a paper dated about 1951: 'In Yugoslavia some evil persons staged a ceremonial burial of the Deity, inviting and securing a great attendance. There came a huge convulsion of the forces of nature, and the terror-stricken people rushed to the local church with frantic cries of repentance and fear, to the scared and pained accompaniment of the actors in the blasphemous orgy. The story comes from a quite reputable source.'

The famous archaeologist Dr Layard, who excavated the ruins of the city of Nineveh, found on the walls there a sculptural picture of the fish god with a man coming out of its mouth! Would this be the clue to what made them scared when Jonah said that God had brought him out of the fish? (See Fig 10.2.)

Do you find it remarkable that although Jonah escaped to sunny Spain to get as far away as possible, God forgave him and even used his waywardness to help his mission? He was made more effective for his mission once he said sorry.

His skin parched white by the whale's gastric juices and the Ninevite's terror of their fish god made Jonah instantly effective. I find that encouraging.

Once we're changed and forgiven, God often uses that as a testimony to his grace. John Newton was once a blasphemous and callous slave trader, but when he allowed himself to be changed by Christ, his testimony helped William Wilberforce to liberate the slaves. John Newton's famous hymn 'Amazing Grace' is even sung in secular circles.

Now this was the very reason why Jonah fled from Ninevah as far as he could. He knew that God would forgive even a wicked nation if it repented. How did he know? He'd read it in Moses' writings written 600 years earlier in Exodus 34, and he quotes it back to God, 'Did I not say, O Lord, while I was in my country, I know you are a gracious God and merciful, slow to anger and of great kindness and who withholds judgement from the repentant. That's why I paid my fare to Gibraltar. I wanted Nineveh destroyed for its cruel sins. I believed your law to Moses.'

Here it is in Exodus 34:6: 'The Lord passed by before Moses and proclaimed, The Lord, The Lord God, merciful and gracious, long-suffering and abundant in goodness and truth, keeping mercy for thousands, forgiving wickedness and waywardness and sin; but will not forgive the unrepentant.'

God replied to Jonah's quoting of Moses: 'You felt sorry because your sunshade plant shrivelled away, leaving you unprotected and sweltering and sorry for yourself. Why should not I feel sorry for one hundred and twenty thousand children who've never been taught right from wrong!'

Has repentance and revival saved nations in more recent history? Abraham Lincoln rescued the United States of America by calling them to repentance and revival. America was facing a debt of millions of dollars, but within a couple of years of gospel revival they were free from debt. I hasten to say that becoming debt-free was not the object of the call to repentance, it was an unexpected outcome of it.

WHY FIREBALLS HIT A CATHEDRAL

York Minster Transept on Fire

In 1984 lightning hit the transept wing of the cathedral in York, England, and demolished it. Someone quipped, 'Can't God look after his property!'

In answer it must be said that there were some mysterious circumstances connected with the incident. The first was the way in which it happened. I had it described to me by one who was standing by the cathedral at the time. He said that there was no thunderstorm about at the time, and none had been forecast. Moreover, it was a fine day, the sun was bright and there was not a cloud in the blue sky. Then a small round cloud appeared from nowhere and came over towards the cathedral, then a series of fireballs shot from the little cloud and hit the turret of the building. He said that this went on for what seemed to be five minutes until the beautiful building burst into flames.

Figure 10.3. York Minster after fireballs attack. Daily Express picture with the newspaper's own comment hinting at the significance.

It really looked as if God had done it deliberately, but whatever for? I remembered that God had destroyed the temple in Jerusalem on two occasions. He said he was going to do it by sending in an enemy army, and the reason was that the priests who ministered there had forsaken God's truth, but surely none had at York Minster!

Well, the *Daily Express* and other national newspapers hinted that they had, for underneath a photo of the ruins was written: 'Firemen hose down the burned-out south transept of England's York Minster

Cathedral *just after a controversial bishop was consecrated there.'*

Some time earlier a heading had appeared in the newspaper: 'Liberal Bishop's Appointment Causes a Stir in England.'

The article went on to announce that this man had been proclaiming widely that he did not believe in the virgin birth of Jesus Christ or that he had risen from the dead. How would such a man be chosen to be a bishop? People are sometimes surprised by the answer – bishops are appointed by the Prime Minister!

Many bishops are very fine faithful men of God, but unfortunately the newspapers don't take much notice of them. It's only when some scandalous utterance is made that it is regarded as news and all the good work of others is spoilt.

There is still more to this story of the fireballs.

That unbelieving bishop was made Bishop of Durham. There was an earlier Bishop of Durham who was a great faithful preacher of the Word of God – Bishop Handley Mowll. A descendant of his heard of the appointment of one who was so different from his relative and was determined to do something about it. This is the story he told to me and later he typed it out as follows:

> The enormity of what was happening in the Church of England struck me very forcibly on Wednesday night, and the thought came that something should be done about it, and that the Lord possibly wanted me to do it. When I discovered that the consecration at York Minster was to happen on Friday, and that I was free to go, I prepared a statement which I intended to read out in the Minster, and got the support of my wardens and of others who were at the Fellowship on Thursday at my vicarage. From the beginning I felt that this was right, and I believe that the Lord helped us.
>
> I set out with a friend early on Friday morning, and we arrived at York at 9.45 am. I got into the Minster, although I had no ticket, and sat on a chair in a block of seats conveniently near the lectern [a stand holding the Bible from which the lesson was read]. I looked at the service sheet and saw that the appropriate time for making my statement was before the presentation of the prospective bishop. He was to be presented to the Archbishop after the creed which would be repeated by all the congregation including the prospective bishop, and who, ironically enough would say with them:
>
> 'I believe . . . in Jesus Christ our Lord who **was conceived by the Virgin Mary** . . . was sentenced to death by Pontius Pilate who died and was buried, but on the third day **He arose from the dead** and ascended into heaven, from whence He will come again to raise the living and the dead . . .'
>
> Meanwhile, my friend was being a great help distributing my statement to people coming in, and looking after my car. I sat in my seat for over half an hour. They should have been expecting a protest, but I was not found out. The service had buoyed me up. The psalm had spoken of God's Word and of David's love for it. The creed had clearly and emphatically

expressed the church's beliefs and faith in the Virgin Birth and in the Resurrection etc., but the sermon, in contrast, was full of liberal theology saying that instead of looking back to the creeds or the Bible as our basic authority we must express our faith in twentieth-century terms, discarding the legends.

As I approached the rostrum where the lectern was, the vicar general was also mounting the rostrum, but fortunately he gave place to me (for which I was very grateful). I asked the dean to allow me less than two minutes and weighed in with my statement which was as follows:

> The Christian faith is about what we as Christians believe. So not to believe in the Virgin Birth and in the Resurrection of our Lord as facts of history is a very grave matter for anyone. How much more so for a man who is about to make solemn vows before God and to be consecrated as a bishop in the Church of England which has its standards of faith in the 39 Articles of Religion and in the Book of Common Prayer, also in the historic creeds of the church, and above all, in the Bible where the apostles gave clear and unequivocal witness to these historic facts, just as the church has always received them. That a would-be bishop who should be a guardian and teacher of the Christian faith is one known to deny these to have in fact happened – thus removing the basis for the two most important doctrines about our Lord which make him unique – is perhaps, in the realm of faith, **the greatest blasphemy possible.**

I got to about as far as here when the head warden asked me to stop and accompany him back to my seat. I still had nine lines to read for the rest of my statement which were as follows:

> That the church can be party to such a thing will, in the eyes of all honest people, deny it the right to speak out on any moral or ethical issue. I beg you to play with words no longer, because this will bring great shame to the church throughout the world, and I ask you to take no further part in this service. I invite you to follow me out of this church as a timely protest against what is happening, or about to happen, and as a protest in favour of the truth.

> *(signed) J.K. Mowll*

It was after this statement, and after the recitation of the creed by the new bishop who did not believe it, and after his consecration, that the fireballs struck the cathedral from a clear sky from a single small cloud. So was God adding his protest to that of John Mowll?

AYOTOLLA'S WRITING ON THE WALL

A strange report appeared in a Grimsby newspaper. It had been reported in an Iran newspaper that a mysterious sign appeared on the wall of the Ayatollah's residence. It was a glowing cross. All attempts to remove it failed. Eventually, they even broke down and removed the wall, but this was unavailing because the glowing cross appeared on the wall behind the one which had been removed.

The Ayatollah was reported as being extremely upset, he being the religious head of Islam. The report was as follows:

> A recent newspaper report has said that the Ayatollah Khomeini of Iran is suffering from liver cancer, and has only three months to live *(Daily Mail,* June 10th, 1988). Now Iranian sources are saying that the Ayatollah had been enraged by a glowing cross which appears on the wall of his room! Khomeini aides at first refused to believe the story, but have now admitted that it is true. The Ayatollah has tried everything in an effort to remove the cross, including knocking down the offending wall – but the cross simply appeared on another wall the next morning. Some international exports claim that the cross, which first appeared some months ago, is responsible for the Ayatollah's decline – they say that after living in a constant stage of rage, he fell into a coma.

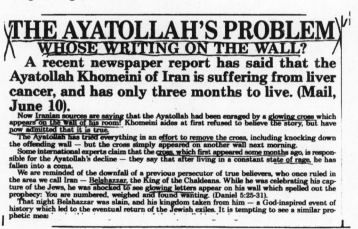

Figure 10.4. Newspaper report of Ayatollah's cross on the wall.
Source: Grimsby Evening Telegraph, *1988*

UNO CONFERENCE AT LAKE SUCCESS (CONFRONTED BY AN ANGEL)

I have doubts as to whether I should bring you the next report. It is so extraordinary. It takes some believing. Yet it is given by a well-authenticated person. It is told by an ABC network reporter Paul Harvey, and it features international figures. It happened at the UNO conference held at Lake Success soon after the Second World War. It was a committee attended by important representatives for each nation and was highly secret. Only the representatives were allowed in. Security measures did not even allow recording secretaries or cameramen into the room. They had to occupy a glassed-in translation loft, so when this unknown figure appeared before the delegates they were astonished.

The delegates were internationally-known names: Dulles and Austin represented USA, Vishinsky for the Soviet Union, Jebb for the United Kingdom, etc. Sir Bengal Rau, the chairman, called them to order to start the meeting and to their amazement this unauthorised stranger suddenly stood before them. How had he got past security? He was a tall thin man dressed in Eastern garments and sandals. That in itself was not uncommon in international meetings. He had a well-groomed beard, and his lips parted to say: 'I have many things to say to you, and to judge to you. I will utter things which have been kept secret from the foundation of the world. And you shall know the truth.'

He was quickly interrupted by the chairman, Bengal Rau, 'Why are you here, Sir?'

The Eastern-clad stranger replied with a soft compelling voice, clear for all to hear without the aid of a microphone: 'There is an evil I have seen under the sun, and it is common among men. With their tongues they have used deceit, and the poison of asps is under their lips, and the way of peace they have not known.'

The eminent audience maintained a dumbfounded silence, and the stranger continued the words which some might recognise as words of Scripture: 'Everyone who doeth evil hates the light. They make clean the outside of the cup, but inside they are full of extortion and excess. The axe is laid to the roots of such trees.'

The Soviet delegate demanded loudly to question the stranger, saying that his delegation refused to listen to the ravings of this warmonger. The stranger spoke sharply to him:

'The day shall come upon you when your enemies will cast a trench about you on every side and will utterly destroy you.'

Mr Austin of the United States waved his little desk flag to gain permission to speak and said:

'In the USA we are hosts to enemies within our own house, and agents of an alien pretend loyalty to our government.'

The stranger raised his hand to intercept with the words: 'No man can serve two masters, for either he will hate the one and love the other, or he will hold to the one and despise the other. Every kingdom divided against itself is brought to desolation.'

'But,' protested Mr Austin, 'those among us say they intend only to alter our government by peaceful means.'

The stranger turned towards Austin and Dulles: 'There is none righteous among you, no not one!'

The chairman rose from his seat, 'Our purpose in coming here was to place the blame on whatever is responsible for international unrest, but you have given each of us our share. But what should we do? Abandon our efforts to seek peace?'

The reply came, 'Be sober, be vigilant. Depart from evil and do good. Execute justice and righteousness. Deliver the spoiled out of the hand of the oppressor, seek peace and pursue it.'

Chairman Rau said, 'You make this sound so simple.'

The stranger looked at him: 'Many righteous men have desired to hear these things which you hear and have not heard them.'

'I'm afraid we do not usually hear them outside our churches,' said Bengal Rau.

The Eastern visitor looked meaningfully at the assembly and said: 'Be not forgetful to entertain strangers, for hereby some have entertained angels unawares.'

Rau replied, 'Thank you sir, could you not write this wisdom in a book to make it available worldwide?'

The stranger's eyes flashed bright: 'My words are already written in a book for all to read.'

Well! What do you make of all that? Whatever your reaction may be, there is much to learn and the question comes to me, is there any similar national confrontation by an incognito angel in the Bible? To my surprise I find there is! It's in the book of Judges chapter two:

'One day, the Angel of the Lord arrived at Bochim, coming up from Gilgal, and announced to the people of Israel, "I brought you out of Egypt into this land which I promised to your ancestors, and I said that I would never break my covenant with you. I told you to destroy heathen altars, why have you not obeyed?" The people burst into tears as the angel finished speaking, so the name of that place was called BOCHIM, meaning where people wept.'

GROTESQUE FIGURES

The next episode was a strange eye-opener to me.

There was a man standing by a lamppost on the other side of the road. He was fairly tall and slim and well dressed in a grey suit and he looked about twenty-nine years of age. I stopped to look at him again as I was sure he was distressed and perplexed and felt that I should go on over to him.

'You seem to be doing some deep thinking,' I said.

He welcomed the approach, and explained that he'd recently lost a brother in an air crash. 'We were very close, and he was a grand guy. His loss is a great shock to me, and I've tried to get in touch with him but it's led to things I don't understand.'

'Tell me!' I said, 'Did you try to contact his spirit?'

'Yes.'

'On your own or through a medium?'

'On my own. I've never been to any seance. It was in my bedroom at home at night. In the dark, I took a notebook and a pencil. I held the pencil loosely and asked my brother to speak to me.'

He went on to describe how the pencil in his hand started to move over the paper for a few minutes as if it were writing something. When it stopped, he switched on the light and saw that a message had been written. All the words were joined because the pencil had remained on the paper as it moved along. The message said that he, his brother was all right and that he was not to worry.

'I wanted to be sure it really was the spirit of my brother who was writing to me, so I said, can you prove you are my brother? Immediately my hand and pencil began to move to and fro in all directions across the paper and when I switched on the light, I was astonished. There on my notepad in dark black pencil shading was a portrait of my brother. It was similar to what an expert portrait artist would draw.'

He pulled it out of his pocket and showed it to me. It was indeed a remarkable block-filled pencil portrait of the head and shoulders of a man.

'Is it really like him?' I asked

He said that it was, but when he continued to ask for messages in the succeeding nights, things seemed to go wrong and get muddled, so he asked the spirit, 'Who is it who is really giving me the messages?' The reply was, 'I am the chief of the letter writers.'

He replied, 'But I thought you were my brother – please draw a picture of yourself.'

The picture that followed was quite astonishing. It was an ugly character of a devil with horns. The young man showed me this drawing and also other drawings that came through to him of the other demons, also with horns. It was later that he showed me all these drawings and the letter with the joined words. The letters all seemed to contradict one another it seemed as though the spirits could not agree on anything for very long.

I said to him, 'It is obvious that these are lying spirits. It is impossible for them to tell the truth. The Bible calls them deceiving spirits and warns you not to be in touch with them.'

The young man explained that when they were no longer claiming to give messages from his brother, he tried to cut off contact, but began to get pains in his back and head and that's when he got worried and perplexed.

I thought he ought to know what God's Word said about trying to contact the dead. It is forbidden in both the Old Testament and the New Testament because of all its dangers. God told the Israelites, through Moses:

Do not defile yourselves by consulting mediums and witches. I am The

Lord I will set my face against anyone who consults mediums and witch-es instead of me. Sanctify yourselves and be holy for I am the Lord your God who cleanses you. (Leviticus 19:31; 20:6)

Later, King Saul consulted a medium at a place called Endor. Because of this Saul was defeated and killed in the next battle.

In the New Testament we read of people who had tampered with evil spirits and become possessed, and Jesus cast out the demons.

Early in his ministry these evil spirits recognised that Jesus was the Son of God. This was long before even his disciples realised it. The following incident – about a disturbance in church where Jesus was preaching – is described early in St Mark's Gospel (Mark 1:23 onwards):

A man possessed by a demon was present [in the synagogue] and began shouting, 'Why are you bothering us, Jesus of Nazareth – have you come to destroy us demons? I know who you are – the holy Son of God!' Jesus curtly commanded the demon to say no more and to come out of the man. At that the evil spirit screamed and convulsed the man violently and left him. (The Living Bible)

Still very early in Christ's ministry even before the apostles were chosen St Mark tells us in chapter 3 that, whenever those possessed by demons caught sight of Jesus they would fall down before him shriek-ing, 'You are the Son of God!' But he strictly warned them not to make him known.

St Paul tells us that:

We are not fighting against people made of flesh and blood, but against persons without bodies – the evil rulers of the unseen world, those mighty satanic beings and great evil princes of darkness who rule this world; huge numbers of wicked spirits in the spirit world. Therefore you need the Lord's mighty power within you.

(Ephesians 6:12)

I turned to the man and said, 'May I pray that you have the mighty power of the Lord in you to stop those evil spirits taking you over?' He was eager that I should, and as I prayed for the Lord's mighty power I laid my hand upon his arm.

Afterwards he said that he felt as though an electric shock went through his arm. That night in his bedroom, he said, it seemed as if all hell had been let loose. The devil did not want to let him go. He joined a Christian church where a group of praying friends achieved his release, and he found a purpose for his life in spite of his bereavement.

I have been asked to add this warning against the occult in case the stories of after death experiences should tempt you in the wrong direction. The Bible warns us that:

> The Holy Spirit clearly says that in the last days some will depart from the faith and give credence to deceitful spirits and doctrines of demons.
> (1 Timothy 4:1)

In the case of horrific shootings of youngsters in schools and cases like the young man at Hungerford who shot eighteen passers-by, the offenders had been dabbling with the occult. In the case of the latter young man, he said that in his occult practices, evil spirits kept telling him to kill. 'Shoot! Shoot and kill!' The voices kept echoing in his head.

In contrast, the Christian message in the Bible is that Christ came to bring life – spiritual life and eternal life to those who believe. Also he urged forgiveness to be practised even towards one's enemies, and to return kindness even to those who are spiteful to you. No one should be considered to be a Christian who encourages hatred, revenge or murder.

'I have come that you may have life and to enjoy it more abundantly.' Jesus is speaking of spiritual life as well, experienced through God's forgiveness and a changed life of love through Jesus.

I hope that my insights into the reasons behind the supernatural interventions give you an understanding of God's hand in history and happenings which are puzzling to you personally.

IS THIS THE MILLENNIUM?

'Of course it is!' I hear one say. 'The year 2000 is here isn't it?'

'That's the calendar millennium!' I would hasten to reply. 'It's Christ's 2,000-year birthday.' Happy birthday Jesus, and thank you for coming – yes, a thousand thanks because it gave me a birthday, my spiritual one, when my life was changed and a real purpose and reason for living came to me.

Yes, the third millennium date-wise is here, but the Bible speaks about another millennium and is very excited about it. The first mention of it is surprisingly early, as early as Moses' time three and a half millennia ago, when things seemed to be going wrong, God says to Moses: 'As surely as I live, all the earth shall see the glory of the Lord!'

Many other passing references are made to it as you read through the Old Testament. Sometimes it is called 'The day of the Lord', but it is the New Testament that tells you that it is to be a thousand-year day (2 Peter 3; and the book of Revelation chapter 20), but in the Old Testament you are given lengthy descriptions about it as many as eight times.

No wonder God is excited about it. It's going to be a wonderful time. All the damage done to the earth by Satan will be rectified, and when the devil is chained in the bottomless pit, mankind will exclaim, 'We never realised that the devil was the cause of all these traumas. We usually blamed God.'

Yes, it's going to be a wonderful time! God tells nearly all the prophets that there are going to be no wars, no fighting, no killing. Tanks are to be melted down to make combine harvesters, armaments for agriculture, gas masks for glowing beauty, illness for long life. There will be universal peace, even the animals will be at peace. There will be no more flesh-eating carnivores, only herbivores, and nature TV programmes will be even more enjoyable, for nature will no longer be 'red in tooth and claw'. That was only brought in by Satan when he rebelled.

'The lion will eat straw like the ox and poisonous snakes will be harmless . . . The wolf and the lamb will feed together. They will not hurt or destroy in all my holy earth,' God told Isaiah in 65:25. So that will end all those blood-dripping programmes about predators!

In another scripture God says:

The wolf will live with the lamb, and the leopard will lie down harmlessly with the kid, and the calf and the lion cub together peacefully and a little child will lead them. The cow and the bear will feed together and their young ones will play together, and the lion will eat straw like the ox.

And here's good news for mothers:

The baby when weaned and crawling about will put its hand on the wasp's nest and not get stung, and the toddler will be unharmed by the adder. They will not hurt or injure in all my holy mountain. For the earth shall be as full of the glory of the Lord as the waters cover the seas. (Isaiah 11:6–9)

The description of this wonderful time goes on and on. Every person will have their fair share of land, food and houses, and the earth will become very fertile. Disease and illness will be banished and people will normally live to over a hundred. Advertisements and billboards will encourage pure, moral and happy living because all the world will put God first in their lives and worship and learn of the Lord, and Bible texts will encourage holiness. Yes, the prayer that Jesus taught will at last have been fulfilled: 'Thy Kingdom come, Thy will be done ON EARTH as it is in heaven.'

So when you are appalled at the terrible state the world is in today remember that the good wonderful time is coming! In fact it's just round the corner, for these horrors were predicted to happen soon before Jesus Christ descends from heaven to reign with great power and to bring in this wonderful time when the earth will be restored to what God had originally intended before Satan fell and mankind rebelled.

Does this calendar millennium have any relationship with the Bible millennium?

This is a question which has confused many down the centuries.

The First Calendar Millennium

You have probably heard of the Doomsday Book, and seen excerpts from its pages. It is a detailed entry, made by William the Conqueror, of every farm and homestead in England. He had it compiled after 1066 so that he could tax everyone accurately, but why did he call it the Doomsday Book?

It was because the first millennium had ended, so people wondered whether doomsday or judgement day was near. Also there was the question of whether the 1,000 years were to be calculated from Christs' birth, or his ministry, or from the fall of Jerusalem in AD 70. So what made them think that the first calendar millennium could be the real millennium? It was far from matching those peaceful descriptions of bliss described by the Scriptures. There had been many ferocious wars and other maladies. It was St Augustine who suggested that the millennium idea could be spiritualised and he wrote his famous book *The City of God.*

In his day, at the end of the fourth century, things looked very rosy for the Christian Church. The Roman empire had taken Christianity to be its state religion and it was made to be compulsory for everybody. What a tremendous change this was from the first 300 years during which believers were tortured and slaughtered for their faith. Had the kingdom come on earth, and without the King? All the Christian writers before Augustine (called the early fathers) had taught that King Jesus would return first to bring in his kingdom, but if the millennium could be spiritualised, then there were other features to apply. The prophecies had said that the saints were to sit on thrones, and so thrones must be placed for the bishops to sit on.

Moreover, the empire had divided into the western empire and the eastern empire, the capital for the west being Rome and that for the east, Constantinople, now called Istanbul, with a very important bishop in each. Should they have a special role? Later on in the seventh century the chief bishop in the eastern empire claimed that he should have jurisdiction over all the Church because Jerusalem was in his area. The Bishop of Rome of the time (Gregory the Great) warned the eastern contender against the claim saying only Christ was the head of the Church.

As the centuries progressed things began to look very unlike a blissful millennium. Poverty and disease spread, and then, in the seventh century, there arose the prophet Mohammed whose policy was to spread Islam by the sword, and so the Muslim invasions almost wiped out the eastern empire Church.

The Second Calendar Millennium

It was a disillusioned Church which had supposed that perhaps the first millennium would be the real one, but hoped the second one could be it. Christ was not here in person, but perhaps the very powerful Bishop of Rome could well represent him. In fact the Cardinal H.E. Manning said, 'In the person of Pope Pious IX, Jesus Christ reigns on earth, and he will reign until he has put all enemies under his feet.' Unfortunately, this millennium was far from answering the Bible description of peace and love. More believers sealed their faith in their blood than in any of the preceding centuries, so that Dr A.J. Gordon, in his book *Behold He Comes,* calls it 'a false millennium'.

Thankfully, the throne of Rome does not support such a claim as Cardinal Manning's today, and welcomes the 'separate brethren' as Rome calls them today, encouraging fellowship with other denominations. The charismatic experience also has overflowed the church boundaries.

The Third Calendar Millennium

So will the third millennium, from the year AD 2000 become the real one?

During the last two centuries the spread of the gospel worldwide achieved epic proportions, so that many became very optimistic that by evangelism the millennium would come in. It has been shown that there are as many born-again Christians alive in the world today as have ever been down through the centuries. This is because the present world population equals all that of the former centuries, and in spite of terrible persecutions more people are coming to Christ than in all the previous centuries. The majority of these are not in Europe. The largest churches are elsewhere, with some congregations numbering hundreds of thousands.

Consequently, some thought that the King would come when all the world was won to Christ – the kingdom first without the King. This was called the post-millennium view. Now that the world has become so full of violence, many have noticed that the Bible says that things will get worse and worse and that will make Christ's return the only hope of the world. They have noticed also that such chapters as Zachariah 14:4 puts the Lord's decent to the Mount of Olives *before* his kingship over all the earth in verse 9, 'Then shall the Lord become king overall the earth'. So instead of things getting better, 2 Timothy

3: 1 says 'In the last days perilous times shall come', and in Luke 21 the Lord said that 'Man's heart will fail for fear in anticipation of what is to befall civilisation, because the powers in uranium [Greek] will be released.' The whole situation is reviewed in my book *Evidence For Truth, Volume 3: Prophecy.*

Birthday Millennium

So the world's real hope is the second coming of Christ bringing in that wonderful real millennium, but what about his first coming? That's what the year 2000 is celebrating. That birthday was prophesied by Isaiah. You've probably sung the carol which quotes the prophecy: 'Unto us a child is born, unto us a son is given. His name shall be called Wonderful, Counsellor, The Mighty God, The Everlasting Father, The Prince of Peace.'

What a remarkable list of titles! They could only be true of Jesus if he was both God and man, and he could only be born as God–man if it was by a virgin-birth with God's Holy Spirit bringing about the conception, and that's what the prophets foretold and what the New Testament records claim did really happen. And why did it have to happen? Because only God could be sinless, and only a sinless man could die for our sins, and that is what Jesus was willing to do for you and me.

So what a 2,000th birthday to celebrate! Have you brought him a birthday present? The present he'd like is yourself so that he can give you new life for the purpose that he put you into this world for. That would be a very happy re-birthday for you as well.

CONCLUSION

In real life today we have seen that individuals and nations have experienced similar miracles and angelic rescues that we read about in the Bible. I hope that all these reported in this book have helped you to become more conscious of the supernatural and to lift your commitment to a higher level, as well as recognising and avoiding the dangers associated with the occult.

Has it helped you to see God's purposes behind world history? That same purpose is behind similar perplexing tests in your own life. Those trials of life will be explained and turned into joy when you come into the presence of the angels and bask in the glory of the King of angels who has his loving hand upon your life. As the Good Book says:

He will come to give you, who are troubled, rest with us when the Lord Jesus is revealed from heaven with his mighty angels. . . . when he comes in that day to be glorified in his saints and to be admired for all that he achieved in those who, believed, because our testimony among you was believed.

Jesus declared many times that there will be this grand angelic finale, 'When the son of man (Jesus) comes in his glory and all the angels with him, then will he sit on his throne. Before him will be gathered all the nations and he will separate them one from another as a shepherd separates the sheep from the goats.' 'Jesus will send out his angels and they will weed out of his kingdom all those making enticements to sin and lawbreakers.' 'He will send out his angels to gather together his chosen ones.'

So you see, 'his mighty angels' will have a very busy time when the *real* millennium is triumphantly trumpeted by the archangel. Is this the reason why the angels seem to have been getting so busy lately?

Evidence for Truth
Science

Dr Victor Pearce

In Volume 1 of the *Evidence for Truth* series, Dr Victor Pearce discusses how scientific knowledge, in many varying disciplines, again and again confirms the truth of the Bible with amazing accuracy.

Dr Victor Pearce sifts through the evidence and gives factual answers to some of the most perplexing questions which have never been fully explained before in an understandable way.

Among the topics covered are:

- The Big Bang theory
- Science confirms Adam and Eve
- The rediscovery of the Garden of Eden
- Charles Darwin's belief in God
- The thousand-year culture gap around the world caused by the Flood
- World-wide evidence for the Flood and its cause.

Dr Victor Pearce is an eminent scientist, archaeologist and theologian. He is well known for his lectures and international broadcasts on United Christian Broadcasters.

0 86347 263 X
320pp

Evidence for Truth
Archaeology

Dr Victor Pearce

Volume 2 in the *Evidence for Truth* series looks at how archaeological findings conclusively support the historical records in
the Bible with devestating accuracy. For example, they reveal
that the dates for the Exodus harmonise with all Middle East discoveries, despite the assertions of some.

Writing in plain non-technical English, Victor Pearce unearths
new evidence from his many international researches in museums, laboratories and archaeological sites which reveal:

* The advanced nature of early civilisations
* Evidencie that proves the dates of the Exodus
* How Hittite law proves Moses wrote the Torah
* How the extra long day happened
* Geological facts hidden in the Bible
* The testimony of the Sphinx
* Matthew's gospel account vindicated
* The great Dead Sea scrolls cover-up
* The genetics of virgin conception

Dr Victor Pearce is an eminent scientist, archaeologist and
theologian. He is well known for his lectures and international
broadcasts on United Christian Broadcasters.

0 86347 264 8
280pp

Evidence for Truth
Prophecy

Dr Victor Pearce

Volume 3 in the *Evidence for Truth* series looks at the controversial subject of prophecy and how the events predicted in the Bible have been fulfilled with stunning accuracy and timing.

Victor Pearce pinpoints facts often overlooked and highlights the significance of present and future events. He reveals how the claims of Christ were confirmed throughout the 1,500 years of prophecies.

The topics covered in the book include:

- God's cosmic timing system explained
- Double fulfilment of prophecy
- The role of Europe and the United Nations
- God's provision for Jews and Arabs
- Jerusalem's destiny as a World Trade Centre
- Prophecies about Christ and by Christ
- What God told Daniel in confidence
- The new millenium and the biblical millenium
- Tribulation and end-time events
- The book of Revelation decoded
- The second coming of Jesus Christ
- Warnings about homosexuality
- Aeroplanes, spacecraft and nuclear bombs predicted

Dr Victor Pearce is an eminent scientist, archaeologist and theologian. He is well known for his lectures and international broadcasts on United Christian Broadcasters.

0 86347 265 6
340pp